THE I TATTI
RENAISSANCE LIBRARY

James Hankins, General Editor

PONTANO

ECLOGUES

GARDEN OF THE HESPERIDES

ITRL 94

GIOVANNI GIOVIANO
PONTANO
✦ ✦ ✦
ECLOGUES

GARDEN OF THE
HESPERIDES

EDITED AND TRANSLATED BY

LUKE ROMAN

THE I TATTI RENAISSANCE LIBRARY
HARVARD UNIVERSITY PRESS
CAMBRIDGE, MASSACHUSETTS
LONDON, ENGLAND
2022

Series design by Dean Bornstein

First printing

*Library of Congress Cataloging-in-Publication Data available from
The Library of Congress at https://lccn.loc.gov/2021051405*

ISBN 978-0-674-27409-9 (cloth : alk. paper)

Contents

꙳꙳꙳

Introduction

⁂

Giovanni Gioviano Pontano (1429–1503) was the leading humanist of Quattrocento Naples, the head of the Neapolitan Academy, and a brilliant humanist Latin poet. He wrote Latin poetry in a range of genres, including didactic, lyric, pastoral, and elegy. He also wrote prose treatises and philosophical dialogues.[1] This volume contains the text and the translation of his *Eclogues* (*Eclogae*) and *Garden of the Hesperides* (*De hortis Hesperidum*), two poetic works written in dactylic hexameters in imitation of ancient pastoral and didactic poetry, respectively, and in particular, of Vergil's *Eclogues* and *Georgics*. The *Eclogues* consist of six poems of varying length on diverse topics set in different places, but predominantly in the Neapolitan countryside. The *Garden of the Hesperides* is a horticultural didactic poem on gardening and the cultivation of citrus trees. The following pages will offer a brief summary of Pontano's life, the broader context of the Neapolitan revival of antiquity, and an introductory discussion of each of the two works featured in the present volume.

Giovanni Pontano was born in Cerreto di Spoleto in Umbria in 1429.[2] His father, Giacomo, was killed in civil conflict while Pontano was still a child, and the family lost all its wealth. Brought up by his mother and his maternal aunt, and subsequently educated in Perugia, Pontano met Alfonso the Magnanimous in 1447 and was brought by Alfonso to Naples in 1448, where he entered into the service of the Aragonese monarchy. Here Pontano opened a school, served as tutor to Aragonese princes, and held high positions of state. Among his many services to the Aragonese, he accompanied King Ferdinand I on an expedition to put down the Barons' Revolt in 1458, participated in a diplomatic mission to

Pope Pius II in 1464, and, as the culminating honor of his career, held the post of head secretary, or "prime minister," to the king in 1486. Pontano's distinguished public career was accompanied by literary accomplishments and success in Neapolitan society. In 1464, Pontano married a young woman from a noble Neapolitan family, Adriana Sassone, and they had three daughters and a son. In terms of literary affiliations, Pontano was associated early on with Antonio Beccadelli, head of the Neapolitan Academy. Later, in 1471, Pontano succeeded Beccadelli as head of the Academy, henceforth known as the Porticus Pontaniana, or Pontano's Academy.[3] Pontano's remarkable successes in his adoptive city were at least partially interrupted by the French invasion of Italy led by King Charles VIII in 1494. Even after the French withdrawal, the Aragonese monarchy never fully recovered its former splendor. Pontano's public career came to an end, and he retreated to his villas and literary pursuits.[4] Pontano also suffered a series of personal losses starting in 1479 with the death of his daughter Lucia and culminating in the closing years of his life: his wife died in 1490, his son-in-law Paolo di Caivano in 1492, and his only son, Lucio, in 1498. The combination of these personal losses and the struggles of the Aragonese monarchy may have contributed to the darker mood of his later poetic works.

A central feature of Pontano's poetry is his adaptation of classical literary motifs to his contemporary Neapolitan world. Pontano imitated a range of poetic modes, including elegiac love poetry and Catullan hendecasyllables.[5] His chief poetic model, however, was Vergil. The two works of poetry included in this volume have Vergilian works as their primary model. Pontano's *Eclogues* imitate Vergil's book of ten eclogues as well as Theocritus, while his *Garden of the Hesperides*, a didactic poem in two books on citrus trees, imitates Vergil's *Georgics* while also drawing from Columella and other ancient didactic works. Especially salient in both works is Pontano's emphasis on Neapolitan locations. The *Eclogues* and

Garden of the Hesperides transfer the literary *loci* of classical pastoral and didactic to the landscapes of the Bay of Naples.

Such innovations in literary geography are related to the sociopolitical circumstances of Aragonese Naples. A major component of the ideology of the Aragonese regime was the revival of antiquity and the promotion of Naples as successor to ancient Rome's political and cultural *imperium*. The Aragonese supported their claims by attracting a stable of top-level humanists, such as Antonio Beccadelli, Lorenzo Valla, Francesco Patrizi, and Pontano himself, who were handsomely rewarded for their association with and services to the Regno.[6] Another major facet of this ideological project was public building. The Aragonese undertook major public building projects with classical associations, including the restoration of the Bolla aqueduct system originally built under classical Rome. The Aragonese monarchs thus deliberately promoted Renaissance Naples as the site of a renewed classicism and restored antiquity.[7] At the same time, Neapolitans also boasted a connection with classical antiquity on the mythic plane. Naples was the site of the tomb of the Siren Parthenope, who drowned herself after her song failed to shipwreck Odysseus' ship. As the land of the Siren, Naples harbored the divine power of song in its very soil.

Pontano's central poetic preoccupations are best understood against this background. Like other Neapolitan humanists, such as Jacopo Sannazaro, Pontano weaves the place-names, natural features, and built structures of Renaissance Naples into a classicizing literary matrix. Repositioning Vergilian poetic genres and places within a Neapolitan topographical framework is an especially notable feature of this humanist project. Pontano's references to the Aragonese villa at Poggioreale furnish a notable example. Designed by Giuliano da Maiano at the behest of Alfonso, duke of Calabria, in 1487, this vast, classicizing villa was built a few miles northeast of Naples at a place called Dogliolo. The villa's gardens included fruit orchards with orange trees as well as splendid fountains.[8] In the opening invocation of the *De hortis Hesperidum*, Pontano mentions the "gardens of Dogliolo" (1.3) in a list of lands and places under the protection of local nymphs. Similarly, in the opening section of Pontano's first eclogue, entitled *Lepidina*, Parthenope, the divine personification of Naples, is depicted bathing "at Dogliolo's spring"" (*Eclogues* 1.30). In both cases, Pontano incorporates into his Vergilian poem an allusion to the Aragonese villa that embodied the regime's aspirations to restore antiquity on Neapolitan soil.

The humanist poet's villa properties furnish a comparable example. In addition to his palazzo on the Via dei Tribunali, Pontano owned a villa on the Vomero hill in the Antignano neighborhood and a villa at Posillipo. In his poetry, Pontano mythologizes these properties as part of his broader strategy of inserting them into the literary matrix of the classical tradition. His property at Antignano is personified as the nymph Antiniana, while his villa at Posillipo becomes the nymph Patulcis.[9] These two topographical nymphs function throughout Pontano's poetry as his personal Muses and divine collaborators. The villas, moreover, were more than just literary symbols. The villa at Antignano was the site of Pontano's citrus orchards, and thus furnished the horticultural corollary of his *Garden of the Hesperides*. The "golden fruit" of this garden brought back to life the legendary gardens of the mythical Hesperides. The villa at Posillipo, like the nearby property of Pontano's fellow humanist Jacopo Sannazaro (1458–1530), was located near the so-called tomb of Vergil, a columbarium tomb at Piedigrotta long mistakenly honored by visitors over the centuries as the site of the classical poet's grave.[10] Sannazaro, whose villa included lemon orchards, also constructed the church of Santa Maria del Parto on his property, which later housed his classicizing tomb monument. Pietro Bembo picked up on the poetic implications of this topographical proximity in an epigram: "Here lies Sincerus [= Sannazaro], closest to Vergil in his poetry as in his tomb."[11] The two humanist poets, like their Aragonese patrons, had a shared interest in citrus orchards, and they celebrated Vergil's sepulchral presence on Neapolitan soil. Gardens, villas, and tombs, for both humanist authors and their Aragonese patrons, formed a nexus of classicizing topographical motifs linking Aragonese Naples with the places and poetry of antiquity.

Just as Pontano's broader poetic project seeks to transfer the prestige of the classical legacy to Aragonese Naples, so too he takes advantage of Vergil's association with Naples in the classical biographical tradition to recast him as a Neapolitan poet. Vergil himself, in his poem's closing *sphragis*, proclaims that he wrote his *Georgics* while in Naples (4.563–64), and the epitaph ascribed to him in the Donatan life identifies Naples as the site of the poet's burial: *nunc me tenet / Parthenope* ("now Parthenope possesses me," *Life of Virgil* 35). Pontano shapes these limited points of contact into a veritable Neapolitan career for Vergil. As Liliana Monti Sabia has argued, Pontano "Neapolitanizes" his revered predecessor, situating the composition of each of Vergil's major works in Naples.[12] Pontano thus becomes Vergil's successor as a poet who moved to Naples permanently after leaving the *patria* of his birth. This Neapolitan genealogy confers, in turn, special significance on these two poems of the land, the *Eclogues* and *Garden of the Hesperides*.

Pontano's Eclogues

Pontano's six eclogues were not originally published as an integral collection (see Note on the Texts).[13] The dating of individual eclogues suggests that Pontano composed them at different times throughout his career.[14] The first eclogue, *Lepidina*, refers to the death of Pontano's daughter in 1479, but not to the death of his wife in 1490; its composition thus probably falls between these two dates. Eclogue 2, *Meliseus*, which focuses on Pontano's mourning of the death of his wife, Adriana, was written sometime after 1490. The occasion of the third eclogue, *Maeon*, is the death of Paolo Attaldi, doctor and member of Pontano's Academy, but we have no secure information about the date of Attaldi's death; recent studies suggest a date of 1496/98.[15] Eclogue 4, *Acon*, alludes to the French invasion and subsequent overthrow of the Aragonese dynasty, and hence may be dated late in Pontano's career, sometime after 1494. *Coryle* has no clear internal indication of dating, but, as suggested by surviving manuscripts, was unfinished and still undergoing revision at the end of Pontano's life. The dramatic date of Eclogue 6, *Quinquennius*, is the fifth birthday of Pontano's son, Lucio, in 1474, but a highly comparable passage in Pontano's late philosophical dialogue *Aegidius* (1501) suggests that this eclogue too may have been written much later, and with retrospective nostalgia, after Lucio's death in 1498.[16] All such indications of dating, however, must be approximate, and, more important, tempered by the awareness that Pontano constantly revised his poems in various phases and only submitted his final corrected autograph manuscripts to his editors near the end of his life.

Pontano's *Eclogues*, then, emerged at different points throughout the humanist's career, and are not all equally bucolic in character. The first four eclogues, however, cohere in their broad outlines, with the definition of pastoral as herdsmen's song in a rural setting. This interest in an idealized rural setting can be understood against the background of broader cultural developments. Quattrocento Italy saw a surge of interest in the aesthetic and ethical value of the countryside and the revival of classical paradigms of rural *otium* (leisure), *secessus* (withdrawal), and villa culture. A vogue for the composition of pastoral poetry formed part of this new interest in the aesthetic possibilities of the countryside. Vergil and Theocritus provided important models, but also the recently rediscovered Calpurnius and Nemesianus. The late medieval and proto-humanist authors Dante, Giovanni del Virgilio, Petrarch, and Boccaccio all wrote Latin pastoral poetry. In the following century, humanists such as Tito Vespasiano Strozzi (1424–1505), Matteo Boiardo (1441–94, Ferrara), Battista Spagnuoli ("Mantuan," 1447–1516), Baldassare Castiglione (1478–1529), Naldo Naldi (1463–1513, Florence), and Jacopo Sannazaro composed pastoral poetry on classical models. The contemporary revival of interest in Statius' *Silvae*, as exemplified by Poliziano's *silva*, entitled *Rusticus*, was a related phenomenon.[17]

Pastoral was a suitable genre for Italian humanists for many reasons.[18] First, according to an interpretation going back to Servius, Vergil's *Eclogues* praised Octavian, and thus pastoral was seen as an appropriate medium for the encomium of princes.[19] Second, the long-standing association between pastoral and allegory provided scope for allegorized autobiography, political commentary, and *epicedia* on the deaths of friends and public figures. The most famous instance of an allegorical reading of pastoral is the interpretation of Vergil's fourth "Messianic" eclogue as a prophecy of the birth of Christ. Furthermore, pastoral was "poetry about poetry," and was especially concerned with the dynamics of competition, imitation, and literary inheritance.[20] For Renaissance humanists involved in the transfer of the classical literary inheritance to modern Italy, the pastoral genre afforded an arena in which to explore their most urgent preoccupations. Finally, pastoral was a genre uniquely focused on the interplay of places, both mythological and real. Italian humanists found in pastoral an ideal literary mode for negotiating the changing meaning of places at the intersection of the real, the mythological, the remembered, and the imagined.

Pontano's *Eclogues* both cohere with these general trends and contribute original elements. Allegory is an especially important feature of Pontano's pastoral world. The herdsman singers within Pontano's pastoral fiction regularly represent members of Pontano's circle, including the poet himself. In Eclogue 2, *Meliseus*, the title character stands for Pontano, mourning his dead wife, Adriana. In inserting himself within his own pastoral realm, Pontano draws on both the centuries-old exegetical tradition that identified Vergil with the herdsman-singer Tityrus and the pastoral allegories of his humanist predecessors such as Petrarch. In Eclogue 3, *Maeon*, the title character refers to Paolo Attaldi, the doctor and humanist colleague of Pontano, while the pastoral interlocutor Syncerius represents Jacopo Sannazaro, also known by his academic name, Actius Sincerus. Both Meliseus and Maeon represent neo-Latin examples of pastoral *epicedion*, as exemplified by the lament for Daphnis in Theocritus' first idyll and Vergil's fifth eclogue.

In Pontano's first eclogue, *Lepidina*, pastoral's allegorical tendencies are combined with the theme of place in a strikingly original way. An ambitious composition divided into seven *pompae* (processions), the eclogue stages the wedding of the Neapolitan river god Sebeto and the siren Parthenope, divine personification of Naples. The divinities who attend the wedding are allegorical representations of the places and natural features of the region, including urban neighborhoods. An encomiastic element informs this scenario: praise of Naples is effectively praise of the magnificence of the Aragonese city, its cultural wealth, and political prestige. As the two focal characters, the shepherdess Lepidina and her husband, Macron, watch the passing processions, they comment on and describe the place-divinities as they pass by. This narrative device allows Pontano to ground the pastoral dialogue in a specific *locus*, as in Vergilian pastoral, even as he opens up a panoramic vision of the topography of the entire region.[21] The poem's overt verbal reminiscences are most frequently Vergilian, and in the epithalamial elements, Catullan. In terms of overall structure, Theocritean pastoral also offers an important precedent. In *Idylls* 15, Theocritus' urban mime on the festival of the Adonia, the lowly dialogue of humble characters similarly facilitates the ecphrastic description of an awe-inspiring public spectacle.

Pontano's *Lepidina* leads the reader on a tour of Neapolitan topography that includes sites associated with the Aragonese monarchy, such as the royal villa at Dogliolo and the fountain of Formiello near Porta Capuana, as well as the places of the poet's own life. Pontano's villa-nymphs, Patulcis and Antiniana, make key appearances,[22] as does the humanist's urban residence in Naples (1.349–55, 395–99). Other passages describe the fearsome personifications of the mountainous and volcanic features of the Bay of Naples, creatures at once sublime and terrifying in appearance (the fifth *pompa*). The seventh and final *pompa* of this most Neapolitan of eclogues reports the words of a place-deity emblematic of Pontano and his poetic achievement: the nymph Antiniana, personification of the site of the humanist's villa at Antignano on the Vomero hill. Speaking in the primeval mythic past, Antiniana voices a prophecy, reminiscent of both Vergil and the song of the *Parcae* in Catullus (64.323–81), regarding the future generations who will extend the Neapolitan lineage of Parthenope and Sebeto. At the culmination of her prophecy of Naples' destiny, she predicts the birth of a great poet: "There will be born one who will come from afar, a stranger, from faraway lands, to these parts, a poor shepherd, with whose words the parched rocks of neighboring Vesuvius will resound" (1.745–47). This poet is Vergil, who, according to Pontano's Neapolitanizing biography, comes to Naples from Mantua as a "stranger" (*advena*) and makes the Campanian landscape resound with his song. Antiniana is not yet finished, however: "There will be born another shepherd, after a long passage of time. He too will be a stranger, but also the sower of his own garden, and he will dare to wear down his tender lip with the reed pipe" (1.757–59). This second shepherd is the work's author himself. Pontano parallels Vergil's praises with his own, employing the Vergilian technique of retrospective prophecy to predict the passing of the pastoral pipes across the centuries to himself, Vergil's Neapolitan successor and competitor.

The sequence of four pastoral poems sent to Aldus, which begins triumphantly with the *Lepidina*, ends on a very different note with the *Acon*, a neo-Ovidian story of transformation: the youth Acon prefers Nape to the Naiads, who therefore poison her out of jealousy; Vertumnus, the Roman god of change and the changing seasons, then transforms her into a turnip (*napus*). This song, cited in the dialogue between Petasillus (broad-brimmed hat) and Saliuncus (Celtic nard), derives from the repertoire of Pontano's pastoral alias, Meliseus. The two speakers are not shepherds (*pastores*), but rather, by another generic innovation, vegetable gardeners (*olitores*),[23] and their discourse is constructed out of references to the garden and its earthy cuisine. The collection ends with a playful rewriting of the closing lines of Vergil's first eclogue, where Tityrus hosts Meliboeus for the evening and offers him a simple shepherd's repast of raw foods to be eaten outdoors on the green grass (1.79–81). Pontano instead brings us into the kitchen of "shaggy-haired Labeo's house grimy with black smoke," who teaches Petasillus and Saliuncus "to mix Falernian [wine] with asparagus and add some pepper, to mix uncooked pear with *boleti*, to add a handful of wild mint, some garlic, and ground thyme, and last of all, to drizzle olive oil into the pan when it starts to sizzle and complain" (4.193–98). Labeo's cooking lesson ends the poem on a meticulously chosen low note, the pan's unmelodic sizzling as the vegetable gardeners learn a new recipe in his smoke-stained dwelling. Pontano once again plays boldly with the possibilities of the genre, offering up new and unexpected combinations of ingredients to his knowing readers.

A similar spirit of innovation characterizes the two final eclogues *not* included in the Aldine sequence, *Coryle* and *Quinquennius*. *Coryle* consists of a hexameter frame and an inset narrative in elegiac couplets — a combination unprecedented in the traditions of Latin poetry. The framing segment tells how the nymph Coryle was transformed into a hazel tree (*corylus*) by the witch Abelle. In the inset narrative, Antiniana, Pontano's villa-nymph, then tells the hazel-tree Coryle how Cupid, asleep by a river bank and vulnerable after being abandoned by the nymph Sebethis, was disarmed, bound, and humiliated by the famous mistresses of classical love poetry, Nemesis, Corinna, Lesbia, and Cynthia. He was then saved by "Ariadne," the poetic alias of Pontano's wife, Adriana Sassone, who is so beautiful that Cupid momentarily mistook her for his mother, Venus. This experimental poem was not included in the pastoral sequence sent to Aldus, and may have been still under revision at the time of Pontano's death.[24]

The final eclogue, *Quinquennius*, has no connection with the pastoral world of herdsmen or the countryside. This dialogue between a "five-year old boy" (*quinquennius*) and his mother, Pelvina — representing Pontano's son (Lucio) and his wife (Adriana) — closely recalls the themes and spirit of Pontano's *Naeniae*, a sequence of elegiac "lullabies" (*ninne nanne*) in the second book of his *De amore coniugali*.[25] Here, the boy first asks about the fearsome sounds of a thunderstorm, and his mother explains that this is the sound of the gods roasting chestnuts over the fire. Then, the conversation turns to the figure of Orcus, a kind of bogeyman who punishes little boys for bad behavior, and finally, to a "benevolent spirit" who "takes care of all things" (6.37–38). Pontano's poem traces the young child's first intimations of divinity, but does so gently and with a graceful naturalism, associating the child's understanding of divine benevolence with his favorite treats (6.39–48). Pontano paints a delicate portrait of the emergence of religious awareness within the intimate rituals of family life. Such a dialogue, of course, has little to do with Vergil's pastoral world of shepherds and flocks. Yet it is not so far from the spirit of Theocritean mime.[26] In *Quinquennius*, as in the *Lepidina*, Pontano seems to be calling the pastoral genre back to its earlier diversity of form and subject matter. He is also infusing it with his own distinctive set of poetic concerns: love, pleasure, the family, and the presence of the divine in the natural world.

The De hortis Hesperidum

Pontano's De hortis Hesperidum (Garden of the Hesperides) is a Vergilian didactic poem in two books on the cultivation of citrus fruit, including oranges, lemons, and citrons.[27] Pontano's correspondence suggests that he was still revising the De hortis Hesperidum in the closing years of his life before sending a final autograph copy to Aldus. The passage on the lemon groves at Jacopo Sannazaro's villa at Mergellina refers to his choice to follow his patron Frederick of Aragon into exile in 1501 (2.297–301); the poet twice refers to his wife's death in 1490 (1.322–26; 2.41–42); and the poem is dedicated to Francesco Gonzaga of Mantua with specific reference to his victory over the French in 1495 at the battle of Fornovo. While these references cohere with a late dating of the poem, Antonietta Iacono has argued that both Pontano's and the Aragonese interest in citrus fruit goes back much earlier, and that the poem had a long gestation period.[28] The dedication to Francesco Gonzaga, on this understanding, was added later in the process of the poem's composition.

The so-called didactic mode was not clearly or formally defined as a genre in antiquity, and in meter and scope of ambition was comparable to heroic epos. In modern criticism, the term didactic refers to works in which the poetic speaker takes on an instructional role and tone, and which treat in a quasi-systematic matter some technical subject matter. While the topics of didactic instruction are potentially infinite, agriculture and astronomy are recurrent areas of focus, and Quattrocento humanist authors gravitated toward these subjects. Basinio da Parma's Astronomicon libri and Lorenzo Bonincontri's *De rebus coelestibus* exemplify astronomical didactic, while Ludovico Lazzarelli's poem on silkworms (*Opusculum de bombyce*) recalls Vergil's bees.[29] In general, neo-Latin poets were slower to take up didactic than pastoral, and despite these earlier Quattrocento efforts, Pontano's three didactic poems — *Urania* (five books, astrology), *Meteororum liber* (celestial phenomena, one book), and *De hortis Hesperidum* — were the first to appear in print (Venice, 1505, Aldus Manutius).

Pontano is the founding figure of a neo-Latin didactic tradition that combines classical literary conventions with modern technical and scientific knowledge. The most important classical model of Pontano's *De hortis Hesperidum* is Vergil's *Georgics*. Vergil does not systematically treat the topic of gardening but alludes to it in a famous digression: "I remember (*memini*) that I saw under the towers of the Oebalian citadel, where the dark Galaesus waters the yellowing crops, a Corycian old man (*Corycium . . . senem*)" (4.125–27). Vergil's old man is a gardener, who leads a self-sufficient existence in the countryside. At the close of the passage, Vergil returns again to the theme of memory. Protesting that he does not have sufficient space to discuss gardening in depth, he leaves it as a topic for later writers: "I pass over these matters and leave them to be remembered by others after me (*praetereo atque aliis post me memoranda relinquo*)" (4.148). In the next century, Columella took Vergil up on this hint, addressing the partially omitted subject of gardens in the tenth versified book of his *De re rustica*. This dynamic of continuation, building on memories of a prior author, is one that deeply informs the dynamic of humanist imitation in general and Pontano's imitation of Vergilian didactic in particular. At the same time, humanist authors were not content simply to continue the work of their predecessors, but sought to innovate and surpass their models, combining memories of previous poets with exciting new subject matter. Pontano, in his *De hortis Hesperidum*, at once continues and strives to surpass the work of Vergil and Columella by expanding the scope of didactic garden poetry to include orange and lemon trees: such fruit, not mentioned by classical authors, represent wholly new material.[30]

There is some uncertainty, however, as to exactly which fruit is to be seen as the prime focus of Pontano's poem. Some scholars have assumed that Pontano is writing about the citron (*citrus*) — the one type of citrus tree known to classical authors and therefore furnished with a classical Latin word — but that fails to explain Pontano's separate and distinct use of the term *citrius*.[31] The poem's title in the Aldine 1505 edition is *De hortis Hesperidum sive de cultu citriorum* (On the Garden of the Hesperides, or, On the cultivation of *citrii*/orange trees), and *De hortis Hesperidum* 2.180–217 is subtitled *Quo differat citrius a citro* (How the *citrius* differs from the *citrus*). The physical traits and differences described by Pontano do seem to correspond to the differences between orange (*citrius*) and citron (*citrus*) trees, respectively. Likewise, lines 2.52–179 ("The citron [*citro*] and its cultivation") are devoted to the citron in particular, just as 2.218–308 are devoted to the lemon ("Lemons [*limonibus*] and their cultivation"). Finally, in two separate passages, Pontano discusses the difference between the sweet and the sour *citrius* (1.336–73, 2.432–99) — a discussion that makes most sense if he is talking about sweet and sour varieties of orange. Pontano, therefore, appears to have invented a new noun derived from the adjectival form *citrius*/*citreus* ("of or pertaining to the citrus"), meaning "orange."[32] Nonetheless, it is not always fully clear when Pontano is referring to orange trees and when to citrus trees in general.

Pontano seems to have anticipated such confusion, when, in the section on grafting, he declares that the different forms of citrus "are not wholly separate species" (2.316). Citrus is one, large, extended family, and its individual branches are related to each other (2.311–22). Under these conditions, perhaps a degree of uncertainty is inevitable. Yet, despite such ambiguities, and consequent difficulties for the translator, there are strong reasons for identifying the orange tree as the main focus of Book 1, and the most insistently foregrounded kind of tree in the work as a whole. First, the orange was a symbol of the Aragonese monarchy. Oranges were cultivated in the splendid gardens at Poggioreale, and the fruit was linked to the monarchy by an attractive play on words (*arangio/Aragonese*).[33] Furthermore, and perhaps most important, oranges satisfy the criterion of literary originality, since, unlike citrons, they were unknown to classical authors. In an interesting passage in Pontano's late dialogue *Aegidius*, the interlocutors are made to emphatically confirm that Pontano's innovative subject matter in his *De hortis Hesperidum* had been "treated by no one previously," and specifically, had not been the subject of any serious investigation by members of the Roman and Florentine Academies.[34]

Pontano's innovative poetic subject matter is accompanied by audacious supplements to the mythic tradition. Pontano recasts the death of Adonis to provide an origins story for orange tree cultivation in Italy. Altering the Ovidian version of Adonis' transformation, and drawing on other Ovidian plant/tree metamorphoses, such as those of Daphne and Hyacinthus, Pontano has Venus transform the dead Adonis into an orange tree to serve as a perpetual memorial of her grief (1.68–101). Oranges thus become the golden fruit of the Hesperides and are subsequently transported to Italian shores by the wandering Hercules (1.102–24). Significantly, the hero first brings them to the towns of Formia and Amalfi in the Bay of Naples region. In a striking reinvention of tradition, Pontano's poem on gardening inserts into classical mythology the origins story of a fruit of which classical authors made no mention. Pontano's bold emphasis on novelty is linked with the Renaissance interest in geographical exploration. In one passage, Pontano refers to the expedition to India undertaken by the Portuguese explorer Vasco da Gama and his importation of sweet oranges (1.346–63). Tracing the path around the coast of Africa with a series of rare neo-Latin toponyms, Pontano notes that Da Gama and his crew, sailing to "unknown places," were struck by "the novelty of things" (*rerum novitate*, 1.354).[35] Pontano's poem reveals a wide-ranging vision of space and time: he recasts classical mythology to account for modern orange and lemon groves and writes a history of citrus fruits that spans the known world.

Even as Pontano's poetic geography broadens its horizons to include Africa and India, Neapolitan places still hold center stage. In the proem to Book 1, Pontano addresses the nymphs and Naiads of the region, asking them to weave fresh garlands for his great predecessor Vergil. He then turns to his Muse, Urania, who inspired his ambitious astrological poem of the same title, and seeks inspiration for the present poem:

> Now, may I find delight in leisure and gardens, in fertile fields and the shores made fruitful by Amalfi's forests, in the glory of the citrus stock, the memorial of the Hesperides sisters, which is your delight as well. Let Thessalian Tempe delight Phoebus, let laurel trees please your brother's heart; may *your* heart be captured by Sebethian citron trees — famous groves — and those which our Antiniana cultivates in her retreat. I sing: you, goddess, inspire and stand by me as I sing, while the age-old rites of the holy bard are renewed. See, charming Patulcis awaits you by the flowing stream. (1.36–45)

Pontano here replaces the emblem (Apollonian laurel) and geography (Thessalian Tempe) of classical poetry with his own modern emblem (the citrus tree)[36] and the geography of contemporary Naples, which includes local places such as Amalfi, the Neapolitan river Sebeto, and Pontano's personified villas, Antiniana and Patulcis. The final lines of the proem honor Francesco Gonzaga, ruler of Mantua, who, through his victory at Fornovo, gives hope to Italian cities, and, like a modern Hercules, drives out enemies of the native land.[37]

The proem to Book 2 includes the same constellation of ideas: Pontano's villa-nymphs, Antiniana and Patulcis, as neo-Latin deities of poetic inspiration; the city and surrounding lands of Naples; the poet Vergil as model and revered presence in Naples; and Francesco Gonzaga as victor and addressee (2.1–51). Here, Pontano also includes explicit references both to Vergil's so-called tomb at Piedigrotta and to the poet's Mantuan origins (2.15–22). These geographical coordinates are indicative of the political and poetic affinities that underlie the connection between Mantua and Naples. Pontano also pays homage to the region north of Mantua, and in particular the town of Verona, birthplace of the poet Catullus, and the Lago di Garda, which includes the island of Sirmione (Latin *Sirmio*), where Catullus owned a villa.[38] Here, too, according to Pontano, the orange tree flourishes, despite the northern climate. He suggests that this exceptional horticultural largesse is Venus' way of honoring Catullus, one of the great love poets of classical antiquity. Poetry coincides once again with citrus. In a modern reprise of the same motif, Pontano praises the lemon groves at the villa of his fellow Neapolitan humanist poet Jacopo Sannazaro, at Mergellina (2.289–308).

The recurrent implication is that citrus fruit and poetry have shared qualities: they are beautiful and redolent with sensual pleasures; they are the products of skilled labor and cultivation; and they are intimately linked with their land of origins. Fruit and trees in classical poetry often have metapoetic significance, and in Vergil's *Georgics*, there is a recurrent parallel between the farmer's *labor* and the poet's: both toil relentlessly in the effort to impose order on their respective worlds. In the closing sections of Book 1, Pontano addresses topics such as "the method of caring for a garden's beauty," "the arrangement of orange trees," and "topiary." A further parallel between poetry and citrus orchards, in Pontano's conception, is the capacity to preserve memory. He repeatedly characterizes the orange tree as a memorial (*monumenta*) of Venus' love and grief for the dead Adonis (1.38, 67, 76, 177, 564). While individual trees are mortal, the species endures over time as a transgenerational collectivity, providing a perpetual reminder of the beauty of the dead Adonis. Such perpetuity comes up as an explicit topic at the end of *De hortis Hesperidum*, Book 1, in the song of the Parcae, or Fates (1.526–80), which, like Antiniana's song in the *Lepidina*, imitates the prophecy of the Parcae in Catullus' Poem 64 (64.323–81). Pontano narrates how the usually pitiless Parcae felt empathy for Venus' grief and, in an extraordinary overturning of their classical identity, attempted to spin the threads of destiny in reverse (*retro*, 1.534) in order to bring Adonis back to life. Venus refused to allow this violation of destiny, instead transforming her dead lover into the orange tree (1.539–40). Whereas, in the Ovidian transformation, Adonis takes the delicate, ephemeral form of the wind-blown anemone (10.717–39), Pontano's plant transformation emphasizes perpetuity and endurance over time, not least through the tree's evergreen foliage: "it is an everlasting species . . . and its beauty is truly everlasting" (1.527–28).

Pontano himself suffered personal losses that left their mark on his poetry, and thus the orange grove as memorial of love and grief (1.75–76) has a further layer of autobiographical meaning. In general, his later works display an increased awareness of monumental commemoration and the status of poems as *monumenta*. This interest extends to architectural monument building. Following the death of his wife in 1490, Pontano began to build a chapel on the Via dei Tribunali in Naples, which still stands today, that was at least partly designed to be in his wife's honor. The structure is classicizing in style and reminiscent of a Roman tomb monument.[39] A comparable instance of the monumental commemoration of love and grief finds poignant expression in a digression in the *De hortis Hesperidum*, where Pontano recalls how he and his wife once worked side by side in the citrus orchard of their villa. He misses her intensely in his current unhappy circumstances, but the space of the garden at Antignano reminds him of their happy times together when she was still alive. In a moving passage, the poet remembers gathering oranges with this wife in their orchard: "My wife too (I recall) was standing near, embracing me, her husband, as I picked flowers for making Idalian perfume and Venus' most delicate gifts; then she sat down in the soft grass and sang and played sweet games with me" (1.318–21). Pontano concludes by addressing his wife: "console me as I lament and gather with me, as we did once, the blossoms of the orange trees" (334–35). With implicit allusion to the epyllion at the close of the fourth book of Vergil's *Georgics* (4.314–558), Pontano assumes the role of the master singer, Orpheus, grieving for his lost wife. At the same time, he also resembles the productive cultivator Aristaeus, who created the "immortal species" (*Georgics* 4.208) of bees from a dead carcass (4.281–314, 540–58). Both gardening and poetry are implicated in the cycle of death and new life.

If Pontano's gardening parallels and stands for his poetic achievement, then it is appropriate that the culminating words of the *De hortis Hesperidum* proclaim his poetic triumph through the figure of his garden villa at Antignano, which, he declares, surpasses the famous gardens and vineyards of antiquity:

> Neither may the Naiads, in return for so great a labor, deny me a green garland made from foliage of willow, nor may my cultivated Antiniana deny me her retreats, with which she outstrips the vineyards of Hermus, the rose beds of Paestum, and the palm groves that produce the fruit of Idumea. (2.577–81)

Pontano's target of emulation, as a series of literary allusions makes clear, is Vergil. It is Vergil who mentions "rose beds of Paestum" in the gardening digression in the *Georgics* (2.118–19), and Vergil who refers to "Idumean" palms (*Georgics* 3.12) in a passage outlining his plans to build an (implicitly literary) temple in honor of Octavian.[40] The humanist's Neapolitan villa-muse thus surpasses the literary and horticultural riches of the classical past.

"Did you know Meliseus, whom Phoebus loved, to whom Antiniana was dear beyond all others?" Thus Giano Anisio, an academician and younger follower of Pontano, recalls his dead master in a touching poetic reminiscence.[41] While Anisio could still climb the slopes of the Vomero hill to visit the villa that belonged to the humanist, today there is only a plaque commemorating Pontano's residence there, an apartment building with shops, and a lively market piazza. Pontano's house on the Via dei Tribunali is also gone, as is the sprawling, once splendid Aragonese villa at Poggioreale. The traces of these buildings remain only in antiquarian writings such as the meandering and melancholy essays of the twentieth-century Neapolitan philosopher and man of letters Benedetto Croce.[42] Such physical disappearances were accompanied by the eclipse of the previously towering literary reputation of Pontano. The rise of the vernacular, and later, Romantic ideas of poetic authenticity doomed Renaissance Latin poetry to a long exile in the literary wilderness.[43] The current revival of interest in the Latin writings of the Italian humanists, encouraged in no small part by the *I Tatti Renaissance Library* editions, allows us to reconsider, and perhaps even take seriously, Pontano's boldest ambition: to rival antiquity.

This book owes several debts of gratitude. James Hankins' comments and keen editorial eye have improved the volume immeasurably. Julia Gaisser, with remarkable generosity and patience, has (again!) saved me from numerous inaccuracies and infelicities, while her deep knowledge of Pontano enriched the notes *passim*.

The staff at the Biblioteca Provinciale S. G. Capone di Avellino kindly permitted me to examine and photograph their manuscript of the *De hortis Hesperidum*. While it is traditional to take personal responsibility for remaining errors, I prefer Pietro Summonte's request to the friendly reader in his 1512 edition of Pontano's *De Fortuna:* "if there is anything I have omitted, please attribute it only to the many demands on my attention."

NOTES

1. Articles on Pontano by the authoritative scholar of his poetry, Liliana Monti Sabia, are collected in Monti Sabia, Monti, and Germano 2010. A selection of his poetic works, including Latin text, facing Italian translation, and commentary may be found in Arnaldi, Gualdo Rosa, and Monti Sabia 1964. Modern texts of the poetry include Oeschger 1948 and Soldati 1902. Tilly 2020 was published online (April 2021), too late to be considered in this edition. Note also Dennis 2006; Gaisser 2012, 2020; and Roman 2014.

2. On Pontano's life, see Pèrcopo 1938; Kidwell 1991; and Monti Sabia 1998. For a more detailed account of Pontano's life and works than in the present volume, see Roman 2014, vii–x.

3. On Pontano and the Neapolitan Academy, see Furstenberg-Levi 2016.

4. The story, in Francesco Guicciardini's *Storia d'Italia* (II.3), that Pontano fell into disgrace with his Aragonese patrons because he received the French into the city has been persuasively rejected by Monti Sabia 1998, 24ff.

5. See Dennis 2006, Gaisser 1993.

6. See Bentley 1987.

7. On Neapolitan antiquarianism and *all'antica* architecture, see, for example, De Divitiis 2012, 2015; on Naples and antiquity, Hughes and Buongiovanni 2015.

8. See Modesti 2014, who reconstructs the architecture of the villa with new evidence.

9. Antiniana and Patulcis often appear in tandem in Pontano's poetry: *Eridanus* 1.40.37–38, 2.22, 2.31.39; *De amore coniugali* 2.5.5, 32; 3.1.32; 3.3 (*passim*); 3.4 (*passim*); *De hortis Hesperidum* 1.42, 1.45, 2.14, 579; *Urania* 5.955; *De tumulis* 1.1.8, 1.18.8; *Baiae* 2.15.13, 2.24.12, 2.37.12; *Lyra* 3.8, 3.10, 4.4, 6.2; *Meteororum liber* 1608. The site, but not any substantial structural remains, of Pontano's villa at Antignano can be seen today at Via Annella di Massimo 9: Kidwell 1991, 104–5; Pèrcopo 1921. On Pontano's urban palazzo, see De Divitiis 2012, 11. The precise site of Pontano's villa on Posillipo is not known, but, according to Pèrcopo 1921, was located in an area of Posillipo called Paturci or *Paturcium* in postclassical Latin (3), hence perhaps "Patulcis." Pontano also had a villa on the island of Ischia: De Divitiis 2010, 111n10.

10. See Trapp 1984.

11. *Carminum libellus* XL, in Chatfield 2005, 104: *hic ille Maroni / Syncerus Musa proximus, ut tumulo.* On Santa Maria del Parto and Sannazaro's villa and tomb, see Croce 1948, 197–217. On the lemon orchards, see Pontano *De hortis Hesperidum* 2.289–308.

12. Monti Sabia 1983. See Pontano's portrayal of Vergil in *Eridanus* 1.14 in Roman 2014.

13. On Pontano's *Eclogae*, see Monti Sabia 1973; Casanova-Robin 2006 and 2011; Tufano 2015. On the dubious pastoral status of the *Quinquennius* and *Coryle*, see Monti Sabia 1973, 8–12.

14. On questions of dating, see Casanova-Robin 2011, xliii–xlv; Tufano 2015, 15–18.

15. See Tilly 2020, 72n195.

16. See Monti Sabia 1973, 134. For the *Aegidius* passage, see Gaisser 2020, section 13.

17. See Fantazzi 2004.

18. Wilson-Okamura 2010, 47–76, offers a good overview. An older monograph, Grant 1965, still retains value.

19. Wilson-Okamura 2010, 56–58.

20. Ibid., 66–69.

21. See Tufano 2015, 29–32.

22. For Antiniana, see *Eclogae* 1.677–87 and the seventh *pompa, passim*. Patulcis appears as a character in the sixth *pompa*. For Formiello, as represented by the nymph Formellis, see *Eclogae* 1.311–26 and n. 30.

23. On this innovation, see Tufano 2015, 21, 31, 39.

24. Monti Sabia 1973, 9–12.

25. *De amore coniugali* 2.8–19 in the edition of Roman 2014.

26. Monti Sabia 1983, 8.

27. On the *De hortis Hesperidum*, see Iacono 2015; Figliuolo 2009; Nuovo 1998; Tateo 1960; Caruso 2013; Ludwig 1982.

28. Iacono 2015, 3. Pontano also corresponded with Gonzaga's wife, Isabella d'Este, who shared Pontano's interests in classical literature and citrus fruit (Caruso 2013, 12).

29. On humanist didactic poetry, see Ludwig 1982; Roellenbleck 1975; Ijsewijn and Sacré 1998, 38–45.

30. On Pontano's claims of poetic originality, see Caruso 2013, 20; Iacono 2015, 11.

31. For the question of the identity of the fruit, see Caruso 2013, 13, 15; Iacono 2015, 1, 39n2.

32. Ludwig 1982, 107, suggests that Pontano originally only planned one book on orange trees, then later added Book 2 with a more wide-ranging discussion of oranges, lemons, and citrons. This might explain some of the confusion as to his precise subject matter.

33. Iacono 2015, 6.

34. See Caruso 2013, 13–15 and *Aegidius* 26 in Gaisser 2020.

35. See Monti Sabia 1993 and my comments on this passage.

36. Cf. Caruso 2013, 20.

37. See Caruso 2013, 11–12.

38. *De hortis Hesperidum* 1.209–31. For Sirmio, see Catullus 31.

39. For the Cappella dei Pontano, see De Divitiis 2012. The structure's resemblance to a Roman tomb monument is discussed ibid., 2–3.

40. "Hermus" refers to the Vomero hill, but also, implicitly, the river Hermus, praised in antiquity for its gold deposits: see on *De hortis Hesperidum* 2.580n42.

41. *Et, nosti Meliseum, inquit, quem Phoebus amavit, / cui cara ante omnes Antiniana fuit?* (*De Antiniano colle*, 53–54). See Pèrcopo 1921, 6.

42. See especially the essays collected in *Storie e leggende Napoletane* (Croce 1948).

43. The arguments of Celenza 2004 regarding a "lost Italian Renaissance" apply perhaps especially to Renaissance Latin poetry.

[JOANNIS JOVIANI PONTANI
ECLOGAE]

GIOVANNI GIOVIANO PONTANO
ECLOGUES

: I :

Lepidina

Cuius pompae septem.

Collocutores Macron et Lepidina.

Macron

Et gravida es, Lepidina, et onus grave languida defers,
Obbam lactis et haec fumanti farta canistro;
Hac, agedum, viridi paulum requiesce sub umbra,
Declinat sol dum rapidus desaevit et aestus.

Lepidina

5 En lactis tibi sinum atque haec simul oscula trado;
Umbra mihi haec veteres (memor es) iam suscitat ignes;
O coniux mihi care, Macron, redde altera, Macron.

Macron

Hic mihi tu teneras nudasti prima papillas,
Hic, Lepidina, mihi suspiria prima dedisti;
10 Tunc Macron, Lepidina, tibi, Lepidina Macroni.

Lepidina

Has inter frondes virgultaque nota latebas,
Cum tibi prima rosam, primus mihi fraga tulisti.

Macron

Hic 'Macron,' Lepidina, 'meus' me prima vocasti,
Et primus 'mea,' te alternans, 'Lepidina' vocavi.

2

: I :

Lepidina

An eclogue in seven processions.

Speakers: Macron and Lepidina.[1]

Macron

You are pregnant, Lepidina, and, fainting, carry a heavy burden, a
pitcher of milk and these sausages in a steaming basket.[2] Come,
rest a little while in this green shade, until the blazing sun begins
to sink and the heat ceases to rage.[3]

Lepidina

Here, I offer you a bowl of milk along with these kisses; this shade 5
is already wakening my flames of old (you remember, yes?): O
Macron, my dear spouse, give me kisses in return.

Macron

Here for the first time you bared your tender breasts for me; here,
Lepidina, you gave me your first sighs. Then, Lepidina, Macron 10
was yours, and Lepidina Macron's.

Lepidina

Amid this foliage and this familiar thicket you used to hide, when
I first brought you a rose and you first brought me strawberries.

Macron

It was here, Lepidina, that you first called me "My Macron," and I
first called you, in response, "My Lepidina."

Lepidina

15 Viximus ex illo gemini sine lite columbi,
     Nox socios vidit, socios lux; oscula iunge
     Mutua, sic gemini servant in amore columbi.

Macron

     Illa, uxor, memini nunc, oscula prima fuere:
     Nostra tuis, tua labra meis haesere, diuque
20 Spiritus alterno huc illuc se miscuit ore.
     Tunc Orcus si nos una rapuisset, amantum
     Una futura anima, una etiam simul umbra futura.

Lepidina

     Quod felix faustumque omen sit! Reice, coniux,
     Hirsutum hunc thalamis, thalami sint omnia fausta,
25 Parthenope thalamo nanque est dignissima fausto.

Macron

     Hirsuti horripilique absint! Age, candida, an ipso
     Visa viro virgo est, heroe et coniuge, digna?

Lepidina

     O Macron, mea cura Macron, illi alba ligustra
     Concedant, collata illi sint nigra colostra.
30 Delioli ad fontem sola ac sine teste lavabat;
     Vidi ego, vidit Anas: viso candore puellae,
     Qui niger ante fuit, nunc est nitidissimus ales,
     Et mihi tum subitus crevit per pectora candor:
     Ipse vides, niveas cerne has sine labe papillas.

Lepidina

We have lived since that time like two doves, without quarrel; 15
night has seen us together, day has seen us together; give me kisses
in return for mine, as two doves are wont to do in love.

Macron

Those were our first kisses, as I now recall, my wife. My lips clung
to yours, yours to mine, and for a long time our breath mingled, 20
now here, now there, in one another's mouths. If Orcus had
snatched us away together at that moment, we two lovers there
would have been united as one soul, one shade.[4]

Lepidina

May the omen be a happy and propitious one! Cast this shaggy
monster out of the wedding celebration, my spouse. Let all marriage omens be propitious, for Parthenope is most worthy of a 25
propitious marriage.[5]

Macron

Shaggy and bristly-haired beasts be gone! Tell me, beautiful wife,
did the maiden seem worthy of having a demigod as husband?[6]

Lepidina

O Macron, Macron my love, white privets would yield before her,
first milk would be black compared to her. At Dogliolo's spring, 30
she bathed alone, hidden from sight. But I saw her, Anas saw her:
he who before was black, now that he has seen the girl's brilliant
whiteness, has become a bird of purest white, and in my heart a
sudden brightness grew.[7] You yourself see it: gaze upon these im-
maculate snow-white breasts.

Macron

35 Quin haec candentes, lux o mea, pascua tauros
Quod nec sueta ferunt, nostrae sunt munera nymphae.
Ipse tuas, mea lux, teneo foveoque papillas,
Nec liquido cedunt argento aut pondere plumbo.
Fige oculos in me, coniux mea, qui mihi lucent
40 Et lychnum et quod nec nigricante cicendula nocte;
Parthenope anne aliis, anne his dea fulget ocellis?

Lepidina

Magnetem gerit illa oculis stellamque supremam:
Venerit ad litus, trahit ad sua lumina pisces,
Iverit in silvas, trahit ad spectacula cervos,
45 Illicet indomiti surgunt ad proelia tauri;
Verterit illa oculos in quem iuvenemve senemve,
Ille perit: miseris haec crescit amantibus error.

Macron

Me miserum, ne oculos in me quoque vertat et ipse
Avellar procul his, procul ah, Lepidina, lacertis!

Lepidina

50 Ne, coniux, ne, care, time; nam sedula mater
Hoc docuit, ter te ut levi pro limine postis
Amplectar, ter rapta tibi simul oscula iungam,
Et dicam: 'Meus es'; tenerum quoque eringion ore
Ferre dedit, dedit atque ederae cum fronde racemum
55 Ferre sinu et geminis te noctu onerare lacertis;
Neu limis, mea lux, dominam spectaris ocellis,
Praesertim si blanda pedem nudarit; ibi illa

Macron

Nay, light of my life, if these pastures bring forth gleaming white   35
bulls contrary to their custom, it is the gift of our nymph. As for
me, my light, I hold in my hands and caress your breasts, which
yield neither to silver in brightness nor to gold in weight. Fix your
eyes on me, my wife, your eyes that shine more brightly for me
than a lamp or a firefly in the dark of night. Do the goddess Par-   40
thenope's eyes shine like yours, or in a different way?

Lepidina

She has a magnet in her eyes, and the loftiest star. If she comes to
the shore, she attracts fish toward her eyes. If she goes into the
forest, she draws deer to come see her; immediately, untamed bulls   45
rise up to fight. If she turns her eyes onto some man, young or
old, he dies of love; this girl lives and thrives to make poor lovers'
wits go astray.

Macron

Alas, wretched me! May she not turn her eyes also on me, may I
not be plucked far away, ah far, Lepidina, from these arms!

Lepidina

Do not be afraid, my dear husband; for my solicitous mother   50
taught me this: I should embrace you three times before the
smooth threshold of the door, three times give you kisses at the
same time, and say: "you are mine." She also gave me a tender
thistle to carry in my mouth and a grape cluster with a leaf of ivy
to carry on my breast, and she told me to make you feel the weight   55
of both my arms at night. Do not, my light, gaze upon our mistress with sideways glance, especially if she enticingly bares her

Retia tendit et insidias parat et fovet ignem:
Quae mihi frater Acon, soror et soror altera dixit.

Macron

60   Haec eadem mihi Naretas et amicus Omason,
Quin maiora ferunt: siccat dum nympha capillum
Ad speculam et niveae ludunt sine veste papillae,
Vidit et: 'O' dixit Saliceni filius 'alis
Utar et ad celsam pennis ferar ipse fenestram!'
65   Annuit et placidis risit dea dulcis ocellis:
Ille volat, celsam pennis petit inde fenestram.
Dic, mea, dic, formosa, canit dum nympha per aestum,
Audierisne deam?

Lepidina

Ad sepem tum forte latebam,
Cum canere inciperet: atrox hic dente pilaster
70   Latrat; ibi ipsa fuga sepem insidiasque reliqui.
Invidia (sic Nicla refert) philomela recessit,
At circum attonitae stupuere ad carmina nymphae.
Ipsa quidem canit (at venti posuere silentes
Strataque pacati requierunt murmura ponti):
75   'Exoptat messemque sator frugemque colonus,
Ver ales, carum virgo desponsa maritum;
Vitis in arboribus, ederae pro rupibus altis,
Coniugis in cupidis gaudet nova nupta lacertis;
Irriguum sitiunt fontem sata, pabula rorem,
80   Nupta sitit socii lusus et gaudia lecti.'
Haec dea. Surgamus, meus hoc, age, personat Hymen.
Pompa venit celebresque vocant Hymenaeon ad aedes.

foot. There she lays out those nets of hers, prepares traps, and kindles fire. My brother Acon, my sister, and another sister told me these things.

Macron

These same things Naretas and his friend Omason told me—nay 60
even greater things: while the nymph dried her hair at the mirror
and her snow-white breasts frolicked without clothing, the son of
Salicenus saw her and said: "O that I might use wings and be
borne on their feathers up to the high window!" The goddess nod- 65
ded her approval and laughed sweetly with gentle eyes. He flew up,
and reached the high window by flapping his wings. Tell, me, my
love, tell me, when the beautiful nymph sang in the summer, did
you hear the goddess?

Lepidina

Once, as it happened, I was hiding by a hedge when she began to
sing. A fierce-fanged dog started barking.[8] I left the hedge and hid- 70
ing place behind in flight. Because of jealousy (so Nicla recounts),
the nightingale flew off. But all around, the astonished nymphs
gaped in amazement at the songs. Indeed, she herself sang (but
the winds fell silent and still, and the roaring of the pacified sea
grew calm and quiet): "The sower yearns for the harvest, the 75
farmer for the crop, the bird for the spring, the betrothed maiden
for her beloved husband. The vine delights in the trees, ivy in the
high rocks, the newly wedded bride in the desirous embrace of her
mate. The crops thirst for the irrigating stream, pastures for dew,
the bride for the games and delights of the shared bed." Such 80
things the goddess sang. Let us arise: this song—come, see—it is
my Hymen that makes this song resound. The procession is arriving, and a crowd of celebrants is calling Hymenaeus to the house.[9]

Pompa Prima

Mares ac foeminae e rure proficiscentes alternis concinunt.

Foeminae

Sperne tuas salices et myrto tempora cinge,
Desere septa, puer, nanque urbs tua gaudia servat.

Mares

85 Pone tuos fastus faciles atque indue mores,
Parthenope, et quid amor, quid sint connubia cura.

Foeminae

Disce, puer, thalamo lusus et coniuge dignos:
Lusus amat thalamos et amant sua ludicra lectum.

Mares

Parce, puella, viro nimium pugnare volenti:
90 Lis thalamis aliena et habent sua foedera lecti.

Foeminae

Est nigris nova nupta oculis, est nigra capillis,
Spirat Acidalios et toto corpore flores.

First Procession

Men and women, arriving from the country, sing in alternation.

Women

Scorn your willows, and garland your forehead with myrtle; forsake your pastures, boy, for the city holds delights in store for you.[10]

Men

Put aside your disdain and assume a more compliant manner,   85
Parthenope, and concern yourself with what love is, what marriage is.

Women

Learn, boy, the games worthy of bedroom and spouse. The bedroom is dear to play; the bed is dear to the bed's games.

Men

Refrain, girl, from fighting too much with the man who desires
you. Quarrelling does not belong in bedrooms, and beds are gov-   90
erned by treaties.

Women

The new bride has black eyes, has black hair, and breathes forth
the perfume of Acidalian flowers from her whole body.[11]

Mares

Et roseo iuvenis ore est roseisque labellis,
Stillat Acidalium roseo et de pectore rorem.

Foeminae

95 Intactum florem maturaque poma legenti
Servat in occultis virgo iam nubilis hortis.

Mares

Poma manu matura leget floremque recentem
Rore novo iuvenis, tenera mulcebit et aura.

Foeminae

Rivulus e tenui manat tofo, exit in amnem
100 Paulatim et ripis crescens decurrit apertis.

Mares

Ex oculi leviore ictu fons stillat amoris,
Paulatimque amnes lacrimarum et flumina volvit.

Foeminae

Fomite de parvo tenuis primum exilit ignis,
Mox auctus versat latis incendia silvis.

Mares

105 Ignescit tenui afflatu fax lenis amorum,
Hinc incensa furit venis et pectora torret.

Men

The young man has a rosy mouth and rosy lips, and from his rosy breast he drips Acidalian nectar.

Women

The maiden, now of marriageable age, keeps in reserve, in her hidden garden, an intact flower and ripe fruit for the one who picks them. 95

Men

The young man will pick the ripe fruit and the blossom fresh with new dew with his hand, and will caress them with a gentle sigh.

Women

A rivulet flows from a narrow channel of tufa, gradually turns into a stream, and growing larger, races between wide banks. 100

Men

The source of love flows from the lightest flick of the eye, and gradually rolls together streams and rivers of tears.

Women

From a small piece of tinder, the slender flame first leaps to life; then, grown larger, it whirls a conflagration throughout the vast forest.

Men

The gentle torch of love catches flame from a light breath; then, 105 once kindled, it rages in the veins and scorches the heart.

Pompa Secunda Nereidum

Collocutores Macron et Lepidina.

Lepidina

Eia agedum, coniux, quaenam procul aequore pompa?
Haud capiunt virides sinuantia litora nymphas:
Nereidum chorus omnis adest. En coerula prima est
110   Pausilipe implexis edera frondente capillis,
Pausilipe mihi nota, vides, procul innuit; haec me
Saepe manu sua ad antra, suos deduxit in hortos
Donavitque apio et odorifero serpillo
Et dixit: 'Tibi mite pirum, tibi praecoqua servo,'
115   Pausilipe nigro sub candida guttura naevo.

Macron

Quam molli incedit passu et sese exerit ore
Quae sequitur, praecincta sinum et pede candida nudo!
An fortasse tibi, coniux nitidissima, nota est?

Lepidina

Ut sese ad choreas, Macron mihi care, resolvit,
120   Ut lepida est, veneres ut toto spirat ab ore,
(An paeto est oculo?) memini, narrare solebat
Crambane mater (eane est?) ea, Mergilline!
Invideant tibi vel digitos Prochyte Capriteque,
Nerine o formosa, o Nereis heroine.
125   O si sim iuvenis, tecum ut coniungere dextram,
Ut tecum hanc libeat choreas flexisse per actam,
O nymphe formosa, o candida Neptunnine!

Second Procession: The Nereids

Speakers: Macron and Lepidina.

Lepidina

Come, look, husband, what is that procession far off on the water? The curving shores can barely contain the crowds of green nymphs; the whole troop of Nereids is here. See, cerulean Pausilype, her 110 hair entwined with leafy ivy, comes first, Pausilype, whom I know — you see, she makes a sign from afar. She often led me by the hand to her grotto, into her gardens; she gave me parsley and fragrant thyme, and said: "I am saving you a ripe pear and apricots" — Pausilype who has a black beauty mark under her 115 white neck.[12]

Macron

With how delicate a gait and with what mild demeanor the next one in the procession comes forth, her garment neatly tucked up, luminous with bare foot! Is she perchance known to you, most elegant wife?

Lepidina

How she abandons herself to the dance, my dear Macron, how 120 charming she is, how she breathes allure from her entire countenance (doesn't she have a flirtatious glance?) — Mother Crambane used to tell me, as I recall — but is it she? Yes, it must be Mergelline. Prochyte and Caprite would envy you your very fingers, O beautiful daughter of Nereus, O divine Nereid![13] O if I were a 125 young man, how I would like to join my right hand with yours, and lead winding dances with you across this shore, O beautiful nymph, O fair Neptunian deity![14] When you dry your hair in the

Dum siccas simul ad solem pectisque capillum,
Tunc ego, tunc niveae pennas imitata columbae
130   Sim volucris, tibi quae cerasi cum tempore primo
Maturos foetus et fraga rubentia rostro
Proiciam in gremium, primos ut ruris honores
Per me prima legas, nostro et sis munere prima!

Macron

Illa illa! Haud aliam vidi gestare puellam
135   Aptius aut pharetram aut intendere fortius arcum.
Atque alio hos arcus, alio tua spicula tende:
Me meus ignis habet et habent mea pectora vulnus.

Lepidina

Me miseram, meus est, alios pete, nympha, iuvencos;
Mi Macron, tege me, collo et tua brachia necte.
140   Ne saevi, Sarniti dea, et tua tela retracta.

Macron

Te teneo, avertit telum dea, fixit et Aulum.
Ah miser, ut madidis vultum demisit ocellis!

Lepidina

O Macron, memini, mater me docta monebat:
'Sarnitim fuge, nata, trucem Sarnitida vita;
145   Fert intinctum oculis, arcu fert saeva venenum,
Non parcit pueris saevitque inimica puellis.'
Hinc videas Satyros passim, hinc languere Napaeas,
Deperit hanc Alcon, octogenarius Alcon,
Insanit Morphe, nonagenaria Morphe,

sun and comb it, O that I might become a bird, imitating the   130
feathered wings of a snow-white dove, and at the onset of spring
cast into your lap ripe cherries and reddening strawberries from
my beak, so that you would be the first to gather the first fruits of
the field because of me, you would be the very first by my gift!

Macron

That girl, that one there! I have never seen another girl either wear   135
a quiver more suitably or stretch a bow with greater strength. But
point that bow elsewhere; aim those arrows somewhere else! I am
possessed by my own flame; my heart already has a wound.

Lepidina

Ah poor me, he is mine! Seek other bullocks, O nymph. Protect
me, my Macron, throw your arms around my shoulders! Don't be   140
cruel, divine Sarnitis; put away your arrows.[15]

Macron

I am holding you; the goddess has turned her bow in another direction and pierced Aulus. Ah the poor boy, how he hung down
his head, his eyes wet with tears!

Lepidina

O Macron, I remember how my wise mother warned me: "Flee
Sarnitis, my daughter; avoid brutal Sarnitis; the cruel woman's   145
bow has a poison on it imbued with her eyes' mortal dose; she
has no mercy on boys and is viciously hostile toward girls."
You may see satyrs and dell nymphs languishing everywhere on
account of her; Alcon perishes for her, the eighty-year-old Alcon; Morphe is mad for her, Morphe who is ninety years old;

150 Deseruit silvas, qui nunc colit aequora, Faunus.
Ecce venit Resina aviae iunctissima nostrae,
Tristior illa quidem patris de clade Vesevi.
Nam teneo, sic lenis anus referebat, amasse
Hanc nunquam, sprevisse procos, at litore solo
155 Moerentem casus exustaque regna parentis,
Tritonis cupidam vix effugisse rapinam.
Ter sese dea surripuit, tria fervidus heros
Oscula compressis liquit signata labellis.
Nunc quoque livor adest; at sunt sine labe papillae,
160 Quis superat nymphas: videas si forte lavantem,
Non tibi candidiora poli sint lactea texta,
Non tibi sit planta crystallus purior alba.
Ex illo, infidum litus fontemque relinquens,
Rura colit dumisque suas studiosa capellas
165 Pascit et errantes servat cum matribus hedos
Quadruplici insignes hirsuta ad tempora cornu.
O Macron, Macron, mihi me, tibi te nova nymphe,
Quae venit, eripiat, cingit quae ad tempora myrtos.
Ipse vides: illi ridet mare, ridet et aër,
170 Cingit quae ad collum caltae florentis honorem,
Illi concedant Dryades, Nereides illi.
O longis praelata comis et lumine peto,
Hercli, superciliis nigris, candente papilla,
Es memor, et meminisse decet, mea nubilis Hercli,
175 Quos mihi corrallos, quae mella liquata dedisti,
Dives corrallis et mellis munere dives;
Sis memor, et niveum tibi me donasse colostrum
Deliciasque rosae primae et vacinia prima.

Macron

Risit et argutos in te dea flexit ocellos.

Faunus has deserted the forests and now dwells in the sea. Look, 150
Resina is coming, a very close friend of my grandmother, quite sad
because of the disaster of her father Vesuvius.[16] For I recollect
(thus the gentle old woman recounted) that she never loved, and
spurned her suitors: yet once, on the lonely shore, grieving her fa- 155
ther's tragedy and the destruction of his realms by fire, she barely
managed to flee the rapacious lust of a Triton. Three times the
goddess pulled herself from his clutches, three kisses the passion-
ate hero left imprinted on her clenched lips. Even now there is a
visible bruise; but her breasts are flawless; with her breasts, she 160
surpasses the nymphs. If perchance you should see her bathing,
you would not think the milky fabric of the firmament more fair,
or crystal more pure, than her white foot. From that time onward,
leaving the untrustworthy shore and font behind, she dwells in the
fields, solicitously pastures her she-goats amid the brambles, and 165
guards, along with their mothers, the straying kids, fine specimens
with four horns sprouting on their shaggy temples. O Macron,
Macron, the new nymph who arrives, her temples garlanded with
myrtle, could steal you away from yourself and me from myself!
You can see her: for her the sea is smiling, the sky is smiling; she 170
wears a necklace of glorious marigold in flower; Dryads would
yield before her, Nereids give way to her. O you who surpass all in
attractiveness with your long hair and flirtatious eyes, Hercli, with
your black eyebrows and fair breasts, you remember—and you
ought to remember—the corals and the liquid honey you gave me, 175
O my nubile Hercli, rich in coral and rich in the gift of honey.[17]
May you also remember that I gave you snow-white first milk, the
enticing pleasure of the first rose, and the first blueberries.

Macron

The goddess smiled and turned her lively eyes toward you.

Lepidina

180 Fallor, an adventat Caprei maris heroine
Praeceditque chorus Tritonum et litora clangunt?
Non capiunt undante salo cava litora puppes.
Haec ipsa est, coniux, Caprei maris heroine;
Circunstant Aequana hinc, illinc innuba Amalphis,
185 Et fidae comites et litoris altera cura.
Illam ego, dum Capreas peterem cum matre, sedentem
Ad scopulum vidi; famulae properare legentes
Ostrea et evulsas lapidoso e margine conchas.
Accepit dea me gremio et donavit echinis.
190 Obstupui ingentemque humero ingentemque lacertis
Atque utero et toto retinentem corpore formam.
Horrebant sed crura nigris et pectora setis,
Purior Aequana cum sit nihil aut sit Amalphi,
Utraque odoriferum spirent et pectore anethum,
195 Litora sed crepuere canitque silentia Triton.

Pompa Tertia

Triton canit dona offerens;
Macron et Lepidina colloquuntur.

Triton

O decus Italidum, longe pulcherrima virgo,
Sirenum genus egregium et dis aequa propago,
En tua coeruleae centum ad connubia nymphae
Dona ferunt auro gravida et Gangetide baca,
200 En tibi odoratos Pancheae mercis honores
Oceanoque advecta ferunt electra Britanno.
Ferte, agite, et plenis haec dona reponite mensis.

Lepidina

Am I mistaken, or is the demigoddess of the sea of Capri arriving? 180
A troop of Tritons parades before her and the shores resound; the
curving shores are not large enough to hold the ships in the salty
waves.[18] She is here, my husband, the demigoddess of the sea of
Capri herself; on one side of her stands Aequana, on the other
unwed Amalfi, her faithful companions and the other darlings of 185
the coast.[19] When I was going to Capri with my mother, I saw her
sitting by a crag. Her serving girls hurried about collecting oysters
and conches, plucking them from the rocky beach. The goddess
took me in her lap and gave me sea urchins. I gazed in amazement 190
to see how she had vast shoulders and arms yet was still beautiful
in her stomach and throughout her whole body. But her thighs
and chest bristle with thick black hairs, for she is not at all more
faultless than Aequana or Amalfi, both of whom waft from their
bosoms the perfume of fragrant anise. But the shores resound as a 195
Triton sings his demand of silence.

Third Procession

A Triton sings while offering gifts;
dialogue between Macron and Lepidina.

Triton

O glory of Italian women, maiden most beautiful by far, noble
child of the Sirens, offspring equal to the gods, behold, a hundred
cerulean nymphs bring gifts weighed down with gold and the pearl
of the Ganges to your wedding; see, they bring the fragrant honors 200
of Arabian merchandise and amber imported from the British
ocean. Come, bring in these gifts and place them on the heaping

En tibi mille ferunt niveae sua serta puellae,
Serta auro intertexta et ramiferis corrallis;
205 En totidem Eois bacata monilia gemmis.
Vos agedum, cultae, capite haec nova dona, ministrae.
En famuli tibi Tritones simul aere canoro
Servitium et volucres propter cava litora currus
Promittunt, iter et placido per coerula cursu,
210 Tercentum iuvenes, tercentum numina ponti,
Et tercentenis dant haec tibi pocula gemmis
Fulva auro, variata smaragdo et iaspide tecta.
Vos haec, o niveae, thalamis servate, puellae.
En Caprei regina maris, cui mille ministrae,
215 Telebois dea dat fulvis radiantia bullis
Cingula Cynipheo ex auro et Garamantide ab ora,
Priscum opus artificisque manus dis nota Faburni.
Haec olim Aenariae Nereus pater, illa sorori
Donat habere, sui monimentum et pignus amoris,
220 Dum migrat sociae confinia ad antra Minervae.
Est illis adamante novo et variata pyropo
Fibula, concordis thalami felicia vincla;
Hac coniux ubi nuda suo cum coniuge vincta est
Accubuitque toro, celeri Discordia passu
225 Diffugit et thalamos subit hinc Concordia notos.
Hac age, nympha, tuum simul et te cinge maritum.
Nunc o nunc, socii, celebres agitate choreas,
Coerulei Tritones, et omina fausta vocate:
Hymen o Hymenaee, Hymen ades o Hymenaee.

Tritones

230 Dicimus: 'O Hymenaee, Hymen ades o Hymenaee,
Felix o Hymenaee, Hymen felix Hymenaee.'

tables. See, a thousand snow-white girls are bringing you their
garlands, garlands interwoven with gold and branching coral; see,   205
they are bringing just as many necklaces adorned with gems of the
Orient. Come, elegant serving girls, receive these new gifts. See,
the Tritons, your manservants, with their sonorous bronze, promise their service, their chariots that fly along the curved shoreline,
and a journey over the azure deep with untroubled course. Three   210
hundred young men, three hundred divinities of the sea, they also
give you these cups yellow with gold and studded with three hundred gems, veined with emerald and covered with jasper. Reserve
these, snow-white girls, for the marriage chamber. See, the divine
queen of the sea of Capri, who has a thousand serving girls, gives   215
a belt gleaming with tawny Teleboan studs made from Cinyphian
gold, brought from the Garamantian shore, an antique artwork
fashioned by the artisan Faburnus, whose hand is known to the
gods.[20] This belt father Nereus once gave to Aenaria, and she gave
it to her sister to keep, a reminder and token of her love when she   220
was moving to the nearby grotto of her friend Minerva.[21] The belt
has a pin made of a novel steel alloy mixed with gold-bronze, the
propitious bond of a harmonious union. When the naked bride is
bound with this to her husband and lies down in bed, Discord
quickly flees and the goddess Concord enters the marriage cham-   225
ber she knows well. Come now, nymph, bind yourself and your
husband with this belt. Now, right now, lead thronging dances, my
companions, O cerulean Tritons, and invoke favorable omens: O
Hymen Hymenaeus, come, O Hymen Hymenaeus.

Tritons

We say: "O Hymenaeus, come, O Hymen Hymenaeus, O propi-   230
tious Hymenaeus, propitious Hymen Hymenaeus."

Lepidina

Desiit ille quidem iuvenis malus; o mihi, Macron,
O Macron, mihi quem incussit malus ille timorem!
Herculis ad fontem mater secura lavabat
235 Gausapium, ipsa udos siccabam sola capillos;
Surripuit mihi supparium, mox innuit et se
Ostentat formosus; ibi per litora praeceps
Eripio meme; sequitur malus; hic mihi dexter
Calceus in summa miserae defluxit arena.
240 Quid non pollicitus ferus hic? Ne nunc quoque tecum
Iam videor secura mihi. Ne respice, coniux:
Quam vereor summa ne nos despectet ab alga!
Litore cedamus; manet illinc altera pompa:
Ipse vides, sociae properant e rure Napaeae.

Pompa Quarta

Macron et Lepidina colloquuntur de nymphis
urbanis et suburbanis.

Lepidina

245 Ecce suburbanis longe praelata puellis,
Ecce venit pingui multum saturata sagina
Butine sociis mecum consueta choreis,
Butine dives hedis, sed ditior agnis,
Et cui sunt primae farcimina pinguia curae.
250 Ut rubicunda nitet plenisque intenta canistris
Nobilis et libis et cognita buccellatis
Ulmia et intortis tantum laudata torallis!
Quae mihi culta placet minus, at de polline vultum
Non nihil alba placet, tamen est ferus ardor amantum.

24

Lepidina

He's finally stopped talking, that nasty youth. O Macron, Macron, what fear that nasty brute struck into me! My mother was washing laundry without a care by the fountain of Hercules, and I was   235
drying my wet hair on my own. He stole my linen robe, then winked at me and showed off how good-looking he was. Then and there, I made a dash for it, running headlong along the shore. The nasty brute followed. At this point, my right shoe slipped off— poor me!—on the surface of the sand. What did that wild beast   240
not promise? Now I do not feel safe even with you by my side. Don't look back, my husband. How I fear he is looking down at us from the heaps of seaweed! Let's leave the shore; over there, another procession awaits. You can see for yourself: my friends the dell nymphs are hurrying from the fields.

Fourth Procession

Macron and Lepidina talk about the nymphs
of the city and surrounding areas.

Lepidina

Behold, the nymph who far surpasses the girls of the city outskirts   245
in beauty: she comes, satiated with rich food, accustomed to attend my companions' dances along with me, Butine, rich in goats, richer still in lambs, whose prime concern is making fatty sausages. How Ulmia gleams with her ruddy complexion, attentive   250
to her heaping baskets, famous for her cakes, known for her biscuits, and highly praised for her twisted *taralli!*[22] She pleases me less when dolled up, but she does please me when her face is white with flour dust; and the passion of her suitors is fierce.

255 Theodocie soror hanc festis nam saepe diebus
Ad choreas vocat, hic dulcem meditatur avenam;
Tum canit, ut taciti stupeant ad pascua tauri:
'Ad fontem duc, Nisa, boves, dum retia tendo.'
Quid cum sola canit frondosae ad culmina villae:
260 'Huc ades, o Amarylli, vocant Amaryllida silvae'?
Hanc, Macron mihi care, (tulit sors) aspice nymphen:
Ad clivum Pistasis adest, en intuba purgat
Rasilibusque onerat calathis et stringit anethum.
Non clivus, non fons, non longi haec litoris acta
265 Vidit ea pictos melius contexere qualos;
Nunc quoque fama refert, liquidum quod in aëre rorem
Cogere apes et mella cavis infundere cellis
Pingit et e vario reddit sua munera iunco.
Forma illi damno est: nulli connubia amantes,
270 Nulli etiam thalamos nymphae petiere iugales,
Quod timeant cupidae simul aspirare rapinae
Hinc Faunos, illinc Laestrygonas et Cyclopas
Correptos facie et candentis honore papillae
Et naevo nigrante nigroque ad tempora cirro
275 Coniurasse tori iura et violare mariti.

Macron

Heu squalet formosa domi, metus urget amantes.
Capparion ubi nunc, ubi Sedigitus Manubrion,
Ausi etiam mediis uxorem avellere claustris
Neptunni? Centum hic Tritones, at ille superbum
280 Excutit aurigam curru et lacerum abicit undis,
Capparion Petroonte, Aeronte satus Manubrion.
Illi, illi heroes et digni ruris alumni,
Et quercu nutriti et castaneis hirsutis,

For her sister Theodocie often invites her to the dances on festive 255
days; there, she composes a sweet melody on the oaten pipe.[23]
Then she sings in such a way that the bulls at pasture stand in silent amazement: "Lead the cattle to the spring, Nisa, while I lay
out the nets." What about when she sings, alone, on the roof of
her cottage surrounded by foliage, "Come here, O Amaryllis, the 260
forests are summoning Amaryllis"?[24] Now look at this nymph, my
dear Macron, since you have the chance: Pistasis is there on the
slope; see, she is picking endive, piling it in smooth baskets, and
plucking anise.[25] No hill, no font, no beach of this long shoreline
has seen anyone weave multicolored wicker baskets better than she 265
does; and it is also said that she makes depictions of bees gathering
liquid dew from the air and pouring honey into the hollow cells,
and that she renders their tasks with differently colored reeds. But
her beauty does her harm: no lovers have sought marriage, none 270
have sought the marriage bed of the nymph, because they fear that
the Fauns on one side, and the Laestrygonians on the other, both
at once aspire to lustful rape, and that the Cyclopes, carried away
by her face and the beauty of her dazzling white breasts, her black
mole, and the black ringlets falling over her temples, have con- 275
spired to violate the rights of the bed and the husband.[26]

Macron

Alas, a beautiful nymph languishes from neglect at home, while
fear overpowers her suitors. Where now is Capparion, where Sedigitus Manubrion, who dared to steal a spouse even from the
midst of Neptune's stronghold? The one knocked aside a hundred
Tritons, while the other knocked the arrogant charioteer from his 280
chariot and cast him, badly wounded, into the waves—Capparion,
son of Petroon, Manubrion, son of Aeron.[27] These are true heroes
and worthy sons of the countryside; they were sustained on oak and

Arbuta quis miliumque liquens abdomen et unctum
285 Miscebant festis convivia lauta diebus.

Lepidina

Pistasis, si qua est, digna est heroe marito,
Cultorem tamen et vitis suspirat et horti
Et cui sit cucumis, sit et unca cucurbita curae;
Est quoque spes agiles sciat ut tornare catinos.
290 At non Hermitis nec Olympias aut Conicle
Haec sibi coniugia aut hos exoptant hymenaeos.
Conicle consueta plagas et retia ferre
Venatorem amat et venantis amore tenetur;
Aucupiis capta est, hinc aucupis uritur igni
295 Hermitis, nec amica colo, sed et apta choreis:
Hae casus mihi saepe suos et vulnera nudant,
Quod felix hymenaeo et quod te coniuge felix.
Notus Olympiadis non est amor: et timet et vult,
Ast prohibet pudor et durae reverentia matris;
300 Ipsa tamen concurrere equum et resonare sub armis
Gaudet et e celsa immoritur spectare fenestra;
Pingit acu tamen, ut credas mugire iuvencum,
In coeno grunnire suem, crepitare cicadas,
Ut, modo cum geminos filo discrevit Amores,
305 Hunc certare avibus risu mitem et tamen alis
Saevire et tacitum stillare in corda venenum,
Illicet insolitum volucres sentire calorem,
Illum arcu facibusque trucem mansuescere in herba,
Sed furtim celeres oculis iactare favillas,
310 Illicet incensos errare per avia tauros.
Est inter natas fecundae prima Labullae
Nomine Formellis: non hac felicius hortos
Ulla colit, nulli concedit munere fusi,

bristly chestnuts; for these men, wild strawberries, crushed millet, and fatty lard made a sumptuous dinner party on festive days!   285

Lepidina

Pistasis, if anyone, is worthy of having a hero as a husband, but she merely sighs for a man to cultivate the vine and the garden, to care for the cucumber and the curved gourd. She also hopes that he might know how to fashion malleable cooking vessels on the potter's wheel. But neither Hermitis, nor Olympias, nor Conicle   290 desires such a marriage for herself or such a union.[28] Conicle, accustomed to carrying nets and snares, loves a hunter, is possessed by love for a man who hunts. Hermitis has been snared by bird catching; hence she is scorched with burning desire for a bird catcher; she is not only inclined to the distaff, but also talented   295 at dancing. These two reveal to me their misfortunes and their wounds because I am happy in my marriage and happy to have you as spouse. It is not known whom Olympias loves: she fears and desires, but modesty and respect for her strict mother hold her back. She herself rejoices in horse competitions and the clank-   300 ing of armor, and pines away, watching from a high window.[29] She embroiders so well, however, that you would believe the bullock was lowing, the pigs grunting in mud, the cicadas droning, and, the moment she has woven two Loves with her thread, you would   305 believe that one of them vies with the birds: he smiles gently yet grows savage in his flight, instilling a silent poison into their hearts, and right away the birds feel an unfamiliar ardor; and you would believe that the other one, fierce with his bow and torches, relaxes calmly in the grass, yet secretly shoots swift sparks from his eyes, and then and there, the bulls, inflamed, wander through the   310 trackless wastes. The first among fertile Labulla's daughters is named Formellis: no woman cultivates gardens more successfully than she does, and she yields to no one in the task of the spindle,

Seu ducat linum, seu mollis vellera lanae,
315 Serica seu digitis promittat fila magistris,
Aurea seu nivea texatur bractea dextra,
Felix sorte sua nymphaque beatior omni.
Illi secretis fons est nitidissimus hortis,
Pomonis donum, matris tutela Labullae,
320 Matris Hamadryadis; et amavit hanc quoque Pomon,
Pomon avus Fragolae, atavus cerealis Acerrae,
Vitiferaeque abavus non certa prole Casullae.
Centum habet hic neptes centumque e stirpe nepotes,
Formellis sed cara illi: non advena fontem,
325 Navita non sitiit, avido quin captus amore
Deserat et patriam et fessos aetate parentes.
Virginis haec nunc fida comes thalamoque ministrat,
Et forma intoleranda et pictis alta cothurnis,
Quos illi suit ex auro miniosus Aluntas,
330 Blanda tamen facilisque et amata ad munera comis.
Mille adsunt huic deliciae et bona commoda ruris;
Una mihi invidiae est cornix, cui noctua Bauli
Cesserit atque oculis Sabuloni gracculus albis.
Haec et 'Ave formosa' et 'Hera o mihi cara' salutat,
335 Observansque fores: 'Quis' ait 'nunc hostia pulsat?'

Macron

Cedam ego turturibus nigris nostraeque columbae,
Sitque semel vidisse deam.

Lepidina

Vel cesseris alno,
Ad quam defossi centum illi ex aere trientes
Servantur. Nunc illa domi parat anxia lactis
340 Candentem florem, misto et cum melle farinam

whether she spins flax or fleece of soft wool, or whether she draws 315
out threads of silk, guiding them with her fingers, or whether she
weaves in gold leaf with snow-white hand; she is happy in her lot
and more fortunate than any other nymph.[30] She has an especially
lovely fountain in a hidden garden, a gift from Pomon, under the
guardianship of her mother Labulla, a Hamadryad; Pomon loved 320
her as well.[31] Pomon was the grandfather of Fragola, the great-
great-great-grandfather of grain-rich Acerra, and the great-great-
grandfather, by uncertain descent, of vine-bearing Casulla.[32] He
has a hundred granddaughters and a hundred grandsons born of
his line, but Formellis is his darling. No foreigner, no sailor ever 325
slaked his thirst at that fountain who did not fall passionately in
love and desert his fatherland and his parents weary with years.[33]
Now she is the faithful companion of the maiden, and attends to
the marriage chamber, irresistible in beauty, raised high on color-
fully decorated boots sewn for her by Aluntas the Red, yet pleas- 330
ant, easygoing, and courteous in carrying out her well-loved tasks.[34]
She has a thousand delights and fine things of the countryside;
but I envy her only a crow, which surpasses Baulus' night owl and
the white-eyed jackdaw of Sabulonus. It greets her: "Hail, pretty
one," and "Hail, my dear mistress"; and watching the door, it says: 335
"Who knocks?"

Macron

I will give up our black turtledoves and our dove, if I may but see
the goddess once.[35]

Lepidina

You might even give up the alder tree at whose foot we keep those
hundred bronze coins buried. Now, flustered, at home, she is preparing the white *fior' di latte*, and then she kneads the flour mixed 340

Mox subigit, succincta sinum, nudata lacertos,
Praestringit violas albas et lilia cana.
Parthenope tum culta manus miratur: ibi illa
Lacteolos et thyrsiculos et oluscula signat,
345   Inde latet forma nimiumque et dote superba.
Verum age et hoc, coniux, (fas est) requiesce sub arcu;
Nam defessa traho vix genua, et inepta canistri
Sarcina me gravat et clivo sudavimus ambo;
Nuper et hic cecinisse ferunt Meliseon et aegras
350   Solantem curas nec mitia fata gementem
Phosphoridos natae: en hic e turribus altis
Fistula dependet, saevi monimenta doloris,
Signaque certa manent numerique per ora feruntur:
'Phosphori nata, quis heu, quis te mihi, Phosphori, ademit?
355   O mecum, o salices, mecum o lugete, myricae.'

Macron

Quin, age, pone et onus et membra labore relaxa,
Nam gravida es, Lepidina, et onus grave languida defers.
Hac quoque pompa venit, via nec capit ipsa Napaeas;
Hic licet et spectare una et requiesse sub umbra.

Pompa Quinta

Colloquuntur Macron et Lepidina; Planuris supervenit,
quae pompam heroum ad nuptias convenientium describit.

Macron

360   Uvidula est, quae prima venit, sed et una rosetum
Fert Paesti, fert et violas haec una Vesevi,
Fuscaque roscidaque et venosis lactea mammis.

with honey, and, with her dress tucked up and her arms bare, binds the pale violets and white lilies. Then lovely Parthenope marvels at her hands: there she traces out little stalks white as milk and miniature vegetables, and then she withdraws, extremely 345 proud of her beauty and her talent. But come now, and rest beneath this arch, my husband, since you may; for I am barely dragging my weary legs, the disproportionate burden of the basket weighs me down, and we both broke into a sweat on the hill.[36] For they say that Meliseus recently sang here, solacing his sorrowful 350 cares and lamenting the cruel fate of his daughter Phosphoris. See, here, from a high tower, his reed pipe hangs, a memorial of cruel pain; certain tokens of him remain and his verses are circulated from mouth to mouth: "Phosphoris my daughter, who, alas, who has taken you from me, O Phosphoris? Mourn with me, O willow 355 trees, mourn with me, tamarisks."[37]

Macron

Nay, come, put down your burden, and relieve your limbs of toil; for you are pregnant, Lepidina, and fainting, carry a heavy burden. The procession also comes by here, nor is the road itself wide enough to contain the crowd of dell nymphs. Here we may watch together and rest in the shade.

Fifth Procession

Macron and Lepidina are in dialogue; Planuris joins them and describes the procession of heroes gathering at the wedding ceremony.[38]

Macron

She is dripping, she who arrives first, but she brings, all by herself, 360 a rose bed of Paestum, she brings, all by herself, the violets of Vesuvius; she is dusky, dew soaked, and has milk-white breasts full of veins.[39]

Lepidina

O coniux, prima haec, prima haec (ne despice) quantum
Et calamis valet et cantu, verum una videri
365 Non formosa cupit, luxum aspernata procosque:
Asparago gaudet fungisque operosa legendis,
Quos et herae, quos et matri dimittat in urbem.
O mihi cara soror (potes et soror ipsa vocari),
Dic, age, qui comites, quos et ducunt hymenaeos,
370 Planuri o generosa soror Leucogidis albae.

Planuris

Descendunt, soror, et nemora et cava flumina currunt
Ad thalamos, mille antra deos vomuere, et ab altis
Montibus indigenae Fauni properantque ruuntque
Ad portas; iter ingentes non explicat Orcos,
375 Quos Acherusiacae fauces nova numina mittunt,
Stagnaque Baulorum quos hostia pinguis Averni
Emisere adytis lacus et fluitantis Araxi.
Mira illis sunt ora, soror, radiantia fronti
Lumina, sulfureis fumus de naribus efflat,
380 Tempora per serpunt rami mentoque rigescunt
Hircosae setae; tum guttura collaque circum
Squalent sulfureae totoque in pectore crustae,
Caetera membra nigror merus occupat et situs et nox.

Lepidina

Me miseram, hine etiam? Procul, ah procul!

Lepidina

O my husband, this first one, this first nymph (don't be scornful)
how skilled she is at playing the pipes and singing; but she alone
does not desire to appear beautiful, disdaining luxury and suitors;   365
she enjoys herself working hard picking asparagus and mushrooms
to send to the city for her mistress and her mother. O my dear
sister (for I can indeed call you my sister), come, tell me who are
your companions, and what wedding rites they carry out, O Pla-   370
nuris, wellborn sister of white Leucogis.[40]

Planuris

Groves and rivers with deep-channeled banks descend and rush to
the wedding; the grottos have spewed forth a thousand gods, and
from the high mountains native Fauns hurry and rush to the gates.
The path is not wide enough to accommodate the vast deities of
the infernal realm, which the jaws of Acheron send forth — unfa-   375
miliar deities — and the still waters of Bauli, which the gates of
rich Avernus released from its inner domain, and the font of un-
dulating Arasso.[41] Their faces are astonishing, sister: they have
light flashing from their eyes on their foreheads, smoke flows out
of their sulfurous nostrils, branches snake over their temples, and   380
goat-like bristles stand erect on their chins; sulfurous incrustations
form a stiff covering over their throats, necks, and entire chests,
and the rest of their bodies is buried in pure black void, decay, and
night.

Lepidina

Wretched me — those deities have come as well? Go away, ah, far
away!

Planuris

O mea, siste:
385   Ad cryptam ferratus adest Aeronius, adsunt
Tercentum rapidi umbrones totidemque molossi.
Ipsi abigent, tecti colla et longa ilia ferro:
Ore latrant, saevum valent qui inhibere Typhoea.
Moverat Aenaria ferus hic et monte revulso
390   Raptabatque iter et litus pede celsus obibat
Intrabatque antrum: ecce Acron, ecce aspera proles
Lancusi, Pelicon et Marsicus Armillatus,
Deturbant antro et femori cava vulnera figunt;
Ille per extremas praeceps vix effugit undas.

Lepidina

395   Et fessa es, mea Planuri, et liquidissimus amnis
It subter: sitienti et aquas et pocula promam;
Proximaque Uranie scorteum et sua poma paravit,
Quae mihi cara soror forma prior et prior annis,
Quodque vides, summa procul innuit alta fenestra.

Planuris

400   Assideo, Lepidina, et poma et pocula sumam:
Mox tibi et heroas referam summosque Oriarchas,
Quos mirere, soror, simul et vereare superbos.
    Primus agit pompam Gaurus cum coniuge Campe,
Ingentemque manu pinum fert; pendet ab alta
405   Hinc leporum grex, inde anatum, post ordine longo
Et damae capreaeque et aper Leboride silva,

Planuris

Do not run away, my dear: ironclad Aeronius stands by the Crypt 385
along with three hundred Umbrian hounds and the same number
of Molossians.[42] They will drive them away, their necks and long
flanks covered in iron: their bark is able to curb the ferocious Typhoeus.[43] This savage giant had come from Ischia, and, after up-
rooting the mountain, was devouring the road, and, a towering 390
figure, was traversing the shore and entering the cave: and behold,
Acron, behold, Lancusus' harsh offspring, Pelicon, and Marsicus
Armillatus thrust him from the cave and inflict deep wounds on
his thigh. He barely escapes, rushing headlong along the extreme
edge of the shore.

Lepidina

You are tired, my Planuris, and an exquisitely clear stream flows 395
down below: I shall bring cups and water to quench your thirst;
nearby my sister Urania, both older and more beautiful than I, has
set out a wineskin and fruits from her orchard. As you can see,
she's making a sign from afar, high up in the topmost window.[44]

Planuris

I am sitting down, Lepidina, and I'll take apples and water. Now I 400
shall tell you about heroes and the lofty Oriarchs, creatures so
haughty that you will at once marvel at them, sister, and fear
them.[45]

Gaurus leads the procession in first place with his wife Campe,
and carries a vast pine tree in his hand:[46] from the top of the pine
hangs a warren of rabbits, a brace of geese, and then, in a long line, 405
deer, she-goats, a boar from the forest of Laboris, a partridge from

Et perdix nemore e Clanii et Vulturnius anser
Ardeaque fuliceque et grus Lucrinide ab alga.
Ipse ebulo pinxitque genas et pectora gypso.
410 At Campe asparago crines redimita virago
Frondentem a radice alnum fert strenua, ubi omnis
Pendet et autumnus matura et fructibus aestas
Pomaque praecoquaque et auro certantia mala
Et viridi cum fronde pira atque cydonia cana;
415 Per medios volitant ramos merulaeque ululaeque,
Pippilat et passer et dulce canit philomele.
　　Ursulon insequitur frontem insignitus echino,
Ipse humeris pedibusque ingens et cornibus ingens;
Cornibus ingentes nutanti pondere cistas
420 Castanea e molli sorbisque virentibus, idem
Fert humero crumeram nucis et mulctralia lactis,
Fert lateri geminas immani ventre lagenas
Sorbino e bimo atque ex anniculo viridisco,
Et dextra hinnuleos querula cum matre gemellos.
425 A leva coniux felici prole Marana
Laeta canit, sociae plaudunt ad carmina nymphae.
Ipsa favos ac mella simul macerumque lupinum
Plurimaque in nitidis fert ova recentia qualis.
Haec illa est felix et coniuge digna Marana,
430 Docta et acu, docta et lino, doctissima lana.
Dos illi ingentes tercentum ad sidera quercus
Tercentumque nuces, quarum tria iugera campi
Brachia protendunt, mille et cum vitibus alni
Tercentumque suum armentum et nemus undique cinctum
435 Arbuteisque comis et nucliferis pinetis,
Et quae se multa circuntegit esculus umbra.
　　Hunc post incedit lentis Misenius heros

the grove of Clanius, a Vulturnian goose, an Ardean waterfowl, and a crane from the algae of the Lucrine Lake.[47] He has painted his cheeks with danewort and his chest with gypsum. But Campe,   410 a woman with masculine strength, her hair wreathed with asparagus, energetically carries a leafy alder tree pulled up from the root, from which hangs all of autumn's harvest, all summer's harvest ripe with fruits: apples, apricots, citrus fruits that vie with gold, pears with green foliage, and pale quinces. Blackbirds and screech   415 owls flit through the midst of the branches; the sparrow chirps and the nightingale sings sweetly.

Ursulon comes next, his forehead adorned with a sea urchin, his shoulders and feet immense, vast horns on his head; hanging from his horns are vast baskets, their heavy mass tottering, made   420 from pliant chestnut and still green sorb-tree wood.[48] On his shoulder he bears a basket of nuts and pails of milk, and on his hip two enormous, potbellied flagons of two-year-old Verdicchio and year-old Asprino, and with his right hand, he carries twin kids along with their mother bleating her complaint.[49] On his left, his   425 fertile wife Marana sings cheerfully while companion nymphs clap to her songs; she herself carries honeycombs, honey, lupine softened in water, and a large number of fresh eggs in neat wicker baskets.[50] This is Marana, happy and worthy of her husband, skilled with the needle, skilled with flax, expert with wool. Her   430 dowry was three hundred huge oak trees that rise as high as the stars, three hundred nut trees, whose branches extend across three acres, a thousand alder trees with their vines, a flock of three hundred pigs, a grove ringed on all sides with the foliage of strawberry   435 trees and cone-bearing pine trees, and a tall oak tree surrounded by thick shade.

After Ursulon comes the hero Misenius with slow steps; he is

Passibus, ipse senex, iuvenum sed viribus usus.
Vectibus hi sublatum alte per brachia cetum
440 Attollunt, caudaque iter et vestigia verrit
Immanis fera et informi riget horrida dorso,
Tum quassat caput et minitanti tergore nutat;
Faucibus at tenebras simul et vomere et simul ipsa
Visa lues pelagusque haurire atque hiscere coelum,
445 Occurrunt trepidoque sinu sua pignora celant
Attonitae matres: pavor hinc, hinc plausus euntum.
Ipsa viam sibi, qua gressum fert, bellua pandit,
At tubicen vocat urgentem ad spectacula turbam,
Cantantis longe ingeminant nemora ardua murmur:
450 'Pastores tellure sati gensque eruta sulcis,
Monstra cavete maris scopuloso et tergore cetum:
Vulnerat et cauda insidians et devorat ore.
Vos, iuvenes, celerate iter et vim afferte lacertis.'
Haec tubicen, turba ingenti clamore salutat
455 Sebethon: 'Nove nupte, nuces para et indue vestem,
Quam tibi Acerranae musco flavente Napaeae
Neverunt, quam pinxit acu Pomelia, ut imo
Fronderet limbo patulis satureia ramis,
Sibilet ut tenui de fronde locusta susurro;
460 Indue et intextum buxo frondente galerum.
In medio telas operosa observat Aragne
Disponitque manu volitantem et captat asilum;
Ille fugam parat, ast tenui interceptus amictu
Implicitatque pedes et passis instrepit alis,
465 Lydaque de tacito prodit tum turgida nido.'
    Hunc iuxta coniux Prochyteia incedit et ore
Et gestu spectanda et pictae tegmine pallae;
Nexilibus cochleis limbus sonat, horrida echinis

an old man, but draws on the strength of young men.[51] These
hold up a whale, hoisted aloft on poles by their arms, and the ter-   440
rible monster sweeps away their footsteps on the path with its tail;
its hideous back is bristly and stiff, it shakes its head, and its spine
undulates in a menacing manner. But as soon as they see this pes-
tilential beast vomiting darkness from its maws, gulping down the
sea, and sucking the sky into its gaping mouth, terrified mothers   445
run up and conceal their children in their trembling arms; some
celebrants in the procession are afraid; some applaud. The beast
opens up a path for itself wherever it goes; the trumpeter summons the crowd surging toward the spectacle, and the tall groves
echo the sound of his song from afar: "O herdsmen sown from the   450
land, people risen from the furrows, beware the monsters of the
sea and the whale with its stony spine: it wounds with its tail, lying in ambush, and devours with its mouth. Young men, hurry on
your way, and use the strength of your arms." So spoke the trumpeter. The crowd hails Sebeto with a loud shout:[52] "Newly mar-   455
ried spouse, prepare the nuts and put on the garment which the
dell nymphs of Acerra interwove with golden moss for you, which
Pomelia embroidered: on the bottom hem, savory grows with
spreading branches, and a locust hums from a leaf with its low
murmur.[53] Also, put on a cap woven from leafy boxwood. In the   460
middle, the industrious spider Arachne keeps watch over her webs,
lays them out by hand, and hunts a flitting gadfly, which tries to
flee, but, intercepted by the fine-spun cloak, gets its legs entangled
and whirs with extended wings, and the Lydian emerges, puffed   465
up, from her silent nest."[54]

Next to Misenius walks his spouse Prochyteia, a sight to behold for her face, her bearing, and the embroidered robe she
wears.[55] The robe's border, with shells tied onto it, makes a clink-
ing sound; her rough belt bristles with sea urchins, and the bosom

Zona riget viridique sinus frondescit in alga.
470 In manicis querulae ludunt per flumina ranae,
Cum subito extremas interstrepit anser ad ulvas:
Tum linquunt mediis convitia rauca sub undis
Attonitae, inde cavos referunt ad carmina rictus
Raucaque limosae meditantur murmura ripae.
475 Auribus hinc oriens radiat sol, splendet at illinc
Luna pruinosis incedens candida bigis.
Ipsa manu speculum dextra fert, cuius in orbe,
Cum sese gemino inclusit Latonia cornu,
Nocte quidem insidias Satyrorum artesque procaces
480 Detegit et cautis aperit nova furta Napaeis:
Illae iter occulto rapiunt per devia passu;
Luce autem, cum sol speculo diffulsit, ibi omnis
Cernere erit curas et facta infida virorum,
Quique paret thalamo fraudem litemque maritus.
485 Hoc fertur dominae rarum ac memorabile donum,
Quo secura sui tueatur foedera lecti.
    Claudicat hinc heros Capimontius et de summo
Colle ruunt misti iuvenes mistaeque puellae.
Omnis amat chorus et iuncti glomerantur amantes;
490 Is lento incedit passu baculoque tuetur
Infirmum femur et choreis dat signa movendis,
Assuetus choreae ludisque assuetus amantum.
Has inter mihi nota Marillia cantat: 'Ad alnum
Cogite oves, amat alnus, amant dominique gregesque.'
495 Responsant: 'Amat alnus, amant dominique gregesque.'
Sparguntur passim e calathis violaeque rosaeque
Et cava Maenalios suspirat tibia versus.
Praecedit gravidis bis septem onerata canistris
Pompa puellarum, pendent mantilia circum

is fringed with foliage of green algae. On the sleeves, frogs croak   470
their complaint and play in the streams, while a goose suddenly
honks from amid the water grass at the river's edge. Terrified, the
frogs abandon their hoarse croaking and plunge into the water's
depths: there, they turn their cavernous gullets back to singing,
and compose deep-sounding rumblings for the slimy bank. On   475
one of her ears, the rising sun shoots rays of light, and on the
other, the white moon shines, traveling across the sky on her dewy
chariot. Prochyteia carries a mirror in her right hand: in the mirror's circle, when Latona's daughter is enclosed between the moon's
two horns, she uncovers the ambushes and wanton strategies of
Satyrs at night and reveals their latest tricks to the cautious dell   480
nymphs: they run off quickly by a hidden course over solitary
paths.[56] But during the day, when the sun is reflected in the mirror, it will be possible to see all the obsessions and unfaithful
deeds of men, to see which husband plans to bring deceit and
quarrels to the bedroom. Prochyteia brings this mirror as a rare   485
and remarkable gift to her mistress Parthenope, so that she may
use it to guard over the pacts of her bed, free from care.

Next, the hero Capimontius comes limping along, and from the
top of the hill a mixed group of young men and girls comes running.[57] The whole troop is in love, and the lovers, joined together,
gather around. Capimontius walks at a slow pace, supports his   490
weak leg on a staff, and gives the sign for the dancing to begin,
accustomed as he is to the dance and lovers' games. Among these
young women, there is one whom I know, Marillia, who sings:[58]
"Drive your sheep to the alder tree: the alder tree is in love, the
flocks and their masters are in love." They respond: "The alder tree   495
is in love, the flocks and their masters are in love." Violets and
roses are strewn everywhere from handbaskets, while the hollow
flute breathes out Maenalian verses.[59] In front, a procession of
fourteen girls walks, weighed down with loaded baskets; on these,

500 Alba quidem, croceis sed flavescentia villis.
    Cuique suus comes haeret amans, cui corniger agnus
    Ex humeris grave pendet onus, sua fistula cuique,
    Plaudit et arguta de valle canentibus echo:
    'Sparge tuas, Sebethe, nuces, en colligit uxor;
505 Parthenope, tua poma sinu (vir seliget) effer.'
    At iuvenum manus usa humeris et pectore hanelans
    Ingentes taurorum armos, ingentia aprorum
    Corpora subvectat duplici pendentia conto,
    Bis septem capita hirta albis nutantia sannis.
510 Ingeminat plausus et vox sonat: 'Exue, nupta,
    Exue gausapinas et nudo corpore ramum
    Excipe, puniceo praefert quem cortice coniux.
    Exue gausapinas, coniux, ramoque valenti
    Sterne aciem, clausis uxorisque ingrue portis,
515 Comminus arma ciens, telumque in sanguine tinge.'
    Fescennina crepant latis convitia campis.
        At lino felix felixque Ansatia fuso
    Ostentat rarum decus ac variabile textum,
    Costalionis opus, telaeque insigne decorum.
520 Hinc illinc fluit amnis opacaque ripa virescit
    Margine cincta suo ruptisque immurmurat undis,
    Apparet certo tenuis sed semita calle,
    Qua nigrum formica agmen trahit ordine longo:
    Festinant aliae, ut plenos populentur acervos,
525 Illa redit rapto gravida atque e pondere fessa
    Invitat sociam in praedam, ac sese ore salutant;
    Pars condit terrae atque hiemi male credit iniquae,
    Emicat agmen agens segetique infertur abactae,
    Ut nunc iam videas, nunc iam vidisse putaris.
530 In medio positis clauduntur ovilia septis,
    Balat ovis vacuam ad mulctram et se calce tuetur,

napkins hang all around, white, but tinged with yellow in their   500
saffron-colored tufts. Each one is accompanied by her lover linger-
ing near; each lover has a lamb, with horns already sprouted,
hanging, a heavy burden, on his shoulders; each one has a flute,
and as the young men sing, from the resounding valley an echo
responds with its applause: "Scatter your nuts, Sebeto; see, your   505
wife gathers them up. Parthenope, proffer apples from your bosom; your husband will pick them." But the band of young men,
using their shoulders' strength, gasping with the effort, carry the
vast flanks of bulls, the vast bodies of boars hanging on two poles,
fourteen shaggy heads bobbing up and down with foaming white
jaws. The applause redoubles and a voice sounds out: "Take off   510
your clothes, O bride, take them off, and with naked body receive
the branch with red bark that your spouse bears before him. Take
off your clothes, groom, and with your strong branch lay low the
enemy's front line, break into the closed gates of your wife's city,
engage in hand-to-hand combat, and dip your weapon in blood."   515
Fescennine verses rattle their abuse across the wide fields.[60]

But Ansatia, happy in her use of thread and spindle, displays
a work of rare excellence, a tapestry varied in color, the work of
Costalio, a fitting tribute to the loom.[61] Here and there a stream   520
flows; the riverbank covered in shade is surrounded by its border
of green, and murmurs as the waves break against it. There appears a narrow path with a sure footway, where an ant leads a
black squadron in a long line: some of them hurry to pillage abundant heaps of grain; one ant returns, weighed down with plunder,   525
and, wearied by its weight, summons a comrade to help carry the
spoils, and they greet each other with a nod of the head. Others
bury their spoils in the ground, not trusting hostile winter. The
ant leading the squadron darts out, then scurries under a pile of
stolen grain, so that now you see it, now you think you have seen
it. In the middle of the tapestry, sheep pens are enclosed by fences,   530
a sheep bleats next to an empty milk pail and defends herself with

Upilio at geminis sudans premit ubera palmis:
Effluit hinc illinc tepidus liquor; adiuvat uxor
Blanditurque viro mulgetque incincta capellam,
535   Et cava fumanti spumant mulctralia lacte;
Filia parva focum bucca excitat: effurit intus
Lactea vis, florem inde legunt trepidantis aheni;
Post, ubi concrevit liquor ac deferbuit humor,
Tunc parco sale contingunt onerantque canistris
540   Decoctusque novo lentescit caseus orbe.
Circunstat pecus ignavum fucusque culexque,
Quos fumo puer aut ramo frondente coercet
Sedulus. Ipsa suo variatur tela colore,
Egregium dominae quondam ac memorabile munus.
545   Non arbor frondosa cavis sic vallibus, hortis
Sic mediis protenta cucurbita, non adeo grex
Altilium, dum scalpit humi sequiturque parentem,
Oblectant oculos et corda liquentia mulcent:
Tale decus telae, talem praescribit honorem.
550   Hos ego, cara soror, vidi novique Oriarchas.
        Murronem fama est cum coniuge Tifatea
Adventare etiam et centum properare quadrigis,
Ilice frondentem caput et colla ilice cinctum;
Hunc centum ciceris grummos totidemque phaseli
555   Convectare fabaeque ingentes volvere acervos
Horreaque annosae cereris; tum praela trecenta,
Et vini fontem atque lacus Lenaeidos undae
Curribus effluere, stagnare liquoribus arva
Baccheis, ipsum ex alta fluitare Caserta
560   Euchion in laticemque Lyaeum abiisse Casoram.
Uxorem vero assuetam Marcinida soli
Et lini cultricem olerumque et cannapis, illam
Et properare iter et rhedas agitare volantes,
Ne qua sit thalamis per se mora. Ne mea, ne tu

her hoof, while the shepherd, sweating, squeezes the udders with both hands: the warm liquid flows out here and there; his wife helps, soothes her husband, and with an apron tied on, milks a she-goat, and the hollow pails foam white with steaming milk.[62]   535
Their little daughter blows on the fire with cheeks puffed out: the milk boils inside; then they skim off the flower from the shaking bronze pot. Afterward, when the moisture has cooled and the liquid has condensed, they sprinkle it with a little salt, put wicker molds on top, and, reduced by boiling, it takes the new shape of a   540
firm round of cheese. Around the lazy herd drones and gnats swarm, which a boy diligently drives away with smoke and a leafy branch. The tapestry itself is richly varied in colors, an exceptional gift for her mistress that will be remembered in time to come. A   545
leafy tree in a hollow valley, a swollen gourd in the middle of a garden, a brood of chicks scraping the ground and following their parent, do not please the eyes and melt the heart with delight as much as this tapestry: such is its splendor, such is the beauty it displays.[63] And these, dear sister are the Oriarchs whom I have   550
seen and come to know.

It is said that Murro with his Tifatean wife is arriving as well, hurrying with a hundred chariots, his head wreathed with leafy holm oak, his neck wreathed with holm oak.[64] He conveys a hundred heaps of chickpeas, the same number of kidney beans, and   555
rolls along vast heaps of fava beans and granaries of stored grain; it is also said that he is transporting three hundred wine presses, and that a fountain of wine and lakes of Lenaean liquid flow from the chariots, the fields are inundated with the juice of Bacchus, the god Euhius himself flows down in streams from high Caserta, and Casora has been transformed into Lyaean nectar.[65]   560
Marcinis, his wife, who is accustomed to cultivate the field, to grow flax, vegetables and hemp, rushes along, driving her carriages at high speed, lest she be the cause of any delay of the wedding.

565 Crede aliam seu vere fabis, aestate phaselo
Fortius insudare atque invigilare colentem.
Ipsa et acu insutas vestes iunco atque genista
Dat dominae, ipse et crateras novum opus Faberontae
Legit herae et triplicem palmae de fronde coronam
570 Fictiliumque operum decus immortale mitellam
Intinctamque croco et frondenti bacchare cinctam.
Et mihi iuncta fide et ceparum Pulvica cura
Hoc et idem mea Panicoclis studiosa lupini
Adventare refert socia cum gente Vesevum,
575 Oblitum cladisque suae veterumque malorum,
Finitimosque heroas et alta ex arce Cicalae
Hircosum Capreonem, hirco nymphaque creatum,
Succinctum rapis et amictum tempora porro.
Curribus hunc corbes atque horrea avellanarum
580 Devehere, ipsum uda referentem carmen avena:
'Rura meam te, Amarylli, tenent, ego vector in urbem;
Dum redeo simul et peponos cole et allia velle.
Ex urbe, o Amarylli, tibi nova munera porto
Fusosque flavamque colum pictosque cothurnos.'
585 Alternant socii atque iterant nova carmina valles:
'Nos dominae siliquas et corna rubentia, felix
Oscula Sebethus feret et feret oscula virgo.
Nos ferimus dulcem peponum et melimela beatis;
Hi peponum et melimela legent thalamoque toroque.'
590   Ipse autem monte e summo sua dona Vesevus
Devectat trivium ad vetus Artusique macellum
Invectusque asino spargit sua munera plebi
Delicias ruris, post et digitalia et aptos
Verticulos fuso et tinnuleas volsellas.
595 Plebs plaudit varioque asinum clamore salutant
Brasiculisque apioque ferum nucibusque coronant.
Mox vecti gravibusque rotant vinalia contis

Do not believe, my sister, that any other woman toils harder over 565
fava beans in the spring or kidney beans in the summer, or is more
watchful a cultivator than she. She gives to her mistress clothing
sewn from rush and broom plant, while he has chosen for his
mistress mixing vessels, newly fashioned by Faberonta, a triple
garland of palm fronds, and an immortal piece of pottery, a miter 570
dyed with saffron and encircled with leafy baccar. Pulvica, joined
to me by trust and our shared cultivation of onions, and my dear
Panicoclis, devoted to growing lupine, both say that Vesuvius is
coming with all his people, forgetful of his catastrophe and mis- 575
fortunes of old, and also the heroes from neighboring lands, including goatish Capreo from the high citadel of Cicala, born of
a nymph and a goat, girded round with turnips, his forehead
wreathed with leek.[66] He transports baskets and granaries of hazelnuts in his chariots, and plays a song on his dew-soaked oaten 580
pipe: "You remain in the country, my dear Amaryllis, whereas I
travel to the city.[67] Until my return, take care of the melons and
pick the garlic. From the city, O Amaryllis, I bring you new
gifts—spindles, a yellow distaff, and decorated boots." The com- 585
panions sing by turns and the valleys echo back the new songs:
"We bring our mistress pulses and red cornel berries; fortunate
Sebeto will bring her kisses, and the maiden will bring him kisses.
We bring sweet melon and honey apples to the happy pair; they
shall harvest the melon and the honey apples in their marriage
chamber and their bed."

But Vesuvius himself brings his own gifts from the top of his 590
mountain to the market of Artusius at the old crossroads, and sitting astride an ass, scatters his gifts among the crowd, delicacies of
the countryside, as well as thimbles, bobbins for the spindle, and
tongs that make a tinkling sound.[68] The people applaud, hail the 595
ass with varied shouts, and garland the beast with little cabbages,
parsley, and nuts.[69] Then, with a lever and heavy poles, they roll
down casks full of the year's wine, full of two-year-old wine, and

Plena horno, plena et bimo, nitrata quadrimo;
Illa ruunt, ipse ex asino sua munera laudat,
600 Laudantem plausu sequitur Vesuina iuventus
Dissultantque cavae, favet et de vallibus echo.

Lepidina

Qua facie, mea Planuri, quo est ore Vesevus?

Planuris

Porticia hoc mihi fida comes narrare solebat,
Carmeli simul ad fontem dum rapa lavamus:
605 Ventre quidem modico, at medio de pectore gibbum
Protendit, quanta est Baviae cretatilis olla,
Qua miscet suibus pultes farcitque catinum;
Quodque pudet, nullas res hic habet et caret illis,
Pro quibus intumuit cucumis niger; inde Napaeae
610 Hunc rident, rident et Oreades; ille superbum
Nutat et inflexo quassat nigra tempora cornu,
Quod longe horrescit setis hinc inde reflexis.
At calvum caput, et nullo vestitur amictu;
Stant mento sentes horrentque ad pectora dumi.
615 Ah vereor, soror, et dicam tamen: huius ab ore
Curvantur geminae sannae, quarum altera pontum
Tetra petit fluctusque ferox et litora verrit,
Altera Sarastris fauces, saxa horrida Sarni,
Ac tantum non . . .

natron-treated casks full of four-year-old wine. The casks rush
down, and Vesuvius himself praises his own gifts from atop the
ass, while the Vesuvian youth follow his praise with their own ap-   600
plause, the grottos tremble, and from the valleys an echo lends its
support.

Lepidina

What is the appearance of Vesuvius, my dear Planuris, what kind
of a face does he have?

Planuris

My trusted friend Porticia would often tell me how he looks,
while we washed turnips together at the fountain of Carmelus:[70]
his stomach is not too large, but protruding from his chest is a   605
hump as large as the clay pot in which Bavia mixes slops for the
hogs and stuffs the vessel full; and (it is embarrassing to speak of)
he has none of *those* things, he lacks *those* things, and in their place,
there swells a dark cucumber. For this reason, the dell nymphs
laugh at him, the Oreads laugh at him; he nods his head pomp-   610
ously, and shakes his black temples with their curved horn, which
bristles all over with coarse hairs bent this way and that. But his
head is bald, and has no covering, while brambles grow on his chin
and thorn bushes bristle on his chest. Ah, I am afraid, my sister,   615
yet I shall tell you nonetheless: two curving tusks descend from his
mouth; one of them, disgusting and ruthless, goes down toward
the sea, skimming the waves and the shore; the other seeks the
jaws of the Sarrastri, the terrible rocks of the Sarno, and it al-
most . . .[71]

Lepidina

Ah soror, ah mea, desine et istos
620   Narrare Oriarchas: en venit aurea pompa,
En cultae Dryades, comptae quoque Oreades adsunt,
Et choreas agitare pares et dicere versus.

Pompa Sexta

Driades atque Oreades alternis concinunt;
Macron et Lepidina colloquuntur.

Driades

Turturibus si certa fides certusque columbis
Est amor, at variat non mutuus ardor amantum.

Oreades

625   Turturibus si certa fides certusque columbis
Est amor, et thalami sunt vincula certa mariti.

Driades

Fert filicem desertus ager, male cultus et hortus;
Non filicem bene aratus ager, non cultior hortus.

Oreades

Non rixam cultus thalamus, non culcitra litem;
630   Fert pacem thalamus cultus, fert culcitra somnum.

Lepidina

Ah, my dear sister, stop telling about those Oriarchs. See, the   620
gleaming procession is arriving; see, the elegant Dryads and the
well-adorned Oreads are here, equally skilled at leading dances and
chanting verses.

Sixth Procession

Dryads and Oreads sing in alternation;
Macron and Lepidina converse.

Dryads

If doves and turtledoves have unwavering loyalty and unwavering
love, so also the mutual passion of lovers is constant.[72]

Oreads

If doves and turtledoves have unwavering loyalty and unwavering   625
love, the bonds of the marriage bed are unwavering too.

Dryads

The abandoned field, the neglected garden, produces the bracken.
The plowed field, the well-cultivated garden, does not produce the
fern.

Oreads

The well-maintained bedroom does not produce quarreling; the
mattress does not produce a brawl. The well-maintained bedroom   630
brings peace; the mattress brings sleep.

Driades

'Somne io, pax dulcis io' cantate, puellae.

Oreades

'Oscula io, amplexus et io' celebrate, sorores.

Lepidina

Has, coniux, mea Planuris sat novit; at illam
Nosse nequit mea fida comes, mihi cara Patulcis,
635 Culta comam, succincta sinus et candida pectus,
Quaeque etiam roseo ver ipsum spirat ab ore.

Macron

Talis eras, cum te primum, Lepidina, sub ulmo
Cantantem vidi, croceis sic ipsa cothurnis
Saltabas, sic ora rosas, sic colla ligustrum
640 Florebant; memini numeros et verba canentis:
'Urit me Macronis amor Neside creati.'

Lepidina

Ipse refers: 'Patula cantat meus ignis ab ulmo,
Ulmus amor Macronis, amor Macronis ab ulmo.'
Alter erat croceus, alter tibi calceus albus,
645 Cingebat crines frondoso e subere ramus,
Et primo tonsore tibi nova barba nitebat.

Dryads

Hail sleep, hail sweet peace! Sing their praises, girls!

Oreads

Hail kisses, hail embraces! Sing their praises, sisters!

Lepidina

These nymphs, my husband, are known sufficiently well to my
dear Planuris: but she, in turn, cannot be known to my faithful
friend, my dear Patulcis, who has elegantly coiffed hair, a garment   635
neatly tucked, and a fair bosom, and who also wafts the fragrance
of spring itself from her rosy mouth.[73]

Macron

You were just like that, Lepidina, when I first saw you singing beneath the elm; thus did you dance in saffron boots, thus did your
face flower with roses, your neck with white privet. I remember   640
the melody and words of your song: "Love for Macron, son of
Nesis, makes me burn."[74]

Lepidina

You responded: "My love sings from an elm tree with spreading
boughs, the elm is Macron's love, Macron's love sings from the
elm." One of your shoes was saffron colored, the other white; a   645
bough from a leafy cork tree wreathed your hair, and your new
beard was sleek after your first shave.

Macron

Ipsa canis, querulae rumpunt tua verba cicadae,
Et dixti: 'Nec amant et sunt sine amore cicadae.'

Lepidina

Ipse arcu querulas stringis de fronde cicadas,
650 Et dixti: 'Querulae rumpant nunc verba cicadae.'
Ut sese ad choreas, Macron, movet apta Patulcis,
Et niveis suris nigrisque Patulcis ocellis!

Macron

Sic, memini, niveas nudasti tum mihi plantas,
Ad fontem cum fessa lavas; ego condor in ulva.

Lepidina

655 Ipsa canit formosa Patulcis, amatque Patulcis;
Me miseram, ut tristes surgunt ad tempora rugae!

Patulcis

Parthenope Sebethon amat, Platamonis Halantum,
Utraque nympha suum tenet et fovet utraque amantem;
Sola Patulcis, amans, sola est sine amante Patulcis:
660 Illum Nisa tenet deserti ad litoris algam
Nigra genu croceisque genis et lumine glauco;
Alba genu roseisque genis et lumine nigro
Oreque puniceo moeret deserta Patulcis
Expectatque deae non seram vindicis iram

Macron

You sang, but the cicadas humming their complaint interrupted your words. You said: "The cicadas do not love; without love are they."

Lepidina

You plucked the complaining cicadas from the foliage with your bow, and said: "*Now* let the complaining cicadas interrupt your words." How skillfully Patulcis dances, Macron; how white her calves, and how black her eyes! 650

Macron

In this way, I recall, you revealed your snow-white feet to my gaze, while you were bathing, weary, at the fountain. I was hiding in the sedge.

Lepidina

It is beautiful Patulcis who sings, Patulcis who is in love. Ah poor me, unpleasant wrinkles are appearing on my forehead! 655

Patulcis

Parthenope loves Sebeto, Platamonis loves Halantus, and each nymph holds and each caresses her lover. Patulcis alone — though in love — Patulcis alone her lover lacks.[75] He is detained near the algae of the deserted shore by Nisa, who has dark knees, yellow cheeks, and grey-green eyes. Patulcis, who has white knees, rosy cheeks, black eyes, and scarlet lips, laments, abandoned by her lover; she awaits the ire (which won't come late) of the avenging 660

665 Et venit ad choreas nec iam desperat amantem:
Nisa, meum tandem reddes mihi, Nisa, Nivanum!

Macron

Ut languet formosa et amari digna puella!
Et sua furta mihi narravit saepe Nivanus;
Nisa illum studiis avium ad sua litora traxit.
670 Tu modo fac viridem ligurim de coniuge Pansae,
(Deperit hanc iuvenis) nunc hoc age perfice, coniux,
Coniuge de Pansae dono ferat ipsa Patulcis:
Non mora, quin retrahat celerem in sua vota Nivanum.
Ipsa Patulcin adi, cura est mihi adire Nivanum.

Lepidina

675 O coniux, o Macron, ego hoc pro munere iam scis,
Scis tibi quid referam; referet sua dona Patulcis.

Macron

Ecce venit formosa, venit decus heroinon,
Et myrto dives serpillisque inclyta virgo,
Clara thymo longeque etiam clarissima melle
680 Antiniana. Ruunt huius fama undique amantes,
Et bona pars sine dote petunt connubia nymphae.
Ipsa seni blandita, senem cupit, huius ab ore
Et choreas agit et carmen meditata per hortos
Laeta canit; stupet ad sepem mirata iuventus.
685 Hinc sola incedit passuque elata superbo
Invitatque senem et suspiria ridet amantum.
Nec nosti, Lepidina, deam?

goddess, goes to dances, and does not yet despair of her lover.   665
Nisa, you will give him back, O Nisa, you will give me back my
Nivanus in the end![76]

Macron

How she languishes, that beautiful girl so worthy of being loved!
Nivanus often told me of his stolen love as well. Nisa drew him to
her shore, taking advantage of his interest in birds. You, make sure   670
that Patulcis herself obtains from Pansa's husband (he is hope-
lessly in love with her), from Pansa's husband — come on, get it
done now, my wife! — a green chaffinch as a gift: in the wink of an
eye, she will bring swift Nivanus back under her control.[77] You go
to Patulcis; it is my job to approach Nivanus.

Lepidina

O my husband, O Macron, for this favor, you already know, you   675
know quite well what I will give you in return; Patulcis will give
you her own gifts.

Macron

Behold, the glory of heroines, a maiden rich in myrtle and celebrated for wild thyme, famous for thyme and by far the most famous for honey, the beautiful Antiniana.[78] Drawn by her fame,   680
lovers come rushing from all directions, and many of them seek to
marry the nymph without a dowry. As for her, she whispers sweet
nothings to an old man, she desires an old man, and at the sound
of his voice, she leads dances and, composing a song, happily sings
amid the gardens. The crowd of young people stands wondering,
astonished, by the hedge. Then she walks on alone, with a proud,   685
elevated gait, calls to the old man, and laughs at the sighs of her
suitors. Did you not recognize the goddess, Lepidina?

Lepidina

Quin, o mea cura,
(Nondum notus eras) sensi sub rupe canentem.
Prima illi vox: 'Eurydice, meaque optima coniux,
690 Eurydice, mihi solus amor.' Tum verba notavi,
Nunc numeros memini; quid amor, iam denique sensi;
Quid sit amor, quid hymen, quid sint connubia nosco.

Macron

Est illi sepostum opus artificis Melidoxi
Fistula, sunt numeri intacti cantoris Hymellae:
695 Despicit hinc et oloris avenam et carmina cygni.
Tum septem nitidae sunt praesto ad munera nymphae,
Sedulaque Uranie scenam atque umbracula tendit.
Illam non alias ederae cinxere virentes
Aptius aut roseis insedit fistula labris;
700 Quin numeros meditata canit nova carmina virgo.

Pompa Septima

Antiniana hymenaeum celebrans feliciter ominatur;
iuvenum ac puellarum chorus recinit;
Macron ac Lepidina colloquuntur.

Antiniana

Dicite 'Io,' iuvenes, et 'Io' geminate, puellae.
Hesperus adveniet fausto cum sidere, nymphae
Qui referet thalamos, qui vincula nectat amantum.
Dicite 'Io,' iuvenes, et 'Io' geminate, puellae.

Lepidina

Why yes, my love, I even heard her (this was before I knew you) singing at the foot of a rock. Her song began: "Eurydice, my best wife, Eurydice, my only love."[79] At that time, I took note of the   690 words. Now I remember the melody. Even back then I felt what love was. What love is, what connubial union is, what marriage is, I now know.[80]

Macron

She has a flute, kept in reserve, the work of the artisan Melidoxus, and untouched melodies of the singer Hymella.[81] She gazes down   695 with disdain on the swan's oaten pipe and the songs of the swan.[82] In addition, there are seven lovely nymphs ready to carry out their tasks, and Urania is diligently setting up the stage and extending the sunshades.[83] On no other occasion has green ivy garlanded her head more elegantly, the pipe rested on her rosy lips more aptly; and now, after composing the melody, the maiden sings her latest   700 songs.

Seventh Procession

Antiniana, celebrating the wedding, offers propitious omens;
a chorus of young men and young women sings in response;
Macron and Lepidina converse.

Antiniana

Sing "Hurrah," young men, echo back "Hurrah," young women. Hesperus will come with his propitious star to bring the nymph her wedding rites and fasten the lovers' bonds.[84] Sing "Hurrah," young men, and echo back "Hurrah," young women.

Chorus

705 Dicimus: 'O Hymenaee, io Hymen Hymenaee!'

Antiniana

Hesperus adveniet, socii qui foedera lecti,
Qui statuat leges, qui deducat Hymenaeum.
Dicite 'Io,' iuvenes, et 'Io' geminate, puellae.

Chorus

Dicimus: 'O Hymenaee, io Hymen Hymenaee!'

Antiniana

710 Hesperus adveniet cari desponsor amoris,
Qui teneros lusus et mutua gaudia monstret.
Dicite 'Io,' iuvenes, et 'Io' geminate, puellae.

Chorus

Dicimus: 'O Hymenaee, io Hymen Hymenaee!'

Antiniana

Interea, adveniet dum Vesperus aureus et dum
715 Flameolum et roseos Hymen parat ipse cothurnos,
Omina dicamus thalamo Geniumque citemus.
Gausapinas virides, nova nupta novusque maritus,
Induite et viridem capiti geminate coronam;
Sint vobis anni virides viridisque iuventus,
720 Et virides horti sint et viridantia rura.
Dicite: 'Io, sic fila neunt, sic stamina volvunt!'

Chorus

We sing: "O Hymenaeus, hurrah, Hymen Hymenaeus!"[85]   705

Antiniana

Hesperus shall come to establish the pacts of the shared bed, make its laws, and lead in Hymenaeus. Say "Hurrah," young men, and echo back "Hurrah," young women.

Chorus

We sing: "O Hymenaeus, hurrah, Hymen Hymenaeus!"

Antiniana

Hesperus, the guarantor of affectionate love, shall come to teach   710 tender games and reciprocal delights. Sing "Hurrah," young men, and echo back "Hurrah," young women.

Chorus

We sing: "O Hymenaeus, hurrah, Hymen Hymenaeus!"

Antiniana

In the meanwhile, until golden Vesper arrives and while Hymen   715 himself prepares the bridal veil and rosy buskins, let us sing the omens for the marriage and call upon the Genius.[86] Newly wedded bride, newly wedded groom, put on green clothing, and double the green garlands on your heads.[87] May you have green years and a flourishing green youth, green gardens and fields that grow   720 green. Sing: "Hurrah, so they spin the threads, so they roll the strands of wool!"[88]

Chorus

Euge io, sic fila neunt, sic stamina volvunt!

Antiniana

Nascetur proles heroo sanguine digna,
Altera, quae tauros domet et sciat ordine plantas
725   Disserere et lentam in quincuncem ponere vitem,
Felix et pratis et felix ubere terrae.
Dicite: 'Io, sic fila neunt, sic stamina volvunt!'

Chorus

Euge io, sic fila neunt, sic stamina volvunt!

Antiniana

Altera, quae telas cum pectine ducat eburno
730   Discernatque, et acu silvas et flumina ducat,
Et fuso docilique manu ingeniosa propago.
Dicite: 'Io, sic fila neunt, sic stamina volvunt!'

Chorus

Euge io, sic fila neunt, sic stamina volvunt!

Antiniana

Nascentur heroes et heroum inclyta pubes,
735   Aclidibusque sparoque verutisque apta iuventus,
Qui monstra oceani, qui saxicolas Tritones
Avertant, terrae Sirenum et litora servent.
Dicite: 'Io, sic fila neunt, sic stamina volvunt!'

Chorus

Hurrah, so they spin the threads, so they roll the strands of wool!

Antiniana

Offspring will be born, worthy of their heroic line: one, who will tame bulls and know how to sow plants in ordered intervals and to   725
arrange the pliant vine in the shape of a quincunx, prosperous in meadows and prosperous in the fertility of the land.[89] Sing: "Hurrah, so they spin the threads, so they roll the strands of wool!"

Chorus

Hurrah, so they spin the threads, so they roll the strands of wool!

Antiniana

And there will be another, who will shape webs with an ivory comb, embroider them, and fashion forests and rivers with the   730
needle, a daughter talented with her skillful hand and spindle. Sing: "Hurrah, so they spin the threads, so they roll the strands of wool!"

Chorus

Hurrah, so they spin the threads, so they roll the strands of wool!

Antiniana

Heroes shall be born, a famous generation of young heroes, youth   735
well suited to darts, hunting spears, and javelins, to drive away the monsters of the ocean, the rock-dwelling Tritons, and preserve the shores of the land of the Sirens.[90] Sing: "Hurrah, so they spin the threads, so they roll the strands of wool!"

Chorus

Euge io, sic fila neunt, sic stamina volvunt!

Antiniana

740 Nascentur qui Mopso et faunigenis Meliboeis
Dent iura et gregibus saltus et pascua monstrent,
Ipsi pastorum reges pecorumque magistri.
Dicite: 'Io, sic fila neunt, sic stamina volvunt!'

Chorus

Euge io, sic fila neunt, sic stamina volvunt!

Antiniana

745 Nascetur qui longinquis procul advena terris
Haec adeat pastor pauper loca, cuius ab ore
Arida vicini resonent et saxa Vesevi,
Ipsae quem pinus, ipsa haec arbusta vocabunt.
Ille alta sub rupe canet frondator ad auras
750 Pastoris musam Damonis et Alphesiboei:
Illi concedant hinc Tityrus, inde Menalcas,
Alter oves, alter distentas lacte capellas,
Et mirata suos requiescent flumina cursus,
Damonis musam dum cantat et Alphesiboei.
755 Dicite: 'Io, sic fila neunt, sic stamina volvunt!'

Chorus

Euge io, sic fila neunt, sic stamina volvunt!

Chorus

Hurrah, so they spin the threads, so they roll the strands of wool!

Antiniana

There will be born men to give the laws to Mopsus and Meli- 740
boeuses descended from Faunus, and show groves and pastures
to the flocks, kings among shepherds, masters of flocks.[91] Sing:
"Hurrah, so they spin the threads, so they roll the strands of
wool!"

Chorus

Hurrah, so they spin the threads, so they roll the strands of wool!

Antiniana

There will be born one who will come from afar, a stranger, from 745
faraway lands, to these parts, a poor shepherd, with whose words
the parched rocks of neighboring Vesuvius will resound, whom
these very pine trees, these very orchards will invoke. Pruning the
trees, at the foot of a high rock, he will sing to the winds the po- 750
etry of the shepherds Damon and Alphesiboeus. Tityrus, on the
one hand, shall yield to him his sheep, and Menalcas on the other,
his she-goats swollen with milk; and the rivers, in amazement, will
bring their currents to a standstill, while he is singing the poetry
of Damon and Alphesiboeus.[92] Sing: "Hurrah, so they spin the 755
threads, so they roll the strands of wool!"

Chorus

Hurrah, so they spin the threads, so they roll the strands of wool!

Antiniana

Nasceturque alius longo post tempore pastor
Advena et ipse quidem, proprii sed consitor horti;
Ausit et hic tenerum calamo trivisse labellum.
760 Hunc et Damoetas et amabit Lyctius Aegon,
Alter oves niveas dono dabit, alter et hedos.
Hic pascet niveos herbosa ad flumina cygnos,
Misceat ipsa suos pascenti Amaryllis olores;
Hic et populea vacuus cantabit in umbra,
765 Uranie intactam cantanti iunget avenam
Et cantum argutae referent ad sidera valles.
Dicite: 'Io, sic fila neunt, sic stamina volvunt!'

Chorus

Euge io, sic fila neunt, sic stamina volvunt!

Antiniana

Succedentque alii Damones et Alphesiboei,
770 Quique etiam tenui musam meditentur avena
Pastores edera insignes et arundine clari.
O mihi tum ut choreas agitare et dicere versus
Compositique senis mutae applausisse favillae,
Ut iuvet et notam tumulo instaurare querelam:
775 Ipse senex tacita positus laetabitur urna.
Dicite: 'Io, sic fila neunt, sic stamina volvunt!'

Chorus

Euge io, sic fila neunt, sic stamina volvunt!

Antiniana

There will be born another shepherd, after a long passage of time.[93] He too will be a stranger, but also the sower of his own garden, and he will dare to wear down his tender lip with the reed pipe. He will be loved by Damoetas and Lyctian Aegon; one will   760
give him snow-white sheep as a gift, the other goats. He will pasture snow-white swans by the grassy riverbanks. Amaryllis herself shall mingle her own swans with his as he pastures them, and he will sing, at leisure, in the shade of poplars. Urania will accompany   765
him on an untouched oaten pipe as he sings, and the clear-sounding valleys will convey his song to the stars. Sing: "Hurrah, so they spin the threads, so they roll the strands of wool!"

Chorus

Hurrah, so they spin the threads, so they roll the strands of wool!

Antiniana

Other Damons and Alphesiboeuses will succeed him, other shep-   770
herds, adorned with ivy and famous for playing the reed, who will also compose poetry on the slender oaten pipe. Oh, how it will delight me then to lead dances and sing verses and applaud the mute ashes of the old man in his grave, how it will delight me to renew the well-known lament on the burial mound! The old man   775
himself, laid away in the silent urn, will rejoice![94] Sing: "Hurrah, so they spin the threads, so they roll the strands of wool!"

Chorus

Hurrah, so they spin the threads, so they roll the strands of wool!

Antiniana

Dicite: 'Io Hymenaee, io Hymen Hymenaee!'

Chorus

Dicimus: 'O Hymenaee, io Hymen Hymenaee,
780 Io Hymen, Hymenaee Hymen, Hymen Hymenaee,
Felix o Hymenaee, Hymen felix Hymenaee!'

Lepidina

O Macron, nympha haec lepido ut sermone locuta est!
Illi mel labris, favus illi stillat ab ore!

Macron

O coniux, nympha haec longe est ditissima melle,
785 Centum habet haec apium tabulata, examina centum.

Lepidina

Nunc agedum (ad thalamos properat nanque undique pompa)
Quae Macron domino, dominae Lepidina loquamur
Conveniat, nanque illa et forma et dote superbit.
Dos illi centumque boves totidemque iuvenci,
790 Tercentum simae Cirnea matre capellae,
Cornigerique hedi totidem, quis fronte sub hirta
Albescunt maculae, sunt caetera corpora fulvi,
Custodes gemini Arctoa de gente Lacones,
Mille Theatinis errant quae montibus agnae;
795 Praeterea decus illud inenarrabile textum
Frondentis zonae cerasi de cortice nexae
Aurato et iunco et purpureis viburnis,
E cuius medio pandens avis altilis alas

Antiniana

Sing: "Hurrah, Hymenaeus, hurrah, Hymen Hymenaeus!"

Chorus

We sing: "O Hymenaeus, hurrah, Hymen, Hymenaeus; hurrah,   780
Hymen, Hymen Hymeneaeus, Hymen Hymenaeus, O propitious
Hymenaeus, O propitious Hymen Hymenaeus!"

Lepidina

O Macron, how gracefully this nymph spoke! Honey drips from
her lips, a whole honeycomb flows from her mouth![95]

Macron

O my wife, this nymph is by far the richest in honey; she has a   785
hundred rows of bees, a hundred swarms of bees.

Lepidina

Come now (for the procession is quickly coming from all directions to the house of the bride and groom), let us speak what is
fitting, you, Macron to your master, I, Lepidina to my mistress;
for she is magnificent in both beauty and dowry. As a dowry she
has a hundred oxen and the same number of bullocks, three hun-   790
dred snub-nosed she-goats of Corsican mother, the same number
of horned goats, that, while tawny otherwise throughout their
bodies, have white spots on their shaggy foreheads, their guardians, two Laconian dogs of northern breed, and a thousand lambs
that wander over the Teatine mountains; in addition, that splendid   795
work of indescribable weave, a belt made from the bark of a leafy
cherry tree interwoven with gilded twigs and purple viburnum: at
its center is a fowl that stretches its wings, scratches at the ground,

Et scalpit terras et pullos evocat ore:
800 Illi triticea tingunt sua rostra farina,
Mox fovet adductis saturos sua mater in alis.
Ergo quid domino, dominae quid uterque loquamur,
Dic, Macron: sua verba suo sint munere digna.

Macron

Qui tuus est et ubique comes, lepor adsit et ipse
805 Cum primis, Lepidina, tibi et venus illa loquenti.

Lepidina

Rura lepos meus is, coniux, colit, effugit urbem,
Forsitan et dominae risum movisse iuvabit.

Macron

Suavia sint quaecumque feres, Lepidina, memento.

Lepidina

Quin etiam geminata illi simul oscula tradam.

Macron

810 Sic dices: 'Cape, nympha, bonum, qui me urit, amorem,
Obbam lactis et haec fumanti farta canistro;
Tercentumque illae Cirnea matre capellae,
Mille Theatinis errant quae montibus agnae,
Bis gravidae fiant anno bis et ubera tendant.'
815 Sic dicam: 'Sume hos culto de margine fructus,
Qui tibi notus amor nostri matrisque patrisque.

72

and calls its chicks by squawking; they dip their beaks in the   800
wheat bran, then, when they are full, their mother keeps them
warm by putting her wings around them.[96] Tell, then, Macron,
what each of us is to say, you to your master, I to my mistress; let
the words in each case be worthy of the gift.

Macron

May you have above all the grace that is yours and that accompa-
nies you wherever you go, and the charm you have when you   805
speak.[97]

Lepidina

That grace of mine, husband, lives in the country, it flees the city,
but perhaps it will be gratifying to make my mistress laugh.

Macron

Let whatever you offer be sweet, Lepidina — don't forget.

Lepidina

Why, I'll even give her two kisses.

Macron

You will say: "Take, nymph, in token of the sincere love with   810
which I burn, a pitcher of milk and these sausages heaped in a
steaming basket;[98] and may those three hundred she-goats born
of a Corsican mother, the thousand lambs that wander over the
Theatine mountains, become pregnant twice a year and twice a
year have udders swollen with milk." I shall say: "Take these fruits   815
from a well cultivated riverbank in token of the love that I, my
mother, and my father bear you, as you well know. May those

Cornigerique illi geminos de coniuge foetus
Suscipiant fronte albentes et tergore fulvos;
Ipse mares videas uno de ventre gemellos,
820   Sis Macron illi, illa suo Lepidina Macroni.'
Haec nos, et properemus et hostia celsa petamus.

horned goats receive from their mates twin offspring with white foreheads and tawny backs; and may you, Sebeto, see two male offspring from a single womb, and may you be Macron to her, she 820 Lepidina to her Macron." Thus will we speak: let us hurry and seek the lofty doors.

Meliseus

A quo uxoris mors deploratur.

Collocutores Ciceriscus et Faburnus pastores.

Ciceriscus

Hic cecinit Meliseus et haec quoque signa doloris
Servat adhuc corylus: 'Vidi tua funera, coniux,
Non, o non perii' caesoque in cortice signat
Populus: 'Ah moriens morientem, Ariadna, relinquis.'

Faburnus

5   Pro facinus, tantumne tibi, Melisee, dolorum?
Cui modo convallesque cavae saltusque querenti
Reddebant: 'Mihi te, quis te mihi, Phosphori, ademit?
O mecum, o salices, mecum o lugete, myricae.'

Ciceriscus

Vox illi gemitusque sonant Ariadnan et antra
10   Responsant Ariadnan; ibi miserabilis: 'Eheu
Te sequor, o coniux' alta et de rupe sonantem
Deturbat, quae cara seni pendebat ab ore
Fistula, dumque cadit fluitans sua reddit arundo,
Et numeros et verba refert vocalis arundo:
15   'Te sequor, o Ariadna, morare, Ariadna, sequentem.'

: II :

Meliseus

Meliseus laments the death of his wife.[1]

Speakers: the shepherds Ciceriscus and Faburnus.[2]

Ciceriscus

Meliseus sang here, and the hazel tree, too, still preserves these
signs of his pain: "I saw your death, wife, but, alas, I did not die."
And on its carved bark the poplar is inscribed: "Ah, dying, Ariadne, you leave behind one who is dying."

Faburnus

Ah, what misfortune! Could there be so much suffering for you,   5
Meliseus? The rolling valleys and groves just recently echoed back
your lament: "Who took you away from me, Phosphoris?[3] Ah,
grieve with me, O willows; grieve with me, O tamarisks."

Ciceriscus

His words, his laments sound out Ariadne's name, and the caves
echo back "Ariadne." Then he wretchedly cries: "Alas, I follow you,   10
O wife," and the old man casts down from the high rock the
sounding flute that hung from his mouth and that he held dear,
and as it falls, fluttering, the reed flute goes on making its music,
and the speaking reed echoes the melody and words: "I am follow-   15
ing you, O Ariadne; wait for me, O Ariadne, as I follow."

Faburnus

Ergo senta iacet spinosisque obsita dumis
Illa quidem et nymphis et Musis cognita avena?
Nec Corydon nec Thyrsis eam nec legit Amyntas?

Ciceriscus

Quin legit, dum spirat adhuc sub rupe, Patulcis,
20 Et dixit: 'Tibi, Daphni, tibi nova munera servo
Cantabisque senem ad tumulum condesque sepulchro.'
Inde levem calamum labris admovit et alto
Corde dedit gemitum cantusque effudit amaros:
    'Severat ipsa suo segetem cum coniuge et una
25 Purgarat valida segetem cum coniuge marra;
Ipsa suo segetem cum coniuge falce secarat
Et gravidos torta culmos religarat avena
Contuderatque suo messem cum coniuge et aurae
Iactarat fragilem socio cum coniuge aristam;
30 Interea socio demulserat aëra cantu,
Mox simul aestiva requierat fessa sub umbra
Carpebatque leves caro cum coniuge somnos.
Ah dolor, abreptamque toro avulsamque lacertis
Coniugis hanc rapuit volucri Proserpina curru,
35 Clausit et aeterno torpentia lumina somno.
Lugeat hanc desertus ager, desertus et hortus
Et deserta teges, desertae et compita villae;
In primis luge, labor, heu, labor irrite, luge,
Et marrae et segetes, fraudataque praemia ruris
40 Et vanam sine fruge operam manuumque boumque.
En squalent prata et sua sunt sine honore salicta
Extinctamque Ariadnan agri, Ariadnan et ipsae
Cum gemitu referunt silvae vallesque queruntur;

78

Faburnus

Does it lie rough with thorns, then, and covered over with brambles, the oaten pipe known to both the nymphs and the Muses?
Neither Corydon, nor Thyrsis, nor Amyntas has picked it up?[4]

Ciceriscus

Why, Patulcis picked it up, while it was still sounding out a tune
under the cliff, and said: "For you, Daphnis, for you I reserve new   20
gifts, and you will sing of the old man by his tomb and you will
bury him in his grave."[5] Then she brought the light pipe to her
lips, from the depths of her heart gave a groan, and poured forth
songs bitter with grief.

"With her husband she had sown the field, and together with
her husband she had cleared the field of weeds with sturdy hoe.   25
With her husband, she had cut down the crops with a scythe, tied
up the abundant stalks with a twisted reed, with her husband
crushed the grain, and with her husband as companion cast the
fragile ears of grain to the wind.[6] Meanwhile, she and her husband   30
had soothed the air by singing together. Then, weary, she had
rested in the summer shade, and with her dear husband, enjoyed
easy sleep. Ah, the grief! Proserpina, in her winged chariot,
snatched her from her husband's bed, tore her from her husband's
arms, and closed her listless eyes in eternal sleep. May the aban-   35
doned field grieve for her, the abandoned garden, the abandoned
cottage, the pathways of the abandoned farm.[7] Above all, lament,
O toil, O ineffectual toil, O crops and hoes, lament the rewards of
the land promised but not given, the vain, fruitless work of men   40
and oxen. See, the meadows lie neglected, her beloved willow
groves lack their beauty, and the fields reecho Ariadne's death, the
very forests report her death with a groan, the valleys lament her

Extinctamque Ariadnam iterant clamantia saxa,
45 Et colles iterant Ariadnam, Ariadnan et amnes.
Conveniant ululae ad questus geminentque querelam
Infelixque Ariadnan avis gemat ore sub imo,
Ipsae etiam querulae iungant suspiria frondes.
    'Duxerat ipsa levi fuso subtegmen et ipsa
50 Tenuia sub celeri versarat pollice fila;
Ipsa sua studiosa manu glomerarat in orbem
Atque hinc vimineis onerarat lecta canistris:
Dum tenui insertas orditur pectine telas,
Unde viro, unde et natis sua texta pararet,
55 Unde sibi cultumque sinum et mantilia cana,
Quis olus intactamque rosam deferret in urbem
Atque arae solitos verno sub tempore flores,
(Ah dolor, ah lacrimae!) verrentem licia et oras
Stringentem telae radiosque et fila trahentem
60 Occupat atra manu truncatque rigentia pensa
Immitis Lachesis crinemque e vertice vellit
Purpureum, et furva circum caput horret in umbra.
Quo radii? Quo pensa? Quis, o quis staminis usus?
Quo telae studium infelix? Quo pecten et orsa?
65 O dolor, o lamenta! Gemat miserabilis "Eheu"
Consuetus dominae turtur, consueta columba.
Illa colum ducebat, ibi vestigia circum
Ludebant geminae volucres, ludentibus ipsa
Et cicer et tenerum spargebat blanda cuminum
70 Mulcebatque manu. Gemat "Heu" miserabilis "Eheu"
De trabe moesta sua nidumque relinquat irundo.
Dum telam stringebat et acre sonantia lina
Et cantu lenibat opus, tum flebilis ales
Iungebat socias lacrimoso carmine voces
75 Miscebatque modos. Gemat "Heu" miserabilis "Eheu,"
"Heu" gemat infelix liguris, cui grata petenti

death, the rocks cry out Ariadne's death again and again, the hills   45
repeat the name of Ariadne, the streams reecho her name. Let the
screech owls come together to lament and redouble their complaint, let the unlucky bird groan Ariadne's name from the depth
of its throat, let the very leaves of the trees sigh, lamenting, in
unison.

"She had drawn the thread with the light spindle, and she her-   50
self had spun the slender threads under her quick thumb. She had
zealously rolled them into balls with her hand, then collected
them and filled wicker baskets with them. She was lining up the
woven thread with the slender comb, out of which she was making
woven garments for her husband and children, and for herself an   55
elegant robe and white cloths for bringing into the city green vegetables, fresh roses, and the flowers that are usually placed on altars in the springtime (ah the grief and tears!); she was brushing
the wool, tightening the edges of the web, and drawing the shuttle
and threads, when pitiless Lachesis seized her with her black   60
hand, cut short the stiffening threads of life, plucked a purple hair
from her head, and a shudder went through her head in the
gloomy shade. To what purpose the shuttles? The day's allotment
of spinning? The use of the threads? The vain exertion of the
loom? The comb and the warp? Ah the grief and lamentations!   65
Let the wretched turtledove that was accustomed to its mistress
moan 'Alas!,' the dove that was accustomed to her lament. She
would be spinning, and there around her feet both birds would
play, and as they played, she would scatter for them chickpea and
tender cumin and stroke them with caressing hand. Alas, let the   70
swallow, in sadness, wretchedly lament from its crossbeam, and
leave its nest. As she tightened the web and the threads that rang
with high-pitched sound, and lightened her task with song, then
the plaintive bird in tearful song would join its notes and mingle   75
its melodies in harmony with hers. Alas, let the unhappy chaffinch

81

Purgabatque nucem contusaque crusta liquabat
Mellis arundinei vitreum et de fonte liquorem.
 'Ad gemitum coeant lacrimosi compita ruris,
80 Pastores Ariadnam, Ariadnam armenta querantur
Extinctamque Ariadnan opacis buccula silvis
Cum gemitu testetur, et antra Ariadnan, et ipsi
Ingeminent montes Ariadnam, Ariadnan et umbrae.
Claudite oves stabulis, stabulis cohibete capellas,
85 Formosae ruris natae innuptaeque puellae;
Dum matres Ariadnam iterant, vos, avia planctu
Implentes, legite intactos et iungite flores
Et solis luctum et pueri lacrimantis amorem
Texite et abscissos Veneris de fronte capillos.
90 Post, ubi: "Io Ariadnan, io Ariadnan!" et ipsum
Implestis clamore nemus, hunc addite honorem
Ad tumulum, pia verba acrem testantia luctum:
"Pro fusoque coloque et vimineis calathiscis
Hos flores atque haec tibi serta, Ariadna, paramus
95 Ad Laurum, tumulo tibi quae iam crescit et ossa
Amplectens densa tumulum mox conteget umbra;
Pro lino telaque et pro subtegmine et orsis
Has lacrimas, Ariadna, atque haec tibi dona vovemus;
En lactis florem ad tumulum et redolentia mella,
100 Placamusque pios manis et condimus umbram,
Aeternum et valeas, Ariadna, aeterna valeto!"
 'Nebat acu tunicam nato indusiumque puellis,
Fundebatque manu latices, dum pingit ab urna
Spargentem Sebethon aquas, dum labitur amnis,
105 Per salices strepit et ripis frondentibus aura,
Murmurat et tenui decurrens lympha susurro;
Ipsa sua lucem dextra insignibat et auras
Spargebat flammis, radiisque micantibus atras
Pellebat tenebras, primo ut sol splendet Eoo

lament, for whom she agreeably used to shell a nut when asked and to soften crushed bits of sugar cane honey in crystalline spring water.[8]

"Let the mourning countryside gather to lament at the crossroads, let the herdsman bewail the loss of Ariadne, the herds bewail Ariadne's loss, let the heifer in the shady woods attest to Ariadne's death with her groaning; let the grottos reecho the name of Ariadne, the very mountains reecho Ariadne's name, the shadows reecho 'Ariadne.' Enclose the sheep in their pens, shut the she-goats in their barn, O beautiful daughters of the countryside, beautiful maidens unwed. As your mothers repeat the name of Ariadne, fill the wilderness with lamentation, pick fresh flowers, join them in a bouquet, and plait together sun's grief with weeping boy's love and locks plucked from Venus' forehead.[9] Afterward, when you have filled the grove itself with your shouting—'Ariadne, hail Ariadne!'—add this homage at her graveside, dutiful words attesting bitter grief: 'Instead of the spindle, distaff and small wicker baskets, Ariadne, we prepare these flowers and these garlands for you by the laurel tree, which already grows on your tomb, and, winding round your bones, will soon cover the burial mound with dense shade; instead of the thread, the web, the woof, and the warp, these tears, Ariadne, and these gifts we vow to you: see, we place fior' di latte and fragrant honey by the tomb; we propitiate your pious spirit and bury your shade; farewell forever, Ariadne, and for all time, farewell.'

"She was sewing a tunic for her son, clothing for her daughters: she produced streams from her hand as she embroidered the Sebeto pouring waters from an urn, while a stream glides by, a breeze murmurs on the grassy banks amid the willows, and water burbles as it flows past with gentle whispering. She was depicting light with her right hand and scattering flames across the sky, driving away dark shadows with gleaming rays as the glittering sun

110 Fulgidus et tremulis intermicat ardor in undis.
　　Ah dolor, ah gemitus! Fleat, o fleat excita silvis
　　Esculus et durae veniant ad funera quercus!
　　Format acu dum quercum et mollibus esculus umbris
　　Dum surgit viridans, procul, ah procul, ingruit acta
115 Tempestas Erebo, vellit quae funditus altam
　　Et quercum et fractis discinditur esculus umbris,
　　Et tunicam et tantos secum rapit Auster honores;
　　Inde repens lucem nox occupat, occidit et sol
　　Et radii; ipsa novis Ariadna offusa tenebris
120 Caligat nocte obscura et circundatur umbra.
　　Crudeles radii, quo lux, quo purpureus sol,
　　Crudelisque dies? Mecum, o mecum ite, puellae,
　　Ad luctum, mecum ite, deae, mecum ite, sorores
　　Naiades, quibus illa choros iungebat et una
125 Nudabat liquidis argentea membra sub undis;
　　Huc, sociae Dryades, simul et celerate, Napaeae,
　　Umbrarum memores choreaeque in montibus actae,
　　Et questus geminate et amarum intendite luctum.
　　　'Sol obiit, tenebrae exortae: non pabula rorem,
130 Non imbrem sitiant segetes, non culta liquorem;
　　In lacrimas abeant rores imberque liquorque,
　　Unde fluant queruli lacrimoso margine rivi,
　　Murmuraque ipsa sonent Ariadnam, Ariadnan et ipsi
　　Suspirent cursus udaeque querantur arenae.
135 Lux periit, tenebrae offusae: iam robora frondes
　　Excutiant foliisque leves spolientur et alni,
　　Ipsa comas, laurus, tristesque avellite, myrti;
　　Dum frondes foliisque comae miscentur et auris
　　Huc illuc agitantur et excitus instrepit aër,
140 Ipse aër, ipsae frondes, folia ipsa comaeque
　　Dum volitant, strepit et miseris conquestibus aura,

shines at rise of dawn and its fire flashes amid the tremulous   110
waves. Ah the grief, the lamentation! May the holm oak come
forth from the forest and weep, ah let it weep, and may the hard
oak trees come to the funeral. While she embroiders the shape of
the oak tree with her needle and the holm oak rises up with green
foliage, casting pleasant shadows, from afar, ah from afar, a storm   115
driven from Erebus assails her, a storm that pulls up the lofty oak
from the roots and splits apart the holm oak, shattering its shade,
and the south wind snatches away the tunic and such fine ornaments. Then sudden night overwhelms the light, the sun and its
rays are eclipsed. Ariadne herself, covered in unfamiliar shadows,
is plunged in night's darkness and enveloped in shadow. Cruel   120
rays, where is your light, the radiant sun, the heartless daylight?
Come with me, come with me to lament, O girls, come with me,
goddesses, come with me, Naiad sisters, whom she used to join in
dancing and with whom she would bare her silvery limbs beneath   125
the crystalline waves; come here quickly, companion Dryads, and
you too, dell nymphs, who keep the memory of shady retreats and
dancing held on the mountains: redouble your laments and intensify the bitterness of your grief.

"The sun has set, darkness has risen: may the grass not thirst
for dew, nor the crops for rain, nor the fields for water; may the   130
dew, the rain, and the water turn into tears; may streams of lamentation flow from them between tearful banks, and may the very
murmuring of the waters resound with the name of Ariadne, the
very currents whisper Ariadne's name, and the moist sands lament.
The light has died, the shadows have spread. Let the oaks cast off   135
their leaves, the slender alders be stripped bare of foliage, and you,
laurel and mournful myrtles, pluck out your locks.[10] While leafy
branches and foliage are mingled with leaves, tossed hither and
thither by the breezes, and the agitated air makes a rustling sound,
and while the air, the leafy branches, the leaves and foliage flutter   140
in the breeze and the wind whistles with pitiful laments, then may

Triste fleant Ariadnam, impulsaque saxa resultent
Flebilibus numeris Ariadnam, Ariadnan, ut ipse,
Ipse senex renovet luctus et prodeat antro.'

145 Finierat lacrimisque genas atque ora Patulcis
Laverat; hic miserae comites et pectora duris
Planxerunt palmis et saxa sonantia longo
Implerunt clamore et foemineis lamentis.
Tum senior gemitum ingentem dedit et scidit albam
150 Caniciem, simul hos effudit pectore questus:
 'Arescat mihi ros et apes sua mella negarint:
Non, o non mihi cara favos quae deliquet uxor;
Torpescant flores, pomum mihi deneget arbos:
Non, o non mihi poma manu quae seligat uxor;
155 Squalescat seges et messem mihi culta negarint:
Non, o non cererem mihi quae mea ventilet uxor;
Arescant horti, frugem mihi deneget hortus:
Non olus o mihi quae, non quae mea tondeat uxor;
Torpescat focus atque ignes focus ipse negarit:
160 Non, o non mihi farra foco quae torreat uxor;
Dispereant fontes et aquas mihi deneget amnis:
Non, o non latices mihi quae mea misceat uxor;
Triste ruat coelo excidium pecudi atque capellae,
Non foetum dent armenta aut mulctralia succum:
165 Non, o non mihi lac quae cara coegerit uxor;
Infelix coelo exitium ruat, ut neque lanam
Vellera dent, nullae veniant ad licia telae:
Non, o non mihi texta manu quae neverit uxor;
Dira lues coelo ruat et ruat altus Olympus
170 Stragem agris, stragem arboribus terraeque ruinam
Det super et mediis tellus internatet undis:
Non uxor mihi cara domi quae sarcula curet,
Non falcem quae acuat messi lignisque securim,
Non socia gratorum operum consorsque laborum,

they sadly weep for Ariadne, and may the rocks when struck re-echo 'Ariadne' in mournful measures, the name of Ariadne, so that the old man, the old man himself, may renew his grieving and come forth from the grotto."

Patulcis had finished singing and bathed her cheeks and face in 145 tears. At this moment, her sad companions struck their breasts hard with their palms and filled the resounding rocks with a lin-gering cry and womanly laments. Then the old man gave a great groan, tore his white hair, and poured out these laments from his 150 breast:

"May the dew dry up for me and the bees refuse me their honey: for I do not, alas, I do not have my dear wife to strain the honeycombs. May the flowers wilt, the tree deny me its fruit: for I do not, alas, I do not have my wife to choose the fruit by hand. May the crop go to seed, and the fields deny me their yield: for I 155 do not, alas, I do not have my wife to fan the grain. May the gar-dens dry up, the garden deny me its yield: for I do not, alas, I do not have my wife to pick the vegetables. May the hearth go cold and deny me fire: for I do not, alas, I do not have my wife to roast 160 the grain on the hearth. May the fonts dry up and the stream re-fuse me its waters: for I do not, alas, I do not have my wife to pour me their waters. May a grim plague fall from the sky onto the flock and the she-goat, may the flocks not produce offspring nor the milk-pails milk: for I do not, alas, I do not have my dear 165 wife to make the milk thicken into cheese. May withering destruc-tion fall from the sky so that neither do fleeces give wool, nor are any webs attached to the loom: for I do not, alas, I do not have my wife to weave the cloth by hand. May dire pestilence fall from the sky and high Olympus cast destruction on the fields, destruction 170 on the trees, cast ruin over the earth and may the earth swim amid the waves, for I do not have my dear wife at home to look after the hoes, to sharpen the scythe for the harvest and the ax for the wood, I do not have a companion to share in pleasing labors and

175 Non, heu, quae defecta senis locet ossa cubili,
Cantanti non quae numeros et verba ministret,
Pulsantem non quae digitis iuvet et iuvet ore,
Non oculos quae claudat amans donetque capillis
Extinctum et lacrimis decoret miseranda sepultum,
180 Quae "Memor, aeternumque vale, vale" ad hostia dicat.'
 Haec Meliseus, et antro sese condit opaco;
Ex illo latet et cura tabescit et annis.
Forsan et ipsa, Faburne, dies solabitur aegrum
Mitescetque malum, nec tanta silentia frustra.
185 Nuper ad extremam, foribus quae proxima, myrtum
Non expressa quidem, tamen est vox reddita: 'Lauri,
Este mei memores; fontemque inducite lauris,
Naiades mihi cultae, et solem arcete hyacinthis.'

Faburnus

Nuper et ad veteres citrios, dum tondet anethum
190 Uxor et ipse simul mentam atque sisimbria purgo,
Suspirantem illum et querula cum voce ferentem
Intenti accipimus: 'Longum o defleta, quid umbra
Nec mihi nocte venis, nec amica occurris imago?'
Huc aures, Cicerisce: vides quid corvus ab ipso
195 Impluvio, consuetus heri ploratibus ales,
Quid corvus secum incrocitet, meditetur et ore:
'Et manes meme fugiunt et vita gravatur;
Cur, o cur nostri non vos quoque poenitet, aurae?'

tasks. I do not have anyone, alas, to settle in bed my enfeebled old 175
man's bones, to supply me with the words and measures as I sing,
to aid me with her voice and with her fingers as I strike the
chords, nor, when I am dead, to close my eyes with loving hands,
to give me an offering of her hair, and, mourning pitiably, honor
my tomb with her tears, and to say, 'Remember me, and farewell, 180
for all eternity farewell,' at the final gate."

Meliseus spoke thus, then hid himself in the shadowy cave.
From that time onward, he has been in hiding, and is consumed
with grief and age. Perhaps, Faburnus, time itself will console his
sorrow, and his pain will lessen, nor will such great silence have
been in vain. Recently, by the myrtle at the very edge nearest to the 185
entrance, the echo of a voice, not fully articulated, was nonetheless
heard: "Laurels, remember me; O Naiads whom I worship, guide
the water from the spring to the laurels, and defend the hyacinths
from the sun."

Faburnus

Recently, by the old orange trees, while my wife was cutting the
anise and, at the same time, I was cleaning the mint and the 190
watermint, intent on our task, we heard him sighing and declaring
in a voice of lamentation:[11] "O long-mourned wife, why, now that
you are a shade, do you not come to me at night, do you not appear before me, a friendly apparition?" Turn your ears this way,
Ciceriscus: do you observe what the crow from the rainwater ba- 195
sin, the bird accustomed to the lamentations of its master, do you
observe what the crow inwardly croaks and murmurs with its
voice: "Even shades flee me and life weighs on me: why, oh why, air
of life, do you too not regret my presence?"

Ciceriscus

Quin aures veterem ad postem, qua ianua hiulca est,
200 Admoveo? Ipse sub haec coryleta, Faburne, maneto.

Faburnus

An potius, qua lotos et alticomae cyparissi
Triste gemunt scriptoque dolent in cortice cedri:
'Parcite, apes: nisi triste nihil de rore legetis,
Infecere mei rores et pabula questus.'
205 Ah dolor, ah desiderium! Non antra nec horti,
Non imae valles, non silvae aut flumina servant
Non monimenta senis; quin hic quoque signa dolorum
Tofus habet memor et lacrimas, quas ebibit ante,
Nunc quoque gutta refert, referunt et saxa dolorem.

Ciceriscus

210 Ille quidem flet adhuc; sed multa, Faburne, levari
Posse monent numerique monent et verba querentis,
Quaeque ipse in vultu speculans et voce notavi,
Dum vacuam in foribus discreto vimine texit
Fiscellam et vario solantem se Orphea cantu
215 Coniuge cum socia pingit memoremque querelam
Quemcunque ad iuncum ingeminans, miseratur amantem.
Mox subit: 'O mea quisnam, heu quis mea vulnera curet?'
En audi: 'Mihi cur, cur o mihi triste minatur
Iris ab exortu, moerent sata, luget et hortus?
220 Tandem, o tandem aquilo nubes disperget et austros:
Quisnam, o quis desiderium et mea vulnera sedet?
Orpheaque Eurydicenque sequentem intexite, iunci,
Dum fiscella levi circunfrondescit acantho.

Ciceriscus

Why don't I move my ears to the old door post, where the door is
ajar? You remain under the stand of hazel-nut trees, Faburnus.   200

Faburnus

Or rather where the lotus and cypresses with their lofty foliage
groan mournfully, and the cedar trees in graven bark express their
grief: "Cease your toils, bees: you will gather nothing except sadness from the dew: my laments have infected the dew and the
pastures." Ah the grief, the longing: there are no grottoes, no gar-   205
dens, no deep valleys, no forests, no rivers that do not preserve the
old man's memorials. Why even this tufa rock bears the marks of
his grieving, and now too the trickle of water recalls his tears that
it once drank in; and the rocks remind of his grief.

Ciceriscus

Indeed, he is weeping still; but many things, Faburnus, suggest   210
that his grief may be lightened—both his rhythms and his words
as he laments, and what I myself noted by observing his expression and his voice while, at the cave's threshold, he wove a basket's
frame out of differently colored reeds: he represents Orpheus,
in company with his wife, consoling himself with diverse song,   215
and he pities Orpheus' love, repeating to every reed his nostalgic
complaint.[12] Soon he adds: "O my love, who, I ask, who could take
care of my wounds?" Listen, he speaks: "Why, oh why, does Iris
bode ill for me since her rising, and why are the crops grieving,
the garden bereaved? One day, ah one day, the north wind shall   220
scatter the clouds and the south winds. Who, ah who, could allay my longing and my wounds? Weave, O reeds, the image of
Orpheus and Eurydice following him, while the basket is encircled
with a ring of slender acanthus leaves. Grim winter rages and a

Saevit hiems dira et pecori ferus ingruit aër
225 Atque apibus, tandem, o tandem mitescet et aër
Et zephyri ver diffundent: quaenam aura, quis aegrum
Solatur veris tepor aut nova mulcet irundo?
Orpheaque Eurydicenque sequentem intexite, iunci,
Dum fiscella levi circunfrondescit acantho.
230 Arescunt coeli vitio atque uredine prata
Et silvis cecidere comae, tandem, o tandem imbres
Restituentque comas silvis et gramina pratis:
Quisnam o restinguitque ignes et vulnera sanat?
Orpheaque Eurydicenque sequentem intexite, iunci,
235 Dum fiscella levi circunfrondescit acantho.'
       Haec senior, suetam interea nec spernit avenam,
Et pateram exornat nymphis et mulctra Vacunae.

Faburnus

Non amnes, Cicerisce, aut haec quae flumina cernis
Decrescunt, non, usta calore, augentur ab imbri;
240 Post coeli tempestates pelagique procellam
Componunt sese fluctus et nubila cedunt.
Tristitiae quoque meta sua est. Meliseus ab antro
Prodibit tandem segetis memor et memor horti,
Diluet et rastris curas et falce dolorem.

Ciceriscus

245 Quin potius, quoniam ver appetit et sua curae est
Insitio, falcemque illi cuneosque paramus?
Cortice quoque etiam lentescat vulnus et udo,
Quae super ipse linens imponat glutina, libro.

pestilent vapor falls upon the flock and the bees, but at last, at   225
long last, the air will grow mild, and the zephyrs pour forth
springtime. Tell me what breeze, what warmth of spring air con-
soles, what newly arrived swallow soothes me in my suffering?
Weave into it, O reeds, the image of Orpheus and Eurydice following him, while the basket is encircled with a ring of slender
acanthus leaves. The meadows are parched with the sky's harmful   230
air and scorching drought, and the leaves have fallen from the
trees; but at last, at long last, the rains will restore leaves to the
trees and grass to the meadows. Ah who extinguishes the flames
and heals the wounds? Weave into it, o reeds, the image of Orpheus and Eurydice following him, while the basket is encircled   235
with a ring of slender acanthus leaves."

So sings the old poet, nor, in the meanwhile, does he spurn the
accustomed oat pipe, and he furnishes a libation bowl for the
nymphs and milking pails for Vacuna.[13]

Faburnus

The streams, Ciceriscus, and these rivers that you see, do not grow
less, nor, burned by the heat, are they increased by the rains.[14]
After the sky's storms and the sea's squall, the waves grow calm   240
again and the clouds recede. Sadness, too, has its limit. Meliseus
will come forth, at last, from his cave, mindful of his crops and
mindful of his garden; he will dilute his troubles with rakes, with
pruning hook dissolve his grief.

Ciceriscus

Why not, instead, since spring approaches and grafting is his care,   245
prepare for him the pruning hook and wedges? Let the wound
become sticky on the bark and the moist inner rind of the tree
that he will smear with glue.[15]

: III :

Maeon

Syncerius et Zephyreus pastores queruntur
apud sepulchrum Maeonis,
mox a dolore in voluptatem conversi
amatoria ac pastoralia quaedam canunt.
Sub ipsius autem Maeonis persona
Pauli Artaldi medici mors deploratur.

Syncerius

Ipse vides, quo tot, Zephyree, inventa, sepulchrum
Cuncta tulit: superat vix, ah, vix est super umbra.

Zephyreus

Synceri, non umbra diu, non fama, nec ipsa
Extabunt monimenta; rogo vix pauca supersunt,
5   Mox eadem nox obscura caligine condet;
Quae tumulo circum increscunt virgulta vel alto
Ignea vis excussa polo aut manus improba perdet,
Ossaque nuda solo sparsa atque ignota iacebunt;
Ne post ossa quidem, nec fabula Maeonis ulla.

Syncerius

10 Haec igitur, Zephyree, dies? Haec summa laborum est?
Quin potius, quoniam nulli sunt Maeoni sensus,
Maeona nec lacrimaeve iuvant aut carmen, eamus.

: III :

Maeon

The herdsmen Syncerius and Zephyreus lament
by the tomb of Maeon;
then, after shifting from grief to pleasure,
they sing some amatory and pastoral songs.
Moreover, under the guise of Maeon,
doctor Paolo Attaldi's death is mourned.[1]

Syncerius

You see with your own eyes, Zephyreus, the tomb whither he took
all his many discoveries: his shade scarcely survives, alas, it scarcely
remains.

Zephyreus

Syncerius, the shade will not last long, nor will fame, nor tomb
monuments themselves. Few things survive the pyre; soon the   5
same night will bury them in darkness. The branches that grow
around the tomb will either be destroyed by the force of fire cast
down from the firmament or cut down by an irreverent hand, and
the bare bones will lie on the ground, scattered and unrecognized.
Not even the bones or any rumor of Maeon will remain.

Syncerius

So this is life on earth, Zephyreus? This is the sum of all our   10
toils? Well then, since Maeon no longer has any consciousness,
since neither tears nor song can help Maeon, let us go. Farewell,

Ara vale, cineres magni pastoris havento;
Nos, Maeon, nos te aeternum salvere iubemus.

Zephyreus

15   Discedens ego, terra, tibi, quae Maeona servas,
    Et desiderium et lacrimas meaque oscula linquo;
    Te zephyri foveant molles, te lenior aura,
    Maeonis et de qua frondescet amaracus, urna,
    Usque fluat liquor ille tibi, quo vulnera et ipse
20   Sanabat, quo Naiadum comebat et ora,
    Fundebatque deum ambrosiam per rura, per hortos,
    Aeris et medica purgabat ab arte venenum,
    Quo fuit et silvis olim tam notus et urbi,
    Et fama superavit Ocrim iugaque alta Matesi.
25   Ipse vale aeternum, Maeon, mihi maxime Maeon.

Syncerius

    Nunc agedum, tenues calami, mea dulcis arundo,
    Di coelo, terris umbrae, nos lenibus auris
    Cantantesque fruamur et ocia laeta sequamur.
    Cura olerum studiumque herbarum artesque medendi
30   Viventem iuvere expressi et Maeona succi,
    Me compressa iuvant labris labra; Phylli, venito,
    Ipse inter frondes coryletaque densa latebo.

Zephyreus

    Oscula me suppressa iuvant; mea Lychni, maneto
    Qua platani strepit umbra, sonat leve murmur aquai.

altar, farewell, ashes of a great shepherd; we bid you farewell for all eternity, Maeon.

Zephyreus

As I leave you, O plot of ground who hold Maeon, I leave you my   15
longing, my tears, and my kisses; may gentle zephyrs, may a mild breeze keep you warm. And for you, O urn of Maeon, from which marjoram grows, may there continually flow that water with which he himself once cured wounds and beautified the faces of Naiads;   20
and he used to pour the ambrosia of the gods over the fields, over the gardens, and he used to cleanse the air of its poison with the art of medicine. This is why he was once so famous both in the woods and in the city: his fame exceeded Monte d'Ocre and the high ridges of the Matese. Farewell for all eternity, Maeon, my   25
dearest, greatest Maeon.[2]

Syncerius

Come now, slender reed, my sweet reed pipes, as the gods rejoice in the sky, the shades in the earth, so let us enjoy the gentle breezes as we sing, let us pursue happy leisure hours. The cultivation of greens, an interest in herbs, the arts of healing, and the   30
extraction of medicinal drafts delighted Maeon when he was alive. I delight in lips pressed together with lips. Come, Phyllis, I will hide amid the leaves and the dense copse of hazels.[3]

Zephyreus

I delight in secret kisses. Stay, my Lychnis, where the shade of the plane tree rustles, where the water makes a gentle murmuring sound.

Syncerius

35 Non me tam levat aura Canis sitientis in aestu,
Spirat Acilla suo quam quod de pectore anethum.

Zephyreus

Me risus fovet, aura Philoenidis, aura cachinni,
Sordeat ut philomela apiumque ad septa susurri.

Syncerius

Vidi ego picta manu selectaque fraga legentem,
40 Innuit et mihi, serta deus dum stringit in umbra:
Hic ibi tum femur hirsutum setosaque menta
Obstupui atque oculos fruticoso in margine fixi.

Zephyreus

Vidit me dum poma lego arrisitque legenti,
Et dixit mihi Nais: 'Amant et poma Napaeae.'
45 His ego tum implevique sinum obstupuique papillas
Pectora dum limis oculis et colla pererro.

Syncerius

Suave per aestatem, ad fontem stat ubi unda, canorum
Agmen et argutas ranarum audire querelas,
Vellera tum crispantem et cornua lata moventem
50 Cirronem spectare, salit dum terga Macillae,
Mox Rufam, mox Albigenam, mox Thyrsan et Hypsan,
Ac iuxta residere, cui tua gaudia narres.

Syncerius

I do not find as much relief in a cool breeze during the heat of the   35
parching Dog as I do in the perfume of anise that Acilla wafts
from her breast.[4]

Zephyreus

I am so caressed by the breeze of Philoenis' laugh, by the breeze of
her laughter, that the nightingale, and the humming of bees by the
hedge, pale by comparison.

Syncerius

I saw the god picking bright red strawberries, choosing them by
hand, and he nodded at me, while he was binding together gar-   40
lands in the shade.[5] Then and there I gaped in astonishment at his
hairy thigh and bristly chin, and fixed my gaze on the shrubbery
on the riverbank.

Zephyreus

A Naiad saw me as I was picking apples, and as I picked, she
smiled at me, and said: "Dell nymphs love apples too." Then I   45
filled her lap with apples, and gazed in astonishment at her nipples
as I scanned her breast and neck out of the corner of my eye.

Syncerius

It is sweet in the summer, by a spring where the water pools, to
listen to a tuneful squadron of birds and the shrill complaints of
frogs, then to watch Cirro with his curly fleece waving his wide   50
horns as he mounts the back of Macilla, then Rufa, then Albigena,
then Thyrsas and Hypsas, and to sit next to someone you can talk
about your pleasures with.

Zephyreus

Suave per hibernum frigus, dum nox silet, ipsum
Ad foenile boum murmur, cum ruminat omnis
55 Grex simul et pastae suspirant pignora matres,
Audire, et saturi distenta sub ubera foetus
Dum ludunt, petit hic socium, fugit ille petentem,
Atque una recubare, cui tua pectora iungas.

Syncerius

Hic aries villosus et hirtis cornibus, aure
60 Quadrifida, cui tergemini lato inguine testes
Horrescunt, hic ipse aries gregis omnis et omnis
Virque paterque gregis; patrem hunc foetura fatetur,
Admissura virum; spes est gregis omnis in uno.

Zephyreus

Miraris taurum hunc; patrem hunc Lucania et unum
65 Iactat habetque virum: armenti laus omnis in uno est.
Ducit ab Herculeo genus et cognomina tauro;
Hunc Dryades mirantur, amatque et deperit illa,
Quae facie tauros, oculis capit aurea cervos.

Syncerius

Sit modus, o Zephyree: instat nox, ite capellae,
70 Ite et oves; age coge, Lacon, age coge, Lycarba,
Latratu et revoca, cessit qui a matre, iuvencum.

Zephyreus

It is sweet in the winter's cold, in the silent night, right next to the
barn, to hear the mooing of oxen, when the entire herd ruminates   55
together, and the mothers, after eating, sigh for their offspring,
and as the little ones, sated, play beneath the swollen teats, one
seeking his companion, the other fleeing his pursuer; and to lie
down together with someone you can hold tight to your breast.

Syncerius

Here is the shaggy ram with bristly horns and ear cloven in four,   60
in whose broad groin triple testicles swell—this same ram is the
husband of all the flock and father of all the flock. He is acknowl-
edged as father of the female who will soon receive him as husband. The hope of the entire flock lies in him alone.

Zephyreus

You gaze in wonder at this bull; Lucania boasts of having him as   65
father and husband, one and the same; the glory of the entire herd
resides in him alone. He derives his name and lineage from Hercules' bull.[6] The Dryads wonder at him, and she, the gorgeous one
who seduces the bulls with her face and the deer with her eyes, is
in love with him, perishes for him.

Syncerius

Time to make an end of it, O Zephyreus: night is coming on; go,
she-goats; time to go, sheep. Come on, Lacon, come on, Lycarba,   70
gather the flock, and call back with your barking the bullock who
has wandered from his mother.

Zephyreus

Synceri, hoc age, lecta sinu dum mespila condo,
In thyrsum dum sorba suis cum frondibus apto.
His gaudet tua Sila, probat mea Rufula sorbum.

Syncerius

75 Eia eia, Saturisca, domum, ad praesepia nota,
Quid segnes? Eia ite, eia; nox advenit, eia,
Ite domum: insidiis nox opportuna luporum est.

Zephyreus

Deal with these things, Syncerius, while I gather the medlars I picked in a sack and fit the sorb apples with all their leaves onto a staff—your Sila loves them, my Rufula likes sorbs.

Syncerius

Ho there, Saturisca, why so slow to trot home to your familiar   75
stable? Ho there, get moving: night is coming, it's time to go
home: night is a time ripe for wolves' stealthy attacks.[7]

: IV :

Acon

Acon adulescens Napen a se amatam nymphis praefert Naiadibus.
Illae veneno ex oculis emisso Napen conficiunt.
Vertunnus eam in napum convertit.
Introducuntur itaque Petasillus et Saliuncus
pastores fabellam hanc referentes, deinde quoque rusticanas
quasdam Melisei cantiones decantantes.

Petasillus et Saliuncus collocutores.

Petasillus

'Cedite, Naiades nymphae, iam cedite, vincit
Pulchra Nape petisque oculis nigroque capillo.'
Verberat his puer acer Acon atque increpat ore.
Illae oculis conceptum atro sub corde venenum
5   Inspirant, quo victa Nape tabescit, ut altis
Tabescunt sub sole nives in montibus, et iam
Ponit humi languentem animam morsque occupat artus.
Hic ter Acon scidit ora comamque a vertice vellit
Et clamore nemus complevit, questibus auras.
10 Clamantem Vertunnus opaco e limite sensit;
Accurrit pueri memor et miseratus amantem
Iniecta tellure Napen tegit. Illa repente
In bulbum conversa solo radicibus haesit;
Vestit eam foliis deus et frondescere iussit:
15 Hinc olus, hinc herbosa Nape turgescit in agris.
     Haec nobis quondam pueris Meliseus ad ignem
Narrabat, cum rapa senex poscamque probaret

: IV :

Acon

The adolescent Acon prefers Nape, whom he loves, to the Naiads.
They kill Nape by shooting poison from their eyes.
Vertumnus transforms her into a turnip.
And so the shepherds Petasillus and Saliuncus
come on the stage, first telling this story,
then singing some of Meliseus' rustic ditties.[1]

Speakers: Petasillus and Saliuncus.

Petasillus

"Yield now, water nymphs, it's time to yield, for beautiful Nape
vanquishes you with her flirty eyes and jet-black hair." With these
words, young Acon lashes them and harangues them. They devise
a poison in their coal-black hearts and blow it into her with their
eyes. Vanquished by it, Nape dissolves, as snows dissolve in the   5
high mountains under the sun, and now she lays her fading life
spirit down on the ground, and death takes her limbs. Here three
times Acon tore his face, ripped his hair from his head, and filled
the grove with groaning, the air with his laments. Vertumnus   10
heard his cries from his shady abode; remembering the boy, he
came running, and pitying her lover, buried Nape with a handful
of dirt. She, suddenly transformed into a root vegetable, clung fast
in the soil with her roots; the god clothed her with leaves and ordered her to sprout green fronds. From then on, Nape, a vegetable,   15
a green plant, has swelled in the fields.

Meliseus told us this tale in front of the fire, long ago when we
were boys, as the old man was tasting turnips and tart vinegar

Contusamque fabam sparsa condiret amurca
Misceretque apio rutam, coriandron aceto.

Saliuncus

20 Non puduit cantorem igitur resonantis avenae,
Cui tot oves, pecoris tantum, mulctralia tanta,
Pellitum pastorem olitorum accumbere mensis
Ulpicaque et veteres ruptare ad prandia cepas.

Petasillus

Illum cepa recens viridisque cucurbita captum
25 Ducebat mentaeque sapor succusque sisimbri,
Munere quo viridi recubans in cespite mecum
Haec cecinit, veteres fassus per carmen amores:
    'Huc ades, o mihi cara, vocant te, Ariadna, ligustra,
Te myrti salicesque vocant, age, cara, venito:
30 Ipse tibi tenerum legi servoque phaselum,
Ipse cicer, tibi sepositis rosa floret in hortis;
En tibi coeruleus cucumis super hamite crescit,
Coeruleus cucumis devectus Arangide terra,
Hic ubi Nigirides ranae certare elephantis
35 Praesidio culicum haud dubitant et irudinis atrae;
Te manet hic cucumis: propera mecumque recumbe.
Quin et Campano de vellere textus et Umbro
Supparus et viridi circum variatus ibisco
Te vocat; hunc suit Alcidamas, distinxit et Alcon,
40 Hic et acu Morco similis, quem mater Acilla
Instituitque colo atque apibus formavit alendis;
Supparus is tibi sepositus blanditur et instat.
Huc ades: en tibi grex, Ariadna, occurrit eunti;
Dum properas, laetae plaudunt de fronde cicadae.'

water, dressing crushed beans with a sprinkling of olive oil dregs, and mixing rue with parsley, coriander with vinegar.

Saliuncus

So the singer of the resounding pipes, who had so many sheep, so   20
great a herd, so many milking pails, a shepherd in garments made
of animal skins, was not ashamed to recline at table with vegetable
gardeners, and belch up leeks and old onions at lunchtime.[2]

Petasillus

Enticed by a fresh onion, a green zucchini, the flavor of mint, and   25
the taste of wild thyme, he sang these words in exchange for the
gift, lying with me on the green grass, confessing his love of old in
song.

"Come here, Ariadne, my beloved, the privets summon you, the
myrtles and willows summon you, come, my darling, come.[3] I   30
myself picked the tender green beans and am saving them for you,
for you I am saving the chickpeas; for you the rose blooms in a
secluded garden. Look a dark green cucumber is growing for you
over the lattice, a dark green cucumber imported from the land of
Arangas, where frogs of the Niger do not hesitate to do battle
with elephants with the help of a garrison of mosquitoes and black   35
leeches.[4] Such a cucumber awaits you: hurry, come lie down with
me. A shawl woven from Campanian and Umbrian wool, embroidered all around with green hibiscus, also invites you here. Alcidamas sewed it, and Alcon did the embroidery, Alcon, who rivals   40
Morcus with the needle, whom his mother Acilla trained to spin
and taught to keep bees. This shawl, specially reserved for you,
wheedles and urges you. Come here, Ariadne—for look! the whole
flock comes to meet you as you approach; as you hasten, happily
from amid the leaves resounds the applause of the cicadas."

45 Haec cecinit Meliseus humique hortensia dona
    Evellens, mentastrum atrox et sectile porrum,
    Sustulit ipse humeris fascem et redolentis anethi,
    Mox sese in montes et pascua nota recepit
    Ad veteres lauros fumosaque tigna Vesevi.
50 Illinc et mihi fiscellas et cymbia lactis
    Mittit, amicitiae memor et trivialis avenae,
    Idem pastorum cultor pariterque olitorum.
    Post dulces quandoque epulas iuvat esse lupinum,
    Esse inulas, asprina iuvant, post lene Falernum;
55 Et mea me quotiens petit ore Biturrica, quantum
    Ruta iuvat, quam labra iuvant redolentia porrum.
    Scilicet ille, satur scrutis et lactibus agni
    Ac sale continctis hedorum clunibus, atrum
    Laudat olus, acres ruptat de gutture bulbos.

                        Saliuncus

60 Et nostri, Petasille, greges sensere canentem
    In silvis Meliseon, adesaque saxa sonorem
    Dum referunt, tacitae cantum stupuere Napaeae;
    Et — mirum — fessae vocem tenuere cicadae
    Prostrataeque solo iacuere ad carmina vaccae,
65 Oblitae cytisum pecudes, satureia capellae.
    Incipit hinc: 'Ariadna piro mihi gratior ipso,
    Quod superat vel odore rosas, vel fraga colore;
    Dum pectus foveoque manu tractoque papillas,
    Non me mulctra iuvant, non lactis plena recocti
70 Fiscina, non hedus dum ludit ad ubera matris,
    Buccula non, cupido dum blanda admugit amanti.'
       Desierat: plausere boves, plausere iuvenci
    Mugitu, socio responsant antra favore

Meliseus sang this song, and plucking the garden's gifts from   45
the ground—bitter-tasting wild mint and many-leaved chives—he
himself raised onto his shoulders a bundle of fragrant anise, and
then retreated to the mountains and familiar pastures, near the old
laurel trees and wooden beams blackened with Vesuvius' smoke.
From there he sends me baskets of cheese and pails full of milk,   50
mindful of our friendship and my humble panpipes—he, who
shows equal honor to shepherds and vegetable gardeners. After
pleasant repasts, it is sometimes nice to have lupine and spring
onions; after mellow Falernian, Asprino gives delight.[5] As for me,   55
whenever my darling Biturrica comes to kiss me, how I take delight in the savor of rue, how I take delight in her lips fragrant
with leek. No surprise that, satiated with lamb sausage and lamb's
intestines, with goat's haunches sprinkled with salt, he praises our
wretched greens, and belches up pungent onions from the depths
of his gullet.[6]

Saliuncus

My flocks too, Petasillus, have heard Meliseus singing in the   60
woods, while the smooth-worn rocks echoed back his resounding
singing, while the dell nymphs gaped in astonished silence at his
song. And, amazingly, at the sound of his songs the weary cicadas
ceased their humming, and the cows lay prostrate on the ground;
the herds forgot their clover, the she-goats their savory. He began   65
from here: "Ariadne delights me more than the pear itself, because
she even surpasses roses in fragrance, strawberries in hue. While I
caress and stroke her breasts with my hand, milk pails do not
please me, nor baskets full of fresh cheese, nor the kid goat that   70
plays at its mother's teats, nor the heifer that moos flirtatiously to
her desirous suitor."

He ceased: the oxen applauded, the bullocks applauded with
their mooing, the grottoes echoed their common approval, and

Convallesque cavae, resono nemora avia cantu.
75 Mox iterum: 'Dulce, in pratis dum gramina tondent,
    Cernere capreolos variato tergore, pictis
    Distinctos maculis; mater vocat usque paventes,
    Sectantur trepidi vestigia matris anhelae,
    Ludunt et saturi circum ubera nota gemelli.
80 Suave per aestatem liquidam mulcentibus auris,
    Dum tectae ramis volucres connubia miscent,
    Pandentemque alas caudamque ad terga rotantem
    Pavonem spectare. Vocat Iunonius ales
    Consortem thalami, speculosa volumina versat,
85 Cauda micat, mediis fulgent sua sidera pennis;
    Venit amans, cupidis miscent simul oscula rostris,
    Iungit amor geminos, geminataque gaudia gliscunt,
    Inter utrosque suos Venus ipsa accendit olores.
    At mea cum liquidos Ariadna recedit ad amnes
90 Albentemque pedem nudatque ad flumina suras
    Genuaque sub vitrea candent argentea lympha
    Et fungis alni candentius et nive corni,
    Populus et niveos quos iactat in aera flores,
    Tunc mihi corda liquant vel mella Sicanidos Hyblae,
95 Mella favis Heliconis et anteferenda Libyscis,
    Et succo Siculae stillant quem cortice cannae.'
        Finierat: simae rupere silentia caprae,
    Ruperunt et oves, simul et cum matribus agni,
    Balatum referunt colles Gaurique recessus
100 Et Cumae vacuae et cryptae graveolentis Averni,
    Antraque Musconis et opaca sepulchra Tuennae.
    Haec ait, et latis humeris quae buccina pendet,
    Inflat eam labris turgentibus: illa frementi
    Involvit coelum gemitu. Quo concita silvis
105 Erumpit clamore suum gens horrida setis,
    Horrida grunnitu et tundentibus aera sannis.

with resounding echo the hollow valleys and inaccessible groves
gave their response. Then he started up again: "It is sweet to look   75
at the roebucks, while they nibble grass in the meadows, marked
out by colored spots on their different-colored backs. The mother
calls them, and always timid, trembling, they follow the footsteps
of their panting mother; and once they have drunk their fill, the
twins play around the well-known teats. It is sweet, amid caressing   80
breezes in summer's bright air, as birds under the cover of branches
join in love, to gaze on the peacock extending his wings and fan-
ning his tail behind his back. The bird of Juno summons his bed
companion and rotates the shimmering layers of feathers; his tail   85
gleams, and amid the feathers, their own stars shine; his lover
comes, they mingle kisses with desirous beaks, love pairs them
together, and their pleasures swell in tandem. Joining their company, Venus herself enflames her swans. But when my dear Ariadne retires to the watery streams, and bares her white foot and   90
calves by the riverbank, and her silvery knees gleam in the crystalline waters with a whiteness more white than mushrooms on an
alder tree, more white than snow on a cherry tree, more white
than the snow-white flowers the poplar scatters into the air, then
my heart melts like the honey of Sicanian Hybla, honey that sur-   95
passes the honeycombs of Helicon and Libya and the sap that Sicilian reeds drip from their bark."[7]

He had finished. Snub-nosed she-goats broke the silence; sheep
broke the silence, the lambs along with their mothers broke the
silence, and the hills echoed back their bleating, as did the recesses
of Gaurus, desolate Cumae, the grottoes of rank-smelling Aver-   100
nus, the caves of Moschiano and the dark catacombs of Tubenna.[8]
After saying these things, he blows with swelling lips on the shepherd's horn that hangs from his broad shoulders: it envelops the
sky in a deep groaning sound. Roused by this din, a family of   105
pigs bursts from the woods, harsh with bristles, harsh with grunting and tusks pounding the air. He himself, scattering acorns from

Ipse manu glandem spargens citat ore crepatque
Ora per et dentes rictu glans hausta voraci,
Lambentes catuli circunstant ubera matrum.
110 Mox abit ad fagos, sequitur simul undique pubes
Armentalis, agris regnat Meliseus in ipsis
Nodoso incumbens baculo et stans imperat; adstant
Umbronum generosa cohors, turmaeque Laconum
Latratu lupos arcent et limine fures.
115 Haec memini, Petasille, iuvat meminisse: vel urnam
Candentis lactis pretium ferat, o mihi siquis
Hunc iterum det vidisse atque audisse canentem,
Det calamos modulare levemque inflare cicutam.

Petasillus

O mihi siquis eum sistat Vulsonis in antro
120 Rursus et ad Mopsi salices aut rura Salenti,
Ille sibi vitulum pretium ferat, eligat agnum
Cornipetam, cui lana pedes descendit ad imos.
Rursus et ipse suos recinat Meliseus amores,
Aut cum Delioli pratis, Minionis ad alnum
125 Haec dolet, et socias ranae iunxere querelas:
    'Ad corylos Ariadna canit subtegmina ducens,
Dum canit, assuetas miscet philomela querelas;
Coniugis absentes haec dum suspirat amores,
Ingeminat memorem nati philomela dolorem;
130 Dumque viri barbam meminit setosaque menta,
Hic philomela gravem sustollit in aera questum;
Dumque torum queritur fraudataque gaudia lecti,
Moesta silet philomela facitque silentia luctus:
Suspirantque dolentque simul, quo carmine captae
135 Formicae tacitum dant laeta per agmina plausum.
Ad fluvios me torret amor, fax urit ad amnes:

his hand, calls to them aloud; the acorns clatter through their mouth and teeth, gobbled by their devouring jaws, and the young pigs stand round and suck their mothers' teats. Then he goes off 110 to the beech grove, and the young cattle follow on all sides. Even in the fields Meliseus reigns supreme, leaning on a knotted staff; standing there, he gives the orders. The noble pack of Umbrian hounds stand by his feet, and troops of Spartan dogs with their barking ward off wolves and thieves from the threshold.[9] I remem- 115 ber these things, Petasillus, and I enjoy remembering them. Ah, if anyone could let me see him again and hear him singing, could let me hear him play the reed pipes and blow on the light flute, he could have a pitcher even of my whitest milk as reward.

Petasillus

Ah, if anyone could do me the favor of placing him once more in the cave of Vulsone, by the willows of Mopsus or Salento's fields, 120 he would take away a calf as reward, he could choose a lamb with butting horns whose wool goes down to the base of his hooves.[10] And once more would Meliseus himself sing of his love, as when, in the meadows of Dogliolo, by the alder tree of Mignone, he 125 would sing these laments, as the frogs added their accompanying complaints:[11]

"By the hazel trees Ariadne sings while spinning wool; as she sings, the nightingale adds her familiar complaints; as she mur- murs about the absence of her loving husband, the nightingale re- doubles her grief in memory of her son.[12] And as she recalls her 130 husband's beard and bristly chin, the nightingale raises her griev- ous lament to the skies; and as she laments being cheated of her marriage and the bed's pleasures, the nightingale goes sadly si- lent—a silence born of grief. Together they murmur their la- ments; captivated with their song, the ants in cheerful squadrons 135 silently applaud. Even by the riverbank I am scorched by love;

O mecum veteres, ranae, renovate querelas!
   'Dum tibi promitto noctem meaque oscula, coniux,
Deliciasque paro gregis et nova munera porto,
140   Dum lavor ad fontem sudataque pectora tergo,
Et filicem necto crines ac tempora circum,
Ecce lupum ad caulas: agnumque ex ubere matris
Eripit et tacitus latebrosa per avia tendit.
Ipse sequor, noctem in nimbis per inhospita duco,
145   Et mea te, coniux, exclamans pectora plango:
O mecum veterem, ranae, revocate dolorem!
   'Dum tibi de viridi fiscellam vimine texo
Virgaque coeruleo miscetur candida iunco
Flavaque supremum circumdat linea textum
150   Et limbum croceo subtexunt flore corymbi,
Ecce per impluvium demisso fune pedumque
Et picturatum buxi de fronde galerum
Fiscellamque, decus texturae et ruris honorem,
Surripiunt fures, ah monstra pudenda Brigantum!
155   Excutior somno trepidus latrante Cynandro;
Dum crudo perone mihi pes sternitur alter,
Ingruit, atra cohors, murmur: subroditur alter
Pero nec a morsu pollex defenditur aegro;
Exclamo lacrimansque genas et pectora tundo.
160   O mecum questus, ranae, geminate recentes!
   'Dum foetus geminos vaccae candentis, adulti
Spem gregis, ad fluvios et prata virentia duco,
Dum mihi promitto soboles, ad aratra iuvencos,
Ad mulctram vitulas, ad dolia dona Lyaei,
165   Dumque sero cytisum vaccis arbustaque pango
Atque serens canto ad sulcos vinetaque pangens
Ad foveas, ipsi mecum experiuntur et agni,
Ludunt ad sentes infirmis cornibus hedi,
Ah dolor, ah lacrimae, sonuere tonitrua coelo,

even beside the streams I am burned by a torch: resume with me,
O frogs, the laments of old!

"As I promise you a night of love and my kisses, O wife, and as
I prepare for you the flock's delicacies and bring you new gifts, and   140
as I wash by the fountain and scrub my sweaty chest, and hang
fern fronds around my hair and temples, look! a wolf at the sheep-
fold—it snatches a lamb from its mother's teat, and is silently
heading toward trackless coverts. I follow him myself, and spend
the night in the rain traveling over desolate places, and beat my   145
chest, crying out your name, my wife. Renew with me, O frogs,
the sorrow of old!

"As I weave for you a basket out of fresh osier: bright twigs are
joined with dark green rushes, a pale-colored thread surrounds the
woven basket's edge, and ivy clusters line the rim with yellow   150
flower—look! thieves, lowering a rope through the *impluvium*,
make off with my shepherd's crook, an embroidered cap made
from box-tree leaves, and the basket, a triumph of woven art and
the glory of the countryside—alas, shameful, monstrous deeds of
brigands![13] I am startled awake in a panic by Cynandro's barking.   155
As I put one foot in a rawhide boot, there is a sudden invasion of
squeaking—grim squadron! The attackers nibble my other boot,
nor can I defend my thumb against a grievous bite. I cry out and
beat my cheeks and chest in tears. Redouble with me, O frogs,   160
recent laments!

"As I lead the two calves of a white cow, the hope of the adult
flock, to the streams and blooming meadows; as I promise myself
offspring from them—bullocks for plowing, heifers for milking,
the gifts of Lyaeus to fill flagons; as I sow clover for the cows   165
and plant vineyards, and as I sing by the furrows while sowing, as
I sing by the pits while planting vines; and as the lambs themselves test their powers of song with me, and the kid goats play by
the brambles with horns still weak—alas, the pain, the tears!—

170 Discurrere faces ignitaque tela coruscant:
De coelo tacti foetus, armenta gregesque
Et tactae vites avulsa et stiva serenti
Attonitu; vix ipse super turbatus et amens
Stragem inter pecorum frugumque relinquor et atris
175 Ambustus flammis iaceo; vix colle propinquo
Lapsa Pales tutatur, humi tollitque iacentem.
O mecum solitas ranae instaurate querelas
Et luctum geminate novosque intendite questus!'
Concidit hic: ipsi simul ingemuere iuvenci
180 Ingemuere et oves cumque ipsis matribus agni,
Ingemuere caprae ipsis et cum matribus hedi,
Demisere comas quercus, liquere palumbes
Et quercus, frondemque nuces posuere, columbi
Deseruere nuces, ramos fregere myricae,
185 Deseruere et aves nidum et cum prole myricas,
Deseruitque et apis flores roremque cicadae
Et ranae mutis facere silentia buccis.

Haec Saliuncus et haec referebat arundine clarus
Et calamis Petasillus, uterque insignis avena.
190 Interea asparagosque legunt fungumque recentem
Boletosque sequuntur et altercantur utrinque,
Conditura suo quae sit miscenda sapore;
Tecta et uterque subit nigro squalentia fumo
Hirsuti Labeonis. Hic et miscere Falernum
195 Asparago docuit, docuit piper, hic boletis
Incoctumque pirum, mentae silvestris acervum
Alliaque adiicere et contritum serpillum,
Postremo querulis oleum stillare patellis.

thunder booms in the sky, torches run in streaks, weapons of 170
flame flash. The calves are struck by fire from the sky, the flocks
and herds are struck, the vines are struck, and the plow handle is
ripped from my hands as I sow, to my astonishment.[14] Confused
and in shock amid the slaughter of flocks and crops, I myself
barely manage to survive, and lie on the ground scorched by the 175
blackening flames. Descending from the neighboring hill, Pales
barely manages to protect me and raise me up from on the ground
where I lie.[15] Begin again with me, O frogs, your customary laments, redouble your lamentation, and intensify fresh songs of
complaint!"[16]

At this point he stopped. The bullocks themselves groaned all
together, the sheep groaned, the lambs along with their mothers, 180
the she-goats groaned, the kids along with their mothers; the oak
trees let their leaves fall, the woodpigeons left the oak trees, the
nut trees let fall their foliage, the doves abandoned the nut trees,
the tamarisks cracked their branches, the birds left their nests and 185
the tamarisks along with their chicks, the bees left the flowers, the
cicadas the dew, and the frogs went silent with uncroaking cheeks.

These things were recounted by Saliuncus, famed for the reed
flute, and Petasillus, famed for the reed pipe, both excellent at
playing the oat pipe. Meanwhile they pick asparagus and hunt for 190
fresh mushrooms and *boleti*, and they argue back and forth over
what condiment should be combined with what flavor.[17] Then
they both go to shaggy-haired Labeo's house grimy with black
smoke. Here he taught them to mix Falernian with asparagus and 195
add some pepper, to mix uncooked pear with *boleti*, to add a handful of wild mint, some garlic, and ground thyme, and last of all, to
drizzle olive oil into the pan when it starts to sizzle and complain.

: V :

Coryle

Coryle transformata et Amor vinctus.

Ad Actium Syncerum Sannazarium.

Hanc Acti (neque enim patula solum aesculus umbra
Grata placet) corylum tueare, nec arbutus una
Carmine nota dei est, Pana aut tegit una canentem
Aestibus in mediis somnos suadente cicada,
5   Verum etiam et corylus nostris est cognita silvis,
Nec tantum Meliseus eam aut tantum una Patulcis
Ornarunt calamis caesoque in cortice versu,
Cum questu commota gravique excita querela
Vertice decuteret frondes et corde sub imo
10 Redderet 'Heu heu'; sed singultibus interrupta
Plena nequit raucas iam vox erumpere ad auras,
Sibilat ipsa tamen: 'Vidi tua funera coniux'
Atque illa: 'Ah moriens morientem, Ariadna, relinquis.'
    Nam iaculo quondam choreisque insignis acuque
15 Praestabat Coryle, nympharum haud ultima forma.
Sed quo non penetrat livor? Dum fessa lavaret
Ad fontem, dum membra fovet Sebethide in unda,
Vertit eam cantu in stirpem Circeis Abelle
Ac densis circum ramis et cortice sepsit.
20 Illa novo latitans sub stipite flevit et ipsos
(Ah miseram) audita est poenam deposcere divos.
    Sic olim puer audieram, dum cantat Amilcon
Ad choreas: nitet alba seni coma deque galero
Cauda lupi et furvis horrent umbracula cirris.

V

Coryle

The transformation of Coryle and the binding of Love.

To Actius Syncerus Sannazarius.[1]

May you watch over this hazel, Actius. For it is not only the broad-canopied winter oak that pleases with its welcome shade; nor is the wild strawberry tree the only one to be made famous by the god Pan's song, or to shelter him as he sings in midsummer, while the cicada's droning induces sleep; but the hazel tree also is 5 known to our woods. Nor were Meliseus and Patulcis the only ones to adorn it with pipes and poetry carved onto its bark, when, shaken by lamentation, moved by grievous complaint, it cast down its leaves from its top, and from its heart's depths, echoed back 10 "alas, alas!" Yet its voice, interrupted by sobs, no longer able to burst forth loud and clear to the hoarse-sounding winds, still whispers: "I saw your death, my wife," and, "Ah, in dying, you abandon me, Ariadne, to my death."[2]

For once there was a nymph named Coryle, preeminent in javelin throwing, dancing, and skill with the needle, and hardly last 15 in beauty among the nymphs. But where does envy not enter? While she, in her weariness, was bathing in a spring, soothing her limbs in Sebeto's waters, Circean Abelle transformed her into a tree with an incantation, enclosing her on all sides with dense branches and bark.[3] Hidden under the newly-formed bark, she 20 wept, and (poor her!) was heard praying to the gods for vengeance.

I had heard this story once as a child when Amilcon was singing at the dances. The old man's white hair gleamed bright; from his cap, a wolf's tail and a brim made from dark tufts of fur bris-

25 Tityrus hunc docuit, sub quo cava fistula primum
Montibus his numeros deduxit et antra canore
Implevit 'Corydona quis aut non novit Alexin,
Pastorum aut musam Damonis et Alphesiboei?'
Inde alii. In primis bifori Corylenus avena
30 Saevum arcu cassumque oculis et pectore Amorem
Optrectare ausus et amaro incessere cantu,
Quod facie minium referens, quod flavus et albo
Pectore, proceros quod late effusus in artus,
Deperit Aridiam, cui sit breve corpus et ater
35 Inficiat livor nigras cum pectore mammas
Torpescantque oculi, albescant et tempora canis,
Assiduus tamen in silvis ad flumina clamet:
'Aridia o mihi cara ades et simul oscula iunge.
En primas tibi castaneas, prima arbuta servo.'
40 Aridiam solae referunt sed inaniter aurae.
    Non igitur tantum Meliseus et una Patulcis,
Verum hedera praecincta virenti et tempora myrto
Ac molli calamos circum complexa labello
Antiniana suos longum est conquesta dolores
45 Ad corylum. Haec solitas lacrimoso murmure voces
Frondibus instrepere ac rupto de cortice visa est
Et questus repetisse gravem et geminasse querelam,
Ut nuper, cum exutum armis vinctumque referret
Immitem Veneris puerum solaque sub umbra
50 Desertum ac tacitas furtim effugisse Napaeas.
Invidia heu tantum potuit visque effera amandi
Victa metu alteriusque tori suspecta libido!

Certabant una genitrix face natus et arcu,
    Ille ferire homines, urere at illa deas.
55 Par erat hinc hominum gemitus, par inde dearum
    Atque hinc atque illinc par quoque vulgus erat.

tled. He was taught by Tityrus, under whom his hollow pipes first 25
led down poetic melodies from these mountains, filling the grottoes with song: "Who does not know Corydon or Alexis, or the
muse of the shepherds Damon and Alphesiboeus?"[4] After him
came others. First among these was Corylenus, who, on his oaten
pipe with two openings, dared to disparage Love for being cruel 30
with his bow and having no sight and no heart.[5] He dared to at-
tack him with bitter song, because he, whose face was as red as
vermillion, who was blond-haired and white-breasted, whose tall
body was drawn out with long limbs, was perishing with love for
Aridia, though she had a short body, her breasts and skin were 35
stained black with a dark tinge, her eyes were lusterless, and her
temples were growing silver with white hair. And yet he still cried
out continually in the woods by the riverbank: "O my darling
Aridia, come, share kisses with me! See, I am saving for you the
first chestnuts, the first wild strawberries." But only the breezes 40
echoed back Aridia's name — an empty echo.

And so not only Meliseus and Patulcis alone, but also Antiniana, her temples encircled with green ivy and myrtle, embracing
the pipes between her soft lips, lamented her sorrows for a long
time by the hazel tree.[6] The hazel, with a mournful groan, seemed 45
to make the familiar cries resound with its leaves, and, from a cleft
in its bark, to renew the lamentations and redouble the grievous
plaint, just as when, not long ago, Antiniana told how Venus' pitiless son, stripped of his weapons, bound, abandoned in the lonely 50
shade, furtively fled the silent dell nymphs.[7] Alas, what great
power was wielded by envy, the savagery of love's force when overcome by fear, the suspicion of desire for another's bed!

"The mother and the son competed against one another, she
with her torch, he with his bow, he in wounding men, she in
scorching goddesses.[8] Equally matched was the groaning of men 55
on one side and goddesses on the other; on both sides, the crowd

Ridebat genitrix, rubuit puer; ille pharetram
    Excutit, accenso haec concutit igne facem.
Tum simul una duas involvit flamma Napaeas.
60   Clamarunt: 'Uno laedimur igne duae.'
Pastores una tris vulnerat ille sagitta,
    Vulnere tres uno congemuere pares.
Fassa est se victam risu dea terque per ora
    Perque genas nato basia anhela dedit.
65 Prima rosas oluere Paphi, Gnidiam altera nardum
    Tertia amaracinas visa referre comas.
Collocat hinc gremio fessum lenemque quietem
    Invitat blando naenia grata sono.
Rorarat teneros artus sopor et tamen ipse
70   Articulos, tanquam spicula tractet, agit.
Mox viola super instratum mollique ligustro
    Ponit ad argutae fluxile murmur aquae
Commendatque suae Sebethidi, moxque sub ipsum
    Tecta nemus longe devia rura petit
75 Diversosque legens non uno e gramine flores
    Nunc sibi, nunc puero serta novella parat.
Nec non et Charites studio mulcente laborem
    Effundunt teneros prata per huda modos.
Admovet interea pueri Sebethis ad ora
80   Ora sua et sensus inficit inde suos.
Illicet huic tacitum serpit per membra venenum
    Sentit et afflatus corde dolente novos.
Deliolum tunc moesta petit soloque sub antro
    Conqueritur flammas nec capit ipsa suas.
85 (Parve Amor, heu deserte Amor, heu puer une sub umbra,
    Nec comes aut custos, non tibi mater adest.
Fraudes insidiaeque assunt, male credite silvis;
    Ah sopor, ah tanto conscia ripa dolo!)

of victims was equally large. The mother smiled, the son blushed:
he brandished his quiver, she shook her torch with fire blazing,
and then one flame engulfed two dell nymphs at once. They   60
shouted: 'One fire harms us both.' The boy wounded three shepherds with one arrow, and all three of them equally groaned together with one wound.

"The goddess, with a smile, admitted her defeat, and gave her
son kisses infused with her breath, three on his mouth and three
on his cheeks. The first was fragrant with the roses of Paphos, the   65
second seemed to recall the nard of Cnidos, the third, hair per-
fumed with marjoram.[9] Then she places her tired son in her lap,
and a sweet lullaby coaxes gentle sleep with its soothing sound.
Sleep had permeated his tender limbs drop by drop, yet he himself
still moved his fingers as if he were shooting darts.[10] Soon she laid   70
him on a bed of violet and soft privet next to the murmuring flow
of clear-sounding water, entrusting him to her dear friend Sebethis, and soon, under the shelter of the grove itself, she sought
fields isolated far away, and, picking various flowers from different   75
meadows, she prepared fresh new garlands, now for herself, now
for her son.[11] And the Charites, too, poured forth delicate melodies over the dewy meadows, lightening her toil with their devoted
song.[12]

"In the meantime, Sebethis touches her lips to the boy's lips,
and thus infects her own senses. Then and there, a poison creeps   80
silently through her body, and she feels unfamiliar influences in
her suffering heart. Then, sadly, she seeks out Dogliolo, and there,
in a lonely grotto, laments the flames she feels, unable to control
them.[13] (Ah, little Love, ah, abandoned Love, ah, boy alone in   85
the shadows, no companion or guardian is there with you, your
mother is not there with you. The woods are full of snares and
deceptions, O my child wrongly entrusted to the woods; ah, sleep,
ah, riverbank, complicit in so great an act of trickery![14]) Nemesis

Hinc Nemesis ruit, inde comis effusa Corinna,
90   Lesbia at hac, illa Cynthia parte volat.
Corripit haec arcus, suspectas illa sagittas
    Et iacit in medios noxia tela rubos,
Illa manus iunco religat, simul altera vittis
    Obstrinxitque oculos occuluitque genas.
95 Mox laetae spoliis redeunt, gratantur euntes
    Quod sit rivalem nulla habitura suam,
Quod nullae invidiae posthac in amore futurae
    Quodque sit et certum quaeque habitura torum
Sitque etiam nullos tandem sensura dolores,
100   Dum nova mutata sorte in amore rota est:
'Unus amor, sua cuique fides, mala philtra valento,
    Nil puer hic quo nos ludere possit habet.'
At puer, ut somno excitus nova vincula sensit
    Atque oculos vitta praepediente tegi,
105 Fletque simul clamatque simul: 'Properate sorores,
    Demite texta oculis, solvite vincla manu.
Heu mater, cui me liquisti, credula mater:
    Me violae aut sertis posthabuisse potes?
Ingratae Charites, somne insidiose nemusque,
110   Et tela et pharetrae num periere meae?
Pastores, genus infidum, infidaeque Napaeae
    Reddite nunc arcus, reddite tela mihi!
Quod si quae vobis iam sint nocitura timetis,
    Reddite quae saltem sint nocitura deis.'
115 Talia per lacrimas iterat puer. Ecce per hortos
    Mota quidem questu pulchra Ariadna venit,
Qualis quae fraudem metuat, quae ferre dolenti
    Quaerat opem: sit opem poscere dignus Amor.
Ut dextram explicuit, 'Mater mea' dixit, et illam
120   Iniicit in teneros pectora blanda sinus;

rushes from this side, from that side Corinna with her hair in
wild disarray, while Lesbia darts in from this direction, Cynthia 90
from the other.[15] One seizes his bow, the other seizes his much-
mistrusted arrows and throws the destructive weapons into the
midst of the bramble bushes. One ties his hands with rushes, the
other blindfolds his eyes and covers his cheeks with a band of
cloth. Then they go back happily with their spoils, and as they go, 95
rejoice that no woman will have a rival, that henceforth there will
be no jealousies in love, that every woman will have a faithful bed,
and, in short, that none will suffer any sorrows at all when fortune 100
changes, and when, in love, the wheel takes a new turn: 'Love is
unchanging, each has her loyal bond: farewell noxious love phil-
ters; this boy no longer has the means to toy with us.'

"But the boy, roused from sleep, felt the new bonds, and sensed
that his eyes were covered, the cloth band binding them. He wept 105
and at the same time cried out: 'Hurry, sisters, remove the cloth
from my eyes, release my hands from bonds. Alas, mother, my too
trusting mother, to whom have you abandoned me? Can you possibly have preferred a violet and garlands to me? O ungrateful
Graces, O snare-laden Sleep and grove, surely my arrows and 110
quiver aren't lost? O shepherds, faithless crew, and you, disloyal
dell nymphs, give me back my bow, give me back my arrows now!
But if you are afraid of the darts that will harm you, return to me
at least the ones that will harm the gods.' These things the boy 115
repeats amid his tears. Look, beautiful Ariadne, moved by his lamenting cry, comes across the gardens, fearing an act of deceit and
wishing to bring help to the boy in pain.[16] May Love be worthy of
asking for help! As soon as he disentangled his hand, he said,
'My mother,' and cast it onto her tender breast, her soothing bo- 120
som; when her breasts convinced him that she was his mother,

Ut matrem suasere sinus, surrisit et inter
　　Verba iacit blandis oscula blanda sonis.
Mutua virgo refert, suasere quoque oscula matrem
　　Dulceque nescio quid oscula Amoris habent.
125　At postquam emicuere oculi et fax illa refulsit,
　　Visus Amor certe est qui fuit ante puer,
Visa sua et puero mater: sic pectora suadent
　　Oraque, ni naevus prima labella notet.
Sed tamen ingeminat: 'Mater da spicula, mater
130　　Redde arcum ac pharetram telaque redde mihi.'
Ecce autem geminae per murmura nota columbae
　　Ostendunt, arcus atque ubi tela latent.
Eruit illa arcus et sentibus abdita tela:
　　Obducunt spinas qua tetigere rubi.
135　Tum puerum accingit pharetra pharetraeque sagittas
　　Indidit, ipsa sua disposuitque manu.
Ridet Amor, gaudetque arcus tractare sinuque
　　Virginis e tenero vulnera sueta parat,
Ore puer, sed fraude senex atque arte magister,
140　　Trux dis, trux homini, trux quoque et ipse feris.
Mox collo implicitus nymphae puerilia iungit
　　Oscula et alternos provocat ore iocos
Paulatimque dolos meditans inspirat amicum
　　Virus et, ah, tacitis inficit ossa notis:
145　'Nec tua non nostrae versabunt pectora curae,
　　Quique sinu teneor, corde fovebor Amor.
Nec vates deerit qui te quoque cantet, et illi
　　Ipse adero, ipsa tibi grata futura parens.'
Haec ait et nitidis coelo se sustulit alis:
150　　Qua volat auratae signa dedere comae.
Ad matrem properat (nam vidit ab aere matrem),
　　Excipitur roseo matris ab ore suae.

he laughed, and between his words, gave her sweet kisses with delightful sounds.[17] The girl gave kisses in return; the kisses too persuaded him she was his mother, and the kisses of Love had a certain indefinable sweetness.

"But after his eyes flashed bright and that famous torch shone again, then he certainly appeared to be Love, who before was but a boy, and to the boy she seemed to be his mother—so her breasts and kisses suggested, if it weren't for a mole that marked the corner of her lips. Yet nonetheless he repeated: 'Mother, give back my darts, give back my bow, mother, and give me back my quiver and arrows.' But see! two doves, with their familiar cooing, showed him where the bow and arrows were hiding.[18] She pulled out the bow and arrows hidden in a briar patch. The bramble bushes, wherever they touched her, hid their thorns. Then she armed the boy with the quiver, put arrows into it, and arranged them herself with her own hand. Love laughed, rejoicing to handle his bow, and from the tender bosom of the maid, prepared his customary wounds—a boy in appearance, but an old man in deceit, a master of artifice, savage to the gods, savage to man, and savage to wild beasts as well. Then, lacing his arms around the nymph's neck, he gave her childish kisses, prompting playful kisses in return, and, contemplating trickery, little by little he breathed into her a sweet poison, and, alas, marked her bones with his silent signs: 'Not even your heart will escape being vexed by my torments. I, Love, held in your bosom, will be cherished in your heart. Nor will you lack a bard to sing your praises. I myself will inspire him, and my mother herself will be grateful to you.'[19] He said these things, and then raised himself up on gleaming wings in the air; his golden hair marked out his path where he flew. He rushed to his mother (for he saw her from the sky), and was welcomed by his mother with a kiss from her rosy mouth.

125

130

135

140

145

150

127

Quae postquam pueri casus et vincula novit,
  Detersit lacrimis quaeque fuere notae
155 Et solata simul, simul et miserata papillas
  Optulit, admovit labra manusque puer.
Deque sinu fluxere aurae, fluxere favoni,
  Atque Arabum afflatu prata oluere nemus.

Haec postquam Antiniana, novum coryleta dederunt
160 Cum plausu gemitum ac veterem indoluere querelam.
Illa iterum solata: 'Quid, o moestissima, dixit,
Nunc corylus, Coryle? Sors haec tua nunc quoque multis
Invidiae est; lacrimae flores, suspiria fructus
Dant tua. Non paucis livor quoque profuit et te
165 Invidia extollet parietque iniuria famam.'

After she learned about the misadventures of the boy, how he was tied up, she washed away what marks there were with her tears, and, at once consoling him and pitying him, offered her breasts,   155 and the boy placed his lips and hands on them. From her bosom, there wafted the breezes and winds of springtime; their breath made the meadows fragrant with the perfume of an Arabian grove."

After Antiniana sang these things, the hazel grove gave a fresh groan along with applause, and felt pain on hearing the old la-   160 ment. She once again offered consolation: "Why, O saddest Coryle, now a hazel tree, why do you lament?" she said. "This lot of yours, even now, makes many people envious: your tears produce flowers, your sighs, fruit. Envy, too, has profited many: jealousy   165 will exalt you, your injury give you fame."

VI

Quinquennius

Institutio ad vitae cultum et religionem.

Quinquennius filius, Pelvina mater.

Quinquennius

Dic, mater Pelvina, fragor quis tantus et unde?
Dolia num stringitque cados vindemia et arctat?
Hei mihi, quam crebri rutilant de nubibus ignes!

Pelvina

Abde sinu te, nate, meo atque amplectere matrem;
5   Ne trepida: di, nate, focis genialibus astant
Castaneasque suo prunis cum cortice torrent.
Illae, ubi sub cinere ardentem sensere favillam,
Displosae crepitant: hinc tanta tonitrua coelo
Disiectique ruunt ignes. Caput exere, nate,
10 Di mensas liquere, neque est metus ullus ab igne.

Quinquennius

Me miserum, properat, procul en vestigia nosco,
Orcus adest atque ore minax ac dente cruentus!
Hunc, mater, mihi pelle manu: trahit horrida crura
Et quassat caput et mento riget hispida barba.
Hunc abigas, Pelvina, mihi.

: VI :

Quinquennius

Elementary instruction in civilized life and religion.

[Speakers:] the son Quinquennius, the mother Pelvina.[1]

Quinquennius

Tell me, mommy, what is that great crashing sound? Where does it come from? It isn't the grape harvesters sealing the barrels and drawing the casks tight, is it? Oh, how the fires from the clouds come down glowing red one after another!

Pelvina

Hide yourself in my bosom, child; hug your mother. Don't be 5
afraid—it's the gods, my son, standing round their pleasant hearths, roasting chestnuts in their shells over the coals. When they feel the embers burning under the ash, the nuts explode and crackle: that's why there are such great thunderings in the sky and forks of flame run down. Raise your head, my son, the gods have 10
left their tables now—no more fear of flame.

Quinquennius

Ah poor me! He is coming quickly—for I recognize his footsteps from afar—Orcus is coming with his menacing jaws, his blood-stained teeth![2] Drive him away from me with your hand, mommy! He drags his hairy legs along the ground, he waves his head back and forth, and a shaggy beard bristles on his chin. Get him away 15
from me, Pelvina!

Pelvina

15   Fuge, saeve: quid audes
In puerum? Fuge, claude: meus iam nocte quiescit,
Inque diem queritur nihil hic meus. I, pete tesqua
Atque famem solare faba ingluviemque lupino.

Quinquennius

Quid, mater? Baculumne quatit ferus et riget aure?

Pelvina

20   Illum ego, nate, antro inclusi scuticaque cecidi.

Quinquennius

Anne etiam zona vinxisti?

Pelvina

Et compede cruda.

Quinquennius

Nunc, mater, tete amplector novaque oscula iungo.

Pelvina

Quinquenni mihi care, tua haec sunt oscula; iunge,
Atque itera.

Pelvina

Off with you, nasty beast: what do you dare to do to my little boy? Off with you, lame beast. My little boy is resting for the night now; he doesn't whine at all during the day, this boy of mine. Go and find wild desolate places; console your hunger with a bean, console your gluttonous maw with lupine.

Quinquennius

What is that, mommy? Is the nasty beast shaking his stick, pricking up his ears?

Pelvina

I closed him up in a cave, my son, and flogged him with a whip.   20

Quinquennius

Did you also tie him up with a belt?

Pelvina

Yes, and with a cruel shackle too.

Quinquennius

Now I'll hug you, mommy, and give you more kisses.

Pelvina

My dear, sweet Quinquennius, here are some kisses for you; kiss me, and kiss me again.

Quinquennius

En itero; dic, o mea, dic, age: quidnam
Hic Orcus deus est?

Pelvina

25   Deus est hic, nate, malignum
Numen et in pueros saevum grassatur. It umbra,
Dentivorax umbra, horrificans noctemque diemque
Et baculo ferit et dextra rapit et trahit unco,
Fauce et hiat puerum, queritur qui nocte, die qui
30   Oblatrat matri mammaeque irascitur; illum
Et dextra fovet et cauda demulcet amica,
Qui ridet matri inque sinu nutricis amatae
Dormiscit, capit absynthi et cum melle liquorem;
Quin cui brasiculae semen placet, huic dat ab ipso
35   Blandus avem nido, dat pictae colla columbae,
Quam tibi pollicitus.

Quinquennius

Num perlita crustula melle
Est quoque pollicitus?

Pelvina

Dabit haec tibi, nate, benignum
Numen et ille deus, cui nos atque omnia curae.

Quinquennius

Dic, mater: deus iste quis est numenque benignum?

134

Quinquennius

Here's another. Tell me, mommy, tell me please: what is this god
Orcus?

Pelvina

This god, my son, is a malevolent spirit, who cruelly attacks little 25
boys. A ghost, he walks abroad, a ghost with devouring teeth, terrifying day and night, and he hits with his club, seizes with his
hand, drags with his hook, and devours with his maws any little
boy who cries at night, who whines at his mother and has a tan- 30
trum with his nurse during the day. Any little boy who smiles at
his mother, falls asleep in his beloved nurse's lap, and swallows
drops of absinth with honey, he caresses with his hand and strokes
affectionately with his tail. And not only that: if a boy likes cabbage seed, he sweetly gives him a bird right from the nest, he gives 35
him the dove with the bright-feathered neck — the one he promised you.[3]

Quinquennius

Didn't he also promise pastries glazed with honey?

Pelvina

He will give you these things, my son — that benevolent spirit, the
god who takes care of us and who takes care of all things.

Quinquennius

Tell me, mommy: who is this god, this benevolent spirit?

Pelvina

40 Qui tenerum lactis florem ac ientacula praebet,
Dum matri puer obsequitur, dum paret alenti;
Qui plena melimela manu croceasque placentas
Dat pueris, dum litterulas et carmina discunt.

Quinquennius

Num det fraga mihi, cerasi num molle quasillum,
45 Ad ferulam cum discipulis si crastinus asto?

Pelvina

Quin et cariculas, quin mitia sorba nucemque
Pineolam et dulci perfusa cydonia musto.
En crustum, en prunum aridulum, en mustacea et offas.

Quinquennius

Num, genitrix, deus hic, panem post, vina canenti
50 Mulsa sacerdoti miscet, dat sorbile et ovum?

Pelvina

Quin et avem: pinguem ipse suum vult esse ministrum.
Det tibi avellanas ficumque uvamque recentem,
Invises quotiens templum et veneraberis aram
Et faris bona verba.

Quinquennius

Monedula si mihi detur,
55 Quive gemat cavea turtur, vel tympana pulsem,
Dum facit antistes rem sacram atque incubat arae.

Pelvina

The one who provides the soft *fior' di latte* and breakfast treats   40
when a little boy listens to his mother, when he obeys his nurse;
the one who gives honey apples with generous hand and golden
cakes to little boys when they learn their first letters and songs.

Quinquennius

Will he give me strawberries, a supple basket of cherries, if tomor-   45
row I stand with the other pupils before the teacher's rod?

Pelvina

Not just that, but also dried figs, ripe sorb berries, a pine cone,
and quinces drenched in sweet unfermented wine; and he'll give a
pastry, a dried plum, must cakes and bonbons.

Quinquennius

Is he the god, mother, who, after the bread, mixes sweet wine for   50
the priest when he sings, and gives him an egg to drink?

Pelvina

Why yes, and a bird too: he wants his own servant to be plump.
He would give you hazelnuts, a fig, and fresh grapes, whenever
you go to church, venerate the altar, and utter pious words.

Quinquennius

If I am given a jackdaw, or a turtledove that moans in its cage, I   55
would even strike the chimes, while the priest carries out the sacred rite and leans over the altar.

Pelvina

His ego citriolum frondenti et praecoqua ramo
Addiderim, nulla in gremium si lotia noctu
Fuderis Unctiliae, tibi quae dedit hubera parvo.
Nunc grandem loti pudeat.

Quinquennius

60   Mihi desine, mater,
Irasci! Sopor ipse gravat; nam saepe per umbram
Ludere cum pueris videor vel litore primo,
Nare simul nassaque leves includere pisces,
Exclusos mox elabi, me subdier amni,
65 Stillare et liquidum madefacto e corpore rorem.
Hoc nato, mater, praesta, ut deus ille benignus
Excitet e somno stupidum exhibeatque matellam;
Cedam ego cariculis siccis dulcique placentae.

Pelvina

Atqui, nate, deus nil esurit; ille matellam
70 Haud curat. Quin dona cape et cape semina, quis tu
Urinam moderere et lotia rara remittas;
Sin aliter, deus ille atrox tibi, nate, flagellum
Incutiet. Volat explorans, quis lintea parvus
Inquinet, urticaeque decem fert se ante maniplos,
75 Et caedit scutica nigroque involvit amictu
Micturientem aliquem tetroque absorbet hiatu.
Mitescit tamen et rictus compescit hiantis,
Pectendum quotiens matri buxoque colendum
Praebueris caput et purgandum lende capillum.
80 Nam secus intortum orditur de vertice funem,
Quo puerum trahit et deserta exponit in alga

Pelvina

I would add to these a cucumber and *percoche* with their leafy
branch, if you don't wet Unctilia's lap with pee-pee at night —
Unctilia, who gave you the breast when you were little.[4] Now that   60
you are a big boy, you should be ashamed of pee-pee!

Quinquennius

Stop getting mad at me, mommy! It is sleep itself that weighs me
down — for often in the dark of night I dream that I am playing
with other boys on the water's edge, swimming and trying to trap
little fish in a wicker basket. Then the fish elude the basket and
glide away. I go under the water's surface, and droplets of water   65
drip from my soaking-wet body. Mommy, do this for your child,
make that benevolent god wake me up, drowsy, from sleep, and
show me the chamber pot. If he does, I will let *him* have the dried
figs and sweet cake!

Pelvina

Ah but the god has no hunger, my child, and the chamber pot is   70
hardly his concern. So take the gifts and the seeds that will help
you hold in your urine, so you only rarely need to pee. Otherwise,
my child, that other nasty god will strike you with his whip. He
flies abroad to find out which little boy soils the linens; he carries
before him ten handfuls of stinging nettle, and flogs with the lash,   75
enfolds in his black cloak, and engulfs in his foul-smelling maws,
any little boy who wets the bed.[5] But he grows gentle and restrains
his gaping jaws whenever you offer your head to be combed and
arranged by your mother with a boxwood comb and your hair to
be cleansed of lice. For otherwise he weaves twisted rope from hair   80
on the child's head, drags off the child with it, leaves him exposed

Invitatque avidas adaperto gutture phocas.
Quare, age, care, mihi cervicem amplectere et ipso
Lude sinu, simul abde oculos et collige somnum.

Quinquennius

85 An, mater, mihi blanditias et carmina dices?

Pelvina

Dicam, nate; etiam cunas modulabor ad ipsas
Naeniolam: cape naeniolam et nigra lumina conde.

on desolate algae, and summons hungry seals with gaping maws
. . . So, dear child, come now, give me a hug around the neck, play
in my lap, and close your eyes and fall asleep.

Quinquennius

Mommy, will you sing me a sweet lullaby?   85

Pelvina

I will, child. I will even rock your cradle to the tune of the lullaby:
listen to your lullaby, and close your black eyes.

IOANNIS IOVIANI PONTANI
DE HORTIS HESPERIDUM SIVE
DE CULTU CITRIORUM
AD ILLUSTRISSIMUM PRINCIPEM
FRANCISCUM GONSAGAM
MARCHIONEM MANTUAE

GARDEN OF THE HESPERIDES OR
THE CULTIVATION OF ORANGE TREES
BY GIOVANNI GIOVIANO PONTANO
TO THE MOST ILLUSTRIOUS PRINCE
FRANCESCO GONZAGA
MARQUIS OF MANTUA

LIBER PRIMUS

Vos o quae liquidos fontis, quae flumina, nymphae
Naiades, colitis, quae florida culta, Napeae,
Deliolosque hortos et litora cognita Musis,
Quae collis Baccho laetos flaventiaque arva
5 Messibus ac summi curatis rura Vesevi,
Quo solem vitetis iniqui et sideris aestum,
Hac mecum placida fessae requiescite in umbra
Gratorum nemorum, Dryades dum munera vati
Annua, dum magno texunt nova serta Maroni
10 E molli viola, e ferrugineis hyacynthis,
Quasque fovent teneras Sebethi flumina myrtos.
Vos gelidi fontes genitalis et aura Favoni
Invitant, vos coeruleo quae litore pictae
Nereides varias ducunt ad plectra choreas
15 Et nudae pedibus fusaeque ad colla capillis.
En ipso de fonte et arundine cinctus et alno
Frondenti caput, ac vitreo Sebethus ab antro
Rorantis latices muscoque virentia tecta
Ostentans, placidas de vertice suscitat auras,
20 Quis solem fugat et salices defendit ab aestu.
Ergo agite et virides mecum secedite in umbras,
Naiades, simul et sociae properate, Napeae,
Quaeque latus Tyrio munitis, Oreades, arcu.
Non hic Pierii cantus, non carmina desint
25 Adventante dea. Summis en collibus offert
Uranie se laeta. Agite, assurgamus eunti
Et dominam comitemur, opaca et rupe sedentem
Et rore Idalio et Syrio veneremur odore
Insignem cithara et stellanti ad tempora serto.

BOOK ONE

You, Naiads, who dwell in flowing springs and rivers, and you, dell
nymphs, who inhabit the flower beds, the gardens of Dogliolo,
and shores known to the Muses, you who care for hills fertile in
wine, fields yellow with crops, and the countryside of lofty Vesu- 5
vius, to avoid the sun and the dog star's excessive heat, rest here
with me, when you are weary, in this soothing shade of pleasing
groves, while Dryads weave annual gifts for the bard, while they
weave fresh garlands for great Maro from soft violet, dusky hya- 10
cinths, and tender myrtles nurtured by the streams of Sebeto.[1]
You are summoned by chill springs and the life-giving breath of
the west wind, by bright-hued Nereids who lead manifold dances
on the azure seashore to the song of the lyre, their feet bare and 15
their hair flowing over their necks. Look, Sebeto, vaunting his
dewy waters and dwellings green with moss, with his head
wreathed in reed and leafy alder branch, from his very source,
from his glass-green grotto, from his eddying waters, stirs up
soothing breezes with which he drives away the sun and protects 20
the willows from the heat. Come, then, and withdraw with me
into the green shade, Naiads, and you too, dell nymphs, hurry
along with them as companions, and you, Oreads, who arm your
sides with Tyrian bow.[2] May Pierian chants and songs be not absent now, for the goddess is arriving. See, on the hilltops Urania 25
gladly shows herself: come, let us rise in her honor as she comes,
and let us accompany our patroness and venerate her with Idalian
ambrosia and Syrian perfume, as she sits on a shady crag, conspicuous with the cithara and a starry garland gleaming on her
temples.[3]

30   O facilis felixque veni, dea. Me per apertos
      Aeris immensi campos summoque vagantem
      Aethere, mox toto numerantem sidera coelo
      Duxisti, legesque deum atque arcana docenti
      Illarum et relegis series et fata recludis
35   Atque ipso rerum causas deducis Olympo.
      Ocia nunc hortique iuvent genialiaque arva
      Quaeque et Amalpheae foecundant litora silvae,
      Citrigenum decus, Hesperidum monumenta sororum,
      Deliciae quoque et ipsa tuae. Peneia Phoebum
40   Delectent Tempe fraternaque pectora lauri;
      Te Sebethiacae capiant nemora inclyta citri
      Et quas nostra suo colit Antiniana recessu.
      Nos canimus: tu, diva, fave atque assiste canenti,
      Dum vatis veteres sacri renovantur honores.
45   En manet irriguum te blanda Patulcis ad amnem.
          At tu, quo Gonsaga domus, quo Mantua gaudet
      Principe, dum canimus, post arma gravisque labores,
      Itala dum spargis Tamarusiaque arva cruore
      Gallorum et victor spolia illa Feretria tentas,
50   Francisce, heroum genus atque Bianore ductum,
      Ne desis neve hortensem contemne laborem,
      Herculeae decus et pretium memorabile clavae.

                Qualis sit arbor citrius, et unde oriunda

      Orbe etenim Hesperio Niasique ad litora quondam
      Oceani auriferis primum sese extulit hortis
55   Citrius arboreae referens praeconia palmae.
      Illi perpetuus frondis decor, inter opacum
      Albescunt nitidi flores nemus, atque ita late
      Spirat odoratus Zephyris felicibus aer.
      Ipsa quidem lauro foliisque et cortice et ipso

Come in favorable and propitious mood, O goddess. As I wan- 30
dered over the open plains of the immeasurable air and in the
highest firmament, as I counted all the stars in the sky, you were
my guide; and as I teach the laws of the gods and their sacred se-
crets, you unravel their order for me and reveal destiny; you lead 35
down the causes of things from Olympus itself.[4] Now, may I find
delight in leisure and gardens, in fertile fields and the shores made
fruitful by Amalfi's forests, in the glory of the citrus stock, the
memorial of the Hesperides sisters, which is your delight as well.
Let Thessalian Tempe delight Phoebus, let laurel trees please your 40
brother's heart; may *your* heart be captured by Sebethian citron
trees — famous groves — and those which our Antiniana cultivates
in her retreat.[5] I sing: you, goddess, inspire and stand by me as I
sing, while the age-old rites of the holy bard are renewed. See, 45
charming Patulcis awaits you by the flowing stream.[6]

But you, Francesco, in whom the house of Gonzaga delights,
whom Mantua delights to have as prince, as you sprinkle the fields
of Italy and the Taro River valley with the blood of the French,
and, victorious after warfare and weighty toils, hold in your hands
the Feretrian spoils, you, who come from a line of heroes that goes 50
back to Bianor, be not absent while I sing, nor despise the labor of
gardens, the glory and memorable prize of Hercules' club.[7]

The nature and origins of the orange tree

Long ago, in the Hesperian realm, by the shores of Ocean near the
Nias, the orange tree first arose in the orchards bearing golden
apples, the orange tree, famed for taking the prize among trees.[8] It 55
has evergreen beauty in its leaves, its bright flowers shine white in
the dark wood, and the air, fragrant with life-giving Zephyrs,
wafts its scent far and wide. It is similar to the laurel in its leaves,

60 Stipite tum similis, tum frondescente iuventa,
    At cono inferior ramisque valentibus impar;
    Nam florum longe candore et odoribus anteit.
    Quin gravida e ramis triplici et distincta colore
    Mala nitent virides primum referentia frondes,
65 Hinc rutilant fulvoque micant matura metallo;
    Flore novo semper, semper quoque foetibus aucta,
    Perpetuum Veneris monumentum at triste dolorum.

De conversione Adonidis in citrium

    Moerebat puero extincto, lugebat amantem
    Scissa comam et lacrimis humebat terra profusis;
70 Humebant lauri, quarum frondente sub umbra
    Et positum ante pedes lamentabatur Adonim,
    Et se oblita deam tundebat pectora palmis.
    Ut vero sese dolor et gravis ira repressit,
    Ac veterum admonuit Daphne Peneia amorum:
75 'Et nostros, inquit, testabitur arbor amores
    Nostrorum et maneant monumenta aeterna dolorum.'
    Ambrosio mox rore comam diffundit et unda
    Idalia corpus lavit incompertaque verba
    Murmurat ore super supremaque et oscula iungit.
80 Ambrosium sensit rorem coma, sensit et undam
    Idaliam corpus divinaque verba loquentis.
        Haeserunt terrae crines riguitque capillus
    Protenta in radice et recto in stipite corpus,
    Lanugo in teneras abiit mollissima frondes,
85 In florem candor, in ramos brachia et ille,
    Ille decor tota diffusus in arbore risit.
    Vulnificos spinae referunt in cortice dentes,
    Crescit et in patulas Aphrodisia citrius umbras.

bark, and even its trunk, as well as its verdant youthfulness; it has 60
a lower apex, and is inferior in strength of boughs, but is superior
by far in the whiteness and fragrance of blossoms.[9] And what is
more, the fruit glisten, hanging in abundance from the boughs, set
off by triple hue, at first resembling green leaves, then growing 65
reddish in color, and then, once ripe, gleaming with a metallic
flash of gold. Always abundant with fresh foliage, always loaded
with fruit as well, the tree is the undying memorial of Venus, the
sad memorial of her grief.

The transformation of Adonis into an orange tree

Venus was in mourning after the boy's death.[10] She tore her hair
and grieved for her lover, and as she poured forth tears, the earth
was getting wet, the laurels were getting wet, and beneath their 70
leafy shade she both lamented the dead Adonis laid out before her
feet, and (forgetting she was a goddess) struck her chest with her
hands. But when her grief and deep anger subsided, and Daphne,
daughter of Peneus, reminded her of an earlier love story, she said,
"My love, too, will have a tree's testimony; may the memorials 75
of my grief endure perpetually."[11] Then with ambrosial dew she
sprinkled his hair, with Idalian ointment bathed his body, mur-
mured indistinct words over him, and gave him a final kiss. His 80
hair felt the ambrosial dew, his body felt the Idalian ointment and
heard the divine words of the goddess' speech.

His locks stuck fast in the earth, his hair grew rigid and extended into a root, his body into an upright trunk; the exquisitely
soft down on his body turned into tender leaves, his white com- 85
plexion into blossoms, his arms into branches, and that beauty of
his was delightfully diffused through the entire tree. The thorns in
the bark were reminiscent of teeth that leave love marks, and Venus' orange tree grew outward into its spreading shade. Then the

Colligit hinc sparsos crines dea mandat et altae
90 Telluri infodiens, tum sic affata: 'Meis heu
Consita de lacrimis nunquam viduabere fronde,
Semper flore novo semperque ornabere pomis
Hortorum decus et nemorum illecebraeque domorum';
Osculaque illacrimans ligno dedit eque capillis
95 Summa sub tellure agitans fibramina ducit,
Hauriat ut sitiens undam atque alimenta ministret.
Illa velut dominae luctum solata recentis
Excussit frondes resupinaque vertice canos
Diffudit florum nimbos, quis pectora divae
100 Implevitque sinum et lacrimas sedavit euntis;
Exin Hesperiis arbor nitet aurea silvis.

De apportatione citrii in Italiam

At postquam Herculeis humeris stetit axis, et Atlas
Prospexit coelo et fessus requievit in antro,
Et iam fata deum Latii et scelera impia monstri
105 Ultricem expectant clavam, procul orbe subacto,
Gerione extincto, spoliis insignis abactamque
Advexit praedam et nostris stetit ultor in arvis,
Idem humeris, idem ipsa arcu clavaque superbus
Devexit simul Hesperio de litore silvas,
110 Hesperidum silvas nemora effulgentia et auro.
Quis post Phormiadum saltus, fragrantia myrto
Litora Caietae fontisque ornavit et hortos
Virginis Hormialae. Venientem ea Tibride ab hudo
Accipit hospitio et thalami simul addit honores.
115 Hinc et ob aetatis florem placidosque hymeneos
Auriferae pretium tulit arboris, inde recenti
Implevit campos nemore et Zephyritide silva,

goddess gathered the scattered locks, entrusted them to the earth, 90
burying them deep, and spoke thus: "Alas, sown from my tears,
you will never be bereft of foliage, you will always be adorned with
fresh leaves and fruit, the splendid ornament of gardens, the enticing charm of houses and groves." Weeping over the trunk, she gave
it kisses; then, drawing down strands from the hair, she guided 95
them just under the earth's surface so that the tree could drink
water when thirsty and distribute nourishment. The tree, as if
consoling its mistress' grief, shook its recently sprouted leaves, and
with its top bent back, poured forth white showers of blossoms,
filling the goddess' lap and bosom with them and checking her 100
tears as they fell. From that time onward, the tree shone with
golden glow in Hesperian groves.

The importation of the orange tree into Italy

After the firmament stood on Hercules' shoulders and Atlas, having made provision for the sky, wearily rested in a cave, the fate of
the gods and the impious crimes of the Italian monster were 105
awaiting his avenging club. Hercules, gloriously adorned with
spoils, having subjugated the far-off region of the Amazons and
killed Geryon, drove and conveyed hither his plunder, and stood,
an avenger, in our fields, confident in the strength of his arms, also
confident in his bow and club.[12] At the same time, he took with
him the orchards from the Hesperian shore, the orchards of the 110
Hesperides, the groves gleaming with gold. Afterward, with these
trees he adorned the groves of the Formian nymphs, the myrtle-
scented shores of Gaeta, and the fountains and gardens of the
maiden Ormiala. As he came from the watery Tiber, she received
him as a guest and added as well the honors of the marriage chamber. Then, because of the flower of her youth and pleasant mar- 115
riage, he brought the reward of the tree bearing golden fruit, filled
the fields with a new grove, the forest of Zephyrium's goddess,

Qua Lestrigonios saltus, saxa horrida, Nereus
Lambit et aequoreae Liris secat arva Suessae
120 Quaque et oliviferis de collibus edita prisco
Nympha Lamo irriguos Fundania prospicit agros
Distinctosque hortos pomis et litora myrtis.
Quin et rura sororis Amalphidos et Sirenum
Ditavit scopulos Niasaei munere mali.

Quae loca sint apta serendis citriis

125 Nunc age, qui cultus citriis, quae certa serendi
Tempora quaeque illis regio magis apta ferendis
Expediam nullique loquar memorata priorum.
Principio apricum ad solem ventosque tepentis
Vergat ager; putres glebae quaeque aequora rastris
130 Molle sonent fluidum facile admissura liquorem.
Nec mihi displiceat salebrosi glarea ruris
Quaeque solo tenui graciles imitatur arenas,
Si modo saepe fimo spargas, si pronior unda
Diluat ipsa super laetusque instillet et himber.
135 Quid non expugnet sollers industria? Non me
Aut pudeat, dum mane suas Philomela querelas
Instaurat seu maiores sol suscitat umbras,
Plena manu liquidis invergere dolia lymphis
Spumantemque cavis inferre canalibus amnem
140 Solari et mollem cantu mulcente laborem;
Aut etiam occasum ad solem primasque tenebras,
Dum nox Oceano nigris sese exerit alis,
Aut tenebris mediis et cum intempesta silet nox,
Nec nocturna negat rorantia lumina Phoebe,
145 Et flumen ruere et fontes mersatilis urnae:
Tantum avet inspergi sese himbre Niasias arbor.

from western lands, where Nereus laps Laestrygonian woodlands — savage coasts — and the Liris cuts through the fields of
watery Suessa Aurunca, and where the nymph Fundania, born of   120
old Lamus, gazes from olive-bearing hills over well-watered fields,
gardens and shores adorned with fruits and myrtles; and he even
enriched the lands of her sister Amalfi and the rocks of the Sirens
with the gift of the Niasaean fruit.[13]

What places are appropriate for planting orange trees

Come now, I shall expound what are the forms of cultivation for   125
orange trees, what are the fixed times for planting them, what climate is more appropriate for growing them, and I shall tell things
that have not been mentioned by any of my predecessors.[14] First of
all, let the field be exposed to the full sun and warm breezes. Let
there be crumbling clods of earth and fields that make a soft   130
sound when struck by hoes and easily absorb flowing water. Nor
would I disapprove of an uneven, gravelly field that imitates fine
sand grains with its thin soil, so long as you often sprinkle it with
manure, so long as water washes down from above and a plentiful
shower pours onto it.[15] What could skillful industry fail to accom-   135
plish? I would not be ashamed, when, in the morning, Philomela
renews her songs of lament, or when the sun casts longer shadows,
to pour out by hand jars full of flowing water, to introduce a foaming stream to the hollowed-out irrigation canals, and to solace the   140
mild labor with soothing song; nor even at sunset and the begin-
ning of the dark, when the night rises from the Ocean on dark
wings, nor when, in the midst of darkness, there is silence in the
dead of night and nocturnal Phoebe offers her dew-glistening
light, would I be ashamed to cast down a stream and waters from   145
irrigating vessel: to such an extent does the Niasaean tree yearn to
be watered.[16]

Quae loca sint evitanda et quibus utendum remediis

Imprimis fuge Sithonii mala frigora coeli,
Afflatus cave Treicios Boreamque nivalem
Quique Lychaonio spirant de vertice Cauri.
150   Quod si non alia poteris ratione malignum
Frigus et Othrisii compescere flamina venti,
Obiicibus cohibe ac summi molimine muri,
Aut olea et multa prudens circuntege lauro
Aut valle occulta vastique crepidine saxi
155   Aut ubi celsa suis obstent fastigia tectis.
Quin et per validas hiemes, per sidera nota,
Cum coelum riget atque gelu coit altior aether,
Tum gelidae noctes concretaque terra pruina
Imprimis metuenda et iniquus Iupiter hortis.
160   Ergo quamprimum coniecto stramine et arctis
Cratibus aut sparsis circum supraque maniplis
Impiger Alpini compesce incommoda coeli
Iratumque Eurum, aut fumos succende volantis,
Aut calcis vivae cumulosque fimumque calentem
165   Insterne et calidis gelidum aera vince favillis.
Ac supplex venerare deos et thura benigno
Ure Iovi, avertat glaciem componat et iras.

Fabula de citriorum reparatione novaque apportatione
in Italiam e media regione

Nanque ferunt ob primitias quandoque negatas
Iunonem indignantem animo graviterque dolentem
170   Immisse et stragem arboribus citriisque ruinam,
Hesperii generis malorum stirpe perempta,
Donec eam Venus e Medorum divite silva
Relliquias relegens per Afrorum pinguia culta

What places are to be avoided and what remedies one should use

Above all avoid the damaging cold of Sithonian weather, beware
Thracian blasts and wintry Boreas, and northwest winds that blow
from Lycaonian heights.[17] But if in no other way you will be able   150
to check the spiteful cold and the blasts of Othrysian wind, enclose the plot with barriers and the laborious undertaking of a very
high wall, or skillfully cover it all around with olive trees and a
good number of laurel trees, or set it in a hidden hollow within a
vast stone enclosure, or where high gables provide shelter with   155
their structures.[18] And also during hard winter seasons, when familiar constellations rise, when the sky is frozen and the upper
firmament contracts with cold, then you must above all fear the
chill nights, the earth congealed with frost, and a Jupiter hostile to
gardens. Therefore as soon as possible, by heaping straw and   160
densely woven wicker all around, or by strewing bundles of hay
around and on top, work hard to limit the damage caused by Al-
pine weather and the rage of Eurus, or kindle fires that send
smoke into the air, or pour heaps of quicklime and steaming manure overtop and subdue the chill atmosphere with warm sparks.   165
Moreover, honor the gods in suppliant fashion and burn incense
to win the favor of Jove, so that he may avert the frost and put
aside his anger.

*A story about the restoration of orange trees, and their fresh importation
into Italy, from the realm of the Medes*

For they say that Juno, indignant in spirit and deeply offended
because the sacrifice of first fruits was neglected on some occasion,
sent down destruction and slaughter on the orange trees, and the   170
stock of fruits of Hesperian lineage was destroyed. But then Venus, gathering up remnants from the rich woodlands of the Medes
and bringing them over the fertile fields of Africa back into Italy,

Rursus in Italiam genti transmisit habendam
175   Aeneadum, quo priscus honos et cura nepotum
In silvis veteres renovaret Adonidis ignes,
Aeternum et maneant monumenta insignia amorum.
    Tu vero, quotiens aestusque et solis iniquum
Fervorem metues rapidi et fera sidera Cancri,
180   Aut glaciem quotiens inimicae et tempora brumae,
Verge iterum latices, iterum fluvialia mersa
Stagna super; sic ipse aestus, sic frigora vinces.
Nanque aestu sitientem alte externoque calore
Arentem madidans sedas aestumque sitimque.
185   At glacie inclusus calor aestuat et furit intus
Flamma vorax. Tum funde himbrem, tum flumine largo
Irrora siccas occulto ex igne medullas,
Quo vigor adversum soles se et frigora duret.

Quod tempus aptum sit serendis citriis

Vere autem et cum sol paribus se temperat horis,
190   Tunc tuto liceat telluri infigere plantas;
Nec toto verear scrobibus committere in anno,
Aestate umbrosis in vallibus; ast hieme et cum
Mollis in aprico mitescit terra recessu,
Si modo perpetuus laticum mihi diffluat humor,
195   Nec desit coniux plena quae diluat urna
Et nunc frondenti ramo defendat ab aestu,
Nunc solem hibernis admittat mensibus et nil
Linquat inexhaustum curaque utatur et arte.

handed the orange tree over to the possession of the race of the
Aeneadae, so that long-maintained honor and the care of her de-   175
scendants would perpetuate her old passion for Adonis in their
forests, and the tokens of her love would endure as memorials for
all time.[19]

But whenever you fear the heat, the excessive blaze of the sun,
and the brutal constellation of fierce Cancer, or whenever you fear   180
ice and the weather of unfriendly winter, pour water once again,
once again pour fluvial pools of water over them; in this way, you
will defeat the heat, in this way, defeat the cold.[20] For when you
water a tree that is profoundly thirsty from the heat and parched
due to external warmth, you allay the burning and the thirst. But   185
heat that is trapped inside by ice rages and a consuming flame
blazes within. In that case, pour a stream of water, irrigate the
marrow that is dried out from hidden fire with a generous dose of
water, so that the tree's vigor may fortify itself against sun and
frost.

What time is appropriate for planting orange trees

In the spring, however, when the sun moderates itself with even
balance of hours, then one may plant shoots safely in the earth.[21]   190
Nor would I fear to entrust them to pits in the soil at any time in
the year, and during the summer, to plant them in shady vales, but
also in the winter when the earth grows soft and mild in a sunny
spot, so long as I have the continual irrigation of water flowing
down, and my wife is there to water with brimming jar, defend the   195
shoots from heat with a leafy branch, let the sun in during winter
months, and leave nothing untried and apply her diligence and
skill.

Quasdam regiones non alere citrios propter frigus

Nec vero Insubrium campis Ticinide terra
200 Quaque Pado alniferis infert sese Abdua ripis,
Ausit se riguis committere citrius hortis,
Nec qua iuncta Pado scindit sua Mincius arva,
Arva virum, heroum, imprimisque feracia vatum.
Arte tamen studioque Cloneia ponitur arbos
205 In rheda, cui pingue solum, cui plurima tellus
Insit et assidua madeat stirps aurea dextra;
Sub Iove quae ferat aestates hiemique malignae
Infertur tectis calidoque fovetur in antro.
Benaci tamen ad ripam Charidaeque recessus
210 Laeta nitet ramisque exultat Adonias arbor.
Munus et hoc, Cytherea, tuum, dum forte canentem
Ad virides Saloi salices tua dulcia furta
Et pueri amplexus teneros et Adonidis ignes
Miraris vatem egregium, cui candida plaudit
215 Verona et liquidis Athesis favet assonus undis.
Ille suas canit ad volucres, sua reddit Adonin
Silva, Dionaeae ludunt ad carmina nymphae.
Ipsa tuos repetis lusus, repetis hymeneos,
Per silvas, per saxa sonat tibi gratus Adonis,
220 Antra per et valles resonat formosus Adonis:
'Huc, o Adoni, ades, huc ades, o mihi dulcis Adoni.'
Addis et his etiam suspiria; suspirarunt
Et tecum salices et tecum flumina, dumque
Et flectunt salices ramos et flumina cursum,
225 Illicet et salices frondis et poma tulerunt
Hesperidum nemoris (nam sic, dea grata, tulisti),
Illicet et fluvii gaudent Cyrenide silva
Delituisse novoque comas nituisse decore,
Gaudet et ipsa suo Verona ornata Catullo,

Orange trees do not grow in some regions because of the cold

To be sure, the orange tree has not dared to entrust itself to well-watered gardens either in the lands of the Insubrians, in the territory of the Ticino, or where the Adda joins the Po with alder-bearing banks, nor where the Mincio cuts through its fields adjoining the Po, fields fertile in men, heroes, and above all, poets.[22] With skill and diligence, however, the Clonian tree can be placed in a wagon that has rich soil and a great deal of earth in it, where the golden slip may be kept wet with continual watering by hand; the kind of tree that endures summers under the open sky is thus both brought under cover against the spiteful winter and nurtured in a warm enclosure.[23] Yet by the bank of lake Benacus and the Graces' retreat, Adonis' tree shines with health and exults in its boughs.[24] This too is your gift, Cytherean goddess; for you admire the extraordinary poet as perchance he sings by the green willow trees of Salò about your sweet, stolen loves, the boy's tender embraces, and the passion of Adonis, the poet whom splendid Verona applauds, harmoniously accompanied by the Adige with its flowing waves.[25] He sings to his birds' melodies; a grove of Adonis' own trees echoes back his name, while the nymphs of Dionaean Venus frolic to the songs.[26] You renew your own love songs, Venus, you renew your wedding songs. Through the forests and over the rocks the beloved name of Adonis resounds for you; beautiful Adonis' name resounds through the valleys and grottoes: "Come here, O Adonis, come here, O Adonis my love." To these words you add sighs as well, and along with you, the willow trees and rivers sighed, and as the willows bent their boughs and the rivers their course, straightaway the willows produced the leaves and fruit of the Hesperides' grove; for in this way, delightful goddess, you brought them forth. Straightaway the rivers delight to hide in the Cyrenean grove, rejoice that the leaves gleam with a new beauty, and Verona itself, glorified by its native son, rejoices in

200

205

210

215

220

225

230 Altisonisque favet reflexa e montibus echo,
    Sirmiaque auratis resplendent rura volemis.

De altitudine scrobium

Sed tamen et scrobibus modus hic erit, ut neque in altum
Desideat nimis, ut quantum radice profunda
Haeserat, hoc paulo iaceat plus eque lacuna
235 Hauriat ut solitos himbris madidumque fluentum;
    Tum baculo aut pedibus facilem calcabis arenam.
    Parce tamen teneris fibris cautusque benignam
    Affer opem indulge et levibus pueriliter annis.
    Haec inter geniumque loci nymphasque sorores
240 Implora auxilio et faveas simul auspice dextra.

Serendas esse citrios nativa cum terra
et palis fulciendas

Quin etiam vellens fosso de gurgite plantam
Rursus et infodiens dextra fautrice videto
Cum tenera radice simulque haurire, simulque
Nativae infodere et multum telluris, ut haerens
245 In patria possit melius consuescere terra.
    Ipse vides puerum materno lacte repulsum
    Indignantem alio ductare e pectore mammas
    Huberibusque aliis dulcis haurire liquores.
    Altera confestim subeat te cura valenti
250 Sistere eam vallo sociisque adiungere truncis,
    Ne venti excutiant teneram, ne verbere torto
    Auferat inducto Boreas immanis hiatu
    Et sublime volet rapidis iactanda procellis.

Catullus, and an echo, reflected back from the deep-sounding 230
mountains, adds its applause, and the fields of Sirmio are resplendent with golden fruit.[27]

The Depth of Pits

Now, the proper measure for a pit shall be such that the tree does
not idle too much in the heights, but rather pushes down a little
further than it has clung fast with its deep root, so that it may 235
drink from the soil's hollow the usual streams of flowing water.
Then you will tamp down the pliable sand with a staff or your
feet. Be careful, however, of the tender roots, carefully bring bene-
ficial aid, and be indulgent of the plant's boyishly tender age. As
you do so, implore the Genius of the place and the sister nymphs
for help, and at the same time, protect the shoot with auspicious 240
right hand.

Orange trees should be planted with their native soil
and propped with stakes

Moreover, as you pluck the plant from the watery pit you have
dug, and then replant it in the ground, see to it that, with protective right hand, you pluck it up together with its tender root and
bury it in a great deal of its native soil, so that, planted in its 245
original earth, it can become better habituated. (You yourself observe that a child driven away from the mother's milk only grudgingly nurses at another's breasts and drinks the sweet milk from
someone else's bosom.) You should then immediately occupy yourself with another concern: to hold the tree in place with a strong 250
palisade and set it next to fellow tree trunks, lest winds tear up the
tender stripling, and savage Boreas, with the lash of his whip, create a gaping hole and carry it off, and it go flying through the air,
cast about by impetuous blasts.[28]

Ferro coercendam esse luxuriem

Ergo et ubi in ramos frondens sese extulit actis
255   Sub terram sparsim radicibus iniice ferrum,
Caede manu, ne in luxuriem fundatur inanem;
Nam veniet quocunque voces. Sed frigora vita,
Neve alte inflictum cera contingere vulnus
Sit pudor, urat ne calor aut ne frigora laedant.

De propaginibus procurandis

260   Atque hinc quo cultu citrii quave arte vel usu
Proveniant, paucis (nam nec sunt multa) docebo.
Partem etenim insitio, partem sibi semina, partem
Vendicat in generis sobolem producta propago.
Ergo ubi subductum felici e matre flagellum
265   Videris, hoc gladio medium feri et iniice saxum
Qua vulnus patet et plagae sic consule hianti.
Inde terebrato per aperta foramina fundo
Fictile coniicias pulla et mox obrue terra,
Nec sit parca manus stillanti infundere gutto.
270   Radicem lento ducet de cortice ramus
Subiicietque novas geminato ex hubere vires.
Ergo ubi in Italiam quater adventaverit ales
Daulias, i, rescinde manu atque excide securi
Frondentem ramum et terrae committe subactae
275   Optatam prolem fibris et fronde vigentem,
Ornet ut excultos et flore et frugibus agros.
Quin etiam cum se felici matris in umbra
Eduxit soboles, ferro diffinde et adactum
Infigas lapidem, ducto mox infode sulco;
280   Crescet in immensum multa radice virago.

Excess growth should be checked with a blade

Therefore, when, putting forth leaves, it has grown upward into branches, and sent roots down into the ground in different direc- 255 tions, apply the blade, hew it by hand, lest it pour forth in pointlessly abundant growth; indeed, it will go wherever you summon it. But avoid the cold, and do not hesitate to sprinkle a deeply cut wound with wax, lest heat burn or cold damage it.

How to care for shoots

Next, I shall teach in few words (for there are indeed not many 260 things to say), by what cultivation, art, or technique orange trees are produced. For some are claimed by grafting, some by seeds on their own, some by the cultivation of a slip to make an offshoot of the species. Therefore, when you see a shoot that has sprouted up from its prolific mother, strike it in the middle with a knife and 265 put a rock in it where the wound lies open, and in this way take care of the gaping injury. Next, guide it into a clay vessel through the open holes of its perforated base and then cover it over with dark soil, and make sure your hand is not sparing in pouring water on it from a dripping vessel. The bough will take root from the 270 pliant bark and supply new strength from redoubled fruitfulness. Therefore, when the Daulian bird has arrived four times in Italy, go and prune the leafy branch by hand, trim it back with a blade, and entrust the desired progeny, flourishing now in leaf and roots, 275 to the plowed earth so that it may adorn the well-worked fields with blossom and fruits.[29] And then, when the offspring has grown up in the prolific shade of its mother, you should split it with iron blade and forcefully drive a rock in, and then plant it in a furrow you have made. The heroic maiden will grow to a vast 280 size, putting down many roots.

De seminio faciendo et colendo

Si tibi seminium curae, primum elige terram
Sole sub aprico nulli quae obnoxia vento.
Hanc validis rastris et duro verbere marrae
Discute et in tenuem redigas studiosus arenam.
285 Hinc semen legito; lectum graviore notatu
Aequatis spaciis serito dextraque fideli
Infodito; infossum solito de more rigato
Et studiosa manus divellat gramina circum.
Non mora: iam toto tollent sese agmina campo
290 Et paribus spaciis aequato et Marte ferentur.
Hinc brevibus vallis sub signum figito et haerbas
Ipse manu legito; lectas sub sole cremato
Saepius et duris agitato bidentibus alte
Frondentem silvam Zephyrosque aurasque cientem.
295   Nec vero non illa tibi sit maxima cura
Et pubi tenerae, et postquam sese extulit arbos,
Sordentis soleas simul et praesegmina tetra,
Illuviem immundam crassisque liquoribus haustam
Ingerere, humorem ut lentum radicibus imis
300 Instillent himbri atque actis fluvialibus undis.
    Praecipue foetus gravidos nitidamque iuventam
Praestabunt infossa canum tibi squalida tabo
Corpora, dum pingues gaudent uligine fibrae
Luxuriantque hieme in media atque arentibus arvis;
305 Nec dubita aggestum cinerem squalentiaque ossa
Mersa solo infodere aut hominum excrementa suumve
Inferre, aut laetis sparsim radicibus urnam
Fundere et humani male olentia flumina loti,
Nocte tamen, ne te petulans vicinia damnet
310 Nidore offensa et graviter spirantibus auris.

· BOOK I ·

The planting of the seed and its cultivation

If planting seed is your concern, first choose a patch of earth with full sun that is not exposed to any wind; break it up with sturdy hoes and hard blows of the weeding hook, and work hard at reducing it to a fine, sand-like consistency. Next, choose seed; after 285 the seed has been chosen by very careful observation, sow it with even spacing, and plant it with steady hand. Once it has been planted, water the seed in the usual way, and with diligent hand pluck up the weeds all around it. No long time to wait: soon squadrons will rise up throughout the whole field, and they will 290 march at even intervals and on equal terms of war. Then, beneath your standard attach them to short stakes, pull up the weeds yourself by hand, and after you have pulled them up, burn them under the sun, and quite frequently with hard mattocks deeply plow up the leafy growth that stirs Zephyrs and breezes.

Indeed, you should take the greatest care to heap on the plant, 295 both in its tender youth, and after it has risen up as a tree, dirty old sandals, bits of refuse, and filth derived from mucky streams to drip slow moisture into the deepest roots, once you have led in 300 rain and river water.

The burial of dogs' bodies, squalid with decay, will be especially effective at providing you with heavy fruit and glistening youthfulness, while the well-nourished fibers rejoice in the moisture and luxuriate in the middle of winter and when the fields are parched. Don't hesitate to plant and bury in the soil heaped-up ash and 305 decaying bones, or to bring in the excrement of people and pigs, or to pour out a jar of bad-smelling streams of human urine all over the prolific roots. (Do this at night, however, lest neighbors petulantly condemn you, offended by the stench and unpleasant- 310 smelling air.)

Evagatio quaedam poetica

Iam tempus legere et cultis disponere in hortis
Et tondere manu et rivos agitare sonantis,
Colligere et plenis redolentia citria ramis
Aestivum ad solem et vento crepitantibus umbris.
315 Colligis ipse manu. Coniux in parte laborum
Dulcis adest, capit expensis de fune canistris,
Et mirata sinum pomis gravioribus implet.
Et (memini) astabat coniux floresque legentem
Idalium in rorem et Veneris mollissima dona
320 Amplexata virum molli desedit in haerba
Et mecum dulcis egit per carmina ludos.
Quae nunc Elisios, o fortunata, recessus
Laeta colis sine me, sine me per opaca vagaris
Culta roseta legens et serta recentia nectis.
325 Immemor ah nimiumque tui studiosa quietos
Umbrarum saltus et grata silentia captas!
Sparge, puer, violas; manes salvete beati:
Uxor adest Ariadna meis honeranda lacertis.
O felix obitu, quae non violenta Brigantum
330 Perpessa imperia, quae non miserabile nati
Funus et orbati senis immedicabile vulnus
Vidisti et patrios foedata sede penates.
Sed solamen ades, coniux; amplectere, neu me
Lude diu, amplexare virum ac solare querentem
335 Et mecum solitos citriorum collige flores.

Fructus citriorum alios dulces esse, alios acrimoniosos

Est vero et duplex citrii genus, et quod amores
Iucundos referat dulcis et Adonidis ignes,
(Sic placitum Veneri) dulce hoc; quodque acre dolores

A poetic digression

Now is the time for choosing plants and arranging them in the cultivated gardens, the time for pruning by hand and conducting trickling streams, for gathering fragrant oranges from the loaded boughs under the summer sun, under the shade of trees rustling in the wind. You yourself gather them by hand. Your sweet wife takes part in the work: she takes the fruit from baskets lowered by a rope, and, in amazement, fills her lap with the heavier ones. My wife too (I recall) was standing near, embracing me, her husband, as I picked blossoms for making Idalian perfume and Venus' most delicate gifts; then she sat down in the soft grass and sang and played sweet games with me.[30] Now, fortunate woman, without me you dwell happily in Elysian retreats; without me you wander amid shady places, gathering roses from well-tended beds and plaiting fresh garlands. Ah, forgetful, and too preoccupied with yourself, you seek out the tranquil woodlands and delightful silences of the dead. Strew violets, lad; hail, blessed spirit; my wife Adriana is here to feel the weight of my embrace. O happy in your death, for you did not endure the arrogant rule of the French, and you did not see the pitiable death of our son, the incurable wound of an old man deprived of his son, and the pollution of our country's *penates* in their very seat.[31] But be present as a consolation, my wife: embrace me, do not deceive me for too long, embrace your husband, console me as I lament and gather with me, as we did once, the blossoms of the orange trees.

315

320

325

330

335

Some fruits of orange trees are sweet, others more sour

There are, in fact, two kinds of orange tree: the sweet kind that recalls the pleasant love and sweet flames of Adonis (so Venus wished it); and the bitter kind that recalls pain, gloomy grief, and

Et tristis luctus et lamentabile funus

340 Sorte refert, suus ut lacrimis ne desit amaror.

Rara sed Ausonio Lamiaeque in litore foetus

Dat dulcis succosque frequens meditatur acerbos.

Contra solis ad ortum atque in Gangetide terra

Sponte sua dulcem victum ac redolentia ramis

345 Mella liquat, fluit eque Indis liquor Atticus hortis.

Nuper enim Hesperio oceano Calletia pubes

Digressa ignotosque locos et inhospita sulcans

Aequora, non solitos tractus, nova litora obivit,

Et procul arentis Libyae penetravit arenas

350 Audax, nec notas pontus quas circuit urbes.

Hinc Austro approperans coeloque intenta cadenti

Sideraque adverso servans labentia mundo,

Incidit obscurum gelidi Aegocerotis in orbem

Attonita et rerum novitate umbrisque locorum.

355 Inde pedem referens Prassi convertit ad oras

Barbaricumque fretum exuperans Rhaptique procellas.

Tandem gemmiferos Indi defertur ad amnes

Litoraque e citriis semper fragrantia silvis,

E quibus Hyblaeosque favos et Hymetia foetu

360 Mella dari dulcemque refert e cortice rorem

Sponte quidem, at succos longe indignanter amaros:

Usque adeo coelique situs solaque abdita terrae

Et soles variant ipsi positusque locorum.

Ergo alibi natura suo se robore firmans

365 Indiga nil opis est nostrae victrixque superbit;

Ast alibi curasque hominum atque inventa requirit

Obsequiturque arti et legum sese arctat habenis.

Nanque haec sponte sua quaedam se in luminis oras

Educunt matrisque suae tolluntur in umbra;

370 Illa hominum expectant operas manuumque laborem,

Naturae tacitum munus; nam prorsus ad artem

the lamentable lot of death, so that tears might not lack their bit-   340
terness.[32] But only the rare tree on Ausonian shores, on the shores
of Lamus' town, produces sweet fruits, and many a one devises
sour juices.[33] By contrast, in the land of the rising sun and the
Ganges, the orange tree of its own accord drips the sweet sustenance of fragrant honey from its boughs, and from Indian or-   345
chards Attic honey flows. Recently, a crew of Galician youths set
out from the Western Ocean, and sailing through unknown places
and inhospitable waters, arrived at unfamiliar regions, unknown
shores, and boldly gained entrance to the arid sands of faraway
Libya and unknown cities surrounded by the sea.[34] Hastening   350
from there toward the south, watching the western sky, and observing the constellations gliding in the opposing hemisphere, they
arrived at the dark region of chill Capricorn, amazed at the novelty of things and darkness of the place. Then, turning back up   355
north, they went to the shores of Prassum, crossing the Indian
ocean and the squalls of Rhapton, and at last they sailed to the
gem-bearing streams of the Indus and the realms ever fragrant
with orange orchards, from which, the crew reports, fruit as sweet
as the honeycombs of Hybla and the honey of Hymettus are
brought forth, and sweet liquid flows from the rind quite willingly,   360
but sour juices only very grudgingly : to such an extent do climate,
the earth's hidden soils, the amount of sun, and the location of
places cause variation.[35]

Therefore, in some places, nature, fortified by its own strength,
is not at all in need of our help, and glories in her victory; but   365
elsewhere, nature needs the attentions and discoveries of men,
submits to the control of art and is held in check by the reins of
laws. For certain things, of their own accord, draw themselves into
the realms of light, and rise up in the shade of their mother. Oth-   370
ers await the exertions of men and the toil of hands — nature's role
is silent. For grafting, to be sure, must be ascribed to the art and

Insitio est referenda humanae et mentis acumen,
De qua post in parte sua suo et ordine dicam.

Quo modo citria fiant crassiora

Sin curae tibi sit grandis educere foetus
375 Et patulas implere manus, age, decute ramis
Crescentem prolem, e multis ut pauca supersint
Poma, sed et maiora loco et magis auspice nata.
Huberiore etenim succo laetabitur haeres
Fraterni lactis, vacua et dominator in aula.

Quo modo citria toto anno insideant in arbore sua

380 Neve autem toto fructus tibi desit in anno,
Carpe manu partem et plenis bacchare canistris;
Quae reliqua est, gravidis sinito gaudere volemis.
Confestim qua parte dolet viduata recentem se
Induit in florem atque implet spe divite ramos;
385 Sic etenim alterno ditescet silva metallo.

De ratione decoris hortensis

Nunc quae sit formae ratio et quae cura docendum,
Undique quo decor ipse sibi et nova gratia constet;
Nec frustra veteres Veneris referentur amores.
Non alias cultu maiore incessit Adonis
390 Venatum, non Niliacas spectatior unquam
In silvas, non ante Venus maiore paratu
Ornarat, quam luce quidem qua fossus ab apro
Concidit et nigras tabo madefecit arenas.
Cingebat crinem myrrhae de palmite ramus,
395 Ad frontem roseus diffulgebat hyacynthus,

170

cunning of the human mind; of this I shall speak later on in its proper order and section.

How oranges become thicker

If it should matter to you to produce abundant fruit and fill your   375
open hands, come now, shake the growing fruit from the branches,
so that, out of many, only a few fruit remain, but those are both
larger and born in a more auspicious place. For the heir of his
brother's milk will rejoice in a richer sap, reigning as lord of an
empty palace.

How oranges may be found in their tree throughout the year

But you should have the enjoyment of fruit the whole year   380
through: pluck part of the harvest with your hand and revel in full
baskets; allow the remaining part of the tree to rejoice with abundant fruit. Right away, in the place where it grieves, bereaved, it
bursts into fresh blossom and fills its boughs with rich hope. For   385
in this way the orchard will be enriched by ore to be mined in al-
ternating turns.

The method of caring for a garden's beauty

Now I must teach what are the care and method for beauty, and
how elegance and fresh loveliness are harmoniously maintained in
all areas; nor will a reference to Venus' ancient love be in vain. At
no other time did Adonis stride forth to hunt with greater adornment, never did he go forth more splendidly into Egyptian forests,   390
never before had Venus ornamented him with a more elaborate
outfit, than on the day when, pierced by the boar, he fell and
soaked the black sand with gore. A branch from a myrrh shoot
encircled his hair, rose-colored hyacinth was gleaming on his brow,   395

Succincta et nitidum velabat purpura pectus,
Collaque fulgentes variabant candida bacae
Sparsim purpureis et coeruleis immistis,
Cingulaque auratis radiabant aspera bullis.
400 Elatis humeris pendebat aheneus ensis,
Ad capulum viridis fulgebat in orbe smaragdus,
Interstincta auro vagina, argentea cuspis,
Crura Cleoneae vestibant laevia pelles
Distinctique auro Tritones et aurea cymba,
405 Qua quondam Paphias Venus ipsa enavit ad arces.
Horrebant manibus duro venabula cornu
Et paribus nodis paribusque nitentia gemmis.
Talibus ornatum in silvas dea mittit opacas
Osculaque in roseis linquit signata labellis;
410 Arboreos igitur cultus dea poscit et ipsis
Ornatu atque auro longe splendescere in hortis.
Quocirca cum primum aetas feret, ipse benigna
Siste manu plantam rectoque in stipite firma:
Siquid et incultum, ferro preme; ferrea cera
415 Vulnera perlinito frigus ne permeet arctus;
In conum crescat facito ramosque fluentis
Sedulus attondeto et legem frondibus indito.
Usque suus puero ne desit lacteus humor,
Tu tenui calicem suspende in palmite filo
420 Imple et aqua tenuemque in aquam mox iniice vittam,
Quae labro emineat pendens, quae stillet et usque
Languentem rorem, laevi qui cortice labens
Ducat limosam gutta fluitante lacunam.
At postquam sese summas subduxit in auras
425 Et felix trunco et ramis frondentibus arbos,
Liberior tibi sit durata et frigore et aestu.
Non omnis tamen aut labor est aut cura neganda;
Nec tu parce oculis, dextrae si parcis, nec te

172

his handsome chest was wrapped in a purple robe, glistening beads added diverse color to his white neck, with dark red and sky-blue ones intermingled here and there, and his belt shone brightly, studded with gilded bosses. A bronze sword hung from his lofty shoulder, a green emerald gleamed on the round of the hilt; the sheath was variegated with gold, the point was silver; Cleonaean skins clothed his smooth thighs, and embroidered on them in gold were Tritons and a golden boat in which Venus herself once sailed to the citadels of Paphos.[36] In his hands bristled hunting spears of hard cornel wood, which gleamed with an equal number of gems as there were knots in the wood. The goddess sent him decked out with such adornments into the shady woods, leaving kisses imprinted on his rosy lips. For this reason, the goddess demands that in gardens too the beauties of trees shine far and wide with golden splendor. Therefore, when its age first allows, with kindly hand cause the plant to stand and support it on a straight stake. If there is any disorderly growth, prune it with iron blade; smear the iron-cut wounds with wax, lest a chill permeate its limbs; make it grow into a cone shape, diligently shear its spreading boughs, and impose law on its leaves. So that it may not lack its continual flow of milky moisture in its youth, hang a cup on its branch with a slender thread and fill it with water; then place a slender fillet into the water, so that it hangs over the lip and continually drips sluggish liquid, which, gliding down the smooth bark, forms a muddy pool with flowing drops. But after the tree has raised itself up into the airy heights, abundant in its trunk and leafy boughs, and has been hardened by heat and cold, you may let it grow more freely. Not all labor and care, however, should be denied; and if you are sparing of the hand, don't be sparing with your eyes. Don't be ashamed to gaze in amazement at the shoot or, as it happens,

400

405

410

415

420

425

Aut sobolem mirari aut ramos forte gravatos
430 Aut pigeat mediis laudare in solibus umbras,
Aut genio indulgentem agitare choros et iniquo
Sole sub appositisque toris mensaque beata
Ludere fumosum puero fundente Falernum.
Interea florum nimbus cadit, et fragrantem
435 Ad praedam coniux, ad praedam nata generque
Surgit laeta toris et flore exultat honesto,
Quem lectum liquat ac thalamos inodorat amorumque
Ipsa viri memor et vestes intingit et ora.
Ergo et frondentem bruma mirabere et aestu
440 Florentem, auratis utroque e tempore malis
Fulgentem; cole sub nivibus, sub sidere Cancri,
Nocturnis neu parce operis, neu parce diurnis.
Quoque modo id facias exempla antiqua monebunt.
Rivus aquae fluat, aut fontes roratilis urnae
445 Muniat elatus paries. Daphneia laurus
Multa tegat super et grato tueatur amictu,
Arceat et fulmen; quotiens et cura vocarit
Sparge fimum, calcis tumulos age, neve nivalis
Sistere per ramos patitor, sed discute nimbos
450 Ingentisque cita fumos et consere pugnam
Flatibus hibernis culmoque et crate saligna.

Post rigidas tempestates non esse amputandas

Sed memini cum nullae artes, non arma dolique
Vim coeli adversam ferrent: periere comantes
Silvae, obriguere gelu nemora omnia, late
455 Irrumpit mors, intereunt decora alta sororum
Hesperidum, sevit Scythicis Aquilonibus aer,
Concreta et solitos sistunt cava flumina cursus.
Quod quando (avertat Venus ipsa) rigentibus Euris

the loaded boughs, or to praise the shade in the midday heat, or,   430
indulging your inclination, lead dances, and while the sun is blazing, set out couches and an abundant board and enjoy yourself as
the servant pours the smoky Falernian.[37] Meanwhile a shower of
blossoms falls, and your wife rises to gather the fragrant spoils,   435
your joyful daughter and son-in-law rise from their couch to
gather the spoils and rejoice in the noble flower. Once it has been
gathered, the wife distills it into a liquid, and perfumes the bedroom, mindful of her love for her husband, and sprinkles it on her
face and clothing. Therefore, you will gaze at it in admiration as it
puts forth leaves in winter, blossoms in the summer, and at both   440
times of year gleams with golden fruit. Take care of it amid snow-
storms, under the sign of Cancer; don't spare efforts at night, don't
spare them in the day. Examples of old will show you how to do it.
Let a channel of water flow or raise up a wall to fence in the water   445
poured from a dew-dispersing urn. Let abundant branches of
Daphne's laurel cover it overtop and guard it with pleasing mantle,
and let it ward off lightning. Scatter manure whenever its care re-
quires; bring heaps of quicklime; don't allow drifts of snow to
stand on the branches, but shake them off, and kindle great bil-   450
lows of smoke and do battle with the blasts of winter with straw
and willow hurdles.

The trees should not be pruned after cold weather

But I remember when no techniques, no weapons and tricks could
withstand the opposing force of the weather. Leafy forests were
destroyed, entire groves were frozen by the chill, death ranged far   455
and wide, the tall glories of the Hesperides sisters perished, the air
howled with Scythian north winds, and deep-bedded rivers, frozen, brought their usual currents to a stop. When this happens as
icy-cold southeast winds blow (may Venus herself prevent it),

Contigerit, neu tu gladio neu caede securi
460 Arentis hortos, sed calce, sed himbre madenti
Affer opem. Hoc saepe ipse hieme, hoc et vere tepenti,
Deceptum nec te fallet labor: ecce repente
Pullulat ab radice, aut summo stipite laeta
Effundit gemmas turgenti et germine frondet.

De dispositione citriorum

465 Si te delectat species quadrata phalangis,
In quadram dispone; acies si forte Latina,
Porrige et in longum; sin et per florida rura
Sparsa manus, decor ipse aurique et gloria frondis
Est eadem. Nitet in mediis stirps aurea lucis,
470 Qualis mane novo cum se fulgentibus astris
Extulit oceani formosus Lucifer unda,
Quocunque inspectat, quoquo sua verterit ora,
Nil illo radiat fulgentius, omnia cedunt
Astra simul, toto exultat Venus aurea coelo.

475 Et quoniam assuetudo mali veterumque laborum
Naturam exuperat tolerando et acerba ferendo,
Iccirco videas silvestri saepe recessu
Non ulla rastrorum opera manuumve labore
Et fructus parere et solidis frondescere campis
480 Hesperiam citrium inculto et dominarier arvo.
Hinc alii, postquam e sulco sese extulit actis
Sub terram late radicibus et stetit arctus
Fixa solo, minus indulgent operamque remittunt,
A teneris quo consuescant nivibusque sitique.
485 Nec vero cultusque soli aut vis falcis ahenae
Aut tantum iuvet undanti de tramite rivus,
Quantum Auster Libycoque ruens de litore flatus
Autumno noceant: perit hic labor omnis et ille,

don't cut the parching orchards with blade or ax, but bring help   460
with quicklime and moistening water. Do this often in the winter,
do this also in the warmth of spring, nor will you be deceived and
cheated of the fruits of your labor. See, the tree sprouts up suddenly from the root, or pours forth buds abundantly from the top
of the trunk, and sends out leaves with swelling shoot.

The arrangement of orange trees

If the square-shaped appearance of a phalanx pleases you, form   465
the trees into a square; if perchance the shape of the Roman battle
line pleases you, stretch it out long. But even if the troop is scattered over flowering fields, the splendor and glory of golden fruit
and foliage remain the same. The golden shoot gleams in the
middle of groves, just as when, at break of dawn, amid the shining   470
stars the lovely Light-bringer rises up from ocean's wave, and
wherever he gazes, wherever he turns his countenance, shines
more brightly than everything, all heavenly bodies yield before
him, and golden Venus exults throughout the entire sky.

Since familiarity with difficulty and past toils, by tolerating and   475
enduring harsh conditions, gets the upper hand over Nature, you
may therefore often see, in a wooded recess, without the help of
any work of rakes or labor of hands, a Hesperian orange tree bear-   480
ing fruit and foliage over an entire tract of land, lording it over an
uncultivated field.[38] Hence some people, after the tree has grown
up from the furrow, sent out roots far and wide under the earth,
and come to a standing position, its limbs fixed in the soil, indulge
it less and put aside their toil so as to accustom it, from its tender
years, to snows and thirst. Nor indeed would the help supplied by   485
cultivation of the soil, the force of the bronze scythe, or water
from an irrigation channel be as great as the damage caused by the
South Wind and blasts rushing from the Libyan shore in autumn.
In this case all the labor is wasted, and all that splendor of fruit

Ah, fructus decor ac frondis squalescit, ut arbor
490 Arescat viduata, ut ramo et fronde perusta
Moereat, heu, liquidis nil proficientibus undis.
Ergo altas saepis praetende et brachia iunge
Densorum nemorum et clypeis ramalibus obsta
Adversae lauri aut quercorum umbrante cohorte.

De opere topiario

495 Quod si nec studium frugis nec cura movebit
Hortensis lucri, nemoris sed sola voluptas
Quaeritur et variis umbracula nota figuris,
Ante locum capias quem fons aut flumina propter
Lapsa fluant, unde et rivus ducatur aquarum,
500 Aut puteus propius scateat, ne forte per aestum
Languescat moriens, mox et rigor asper adurat,
Et labor et silvae pereant incepta superbae.
Parietibus mox obde futuras ante procellas
Avertens; post hinc quadras age, dirige fossas
505 Et dispone locos et vallis agmina cinge.
Infode dehinc teneram prolem et sere tramite certo
Et vinclis obstringe, obeunda ut munera discant
A pueris, sed quisque suo spacioque locoque;
Inde ubi et assiduo cultuque operaque magistri
510 Porrigit et ramos et frondis explicat arbos,
Ad munus lege quanque suum et dispone figuras,
Gratum opus, informemque gregem ad speciosa vocato.
Haec altam in turrim aut in propugnacula surgat,
Haec arcum intendatque et spicula trudat, at illa
515 Muniat et vallo fossas et moenia cingat,
Illa tuba armatos ciat et vocet agmen ad arma,
Altera tormento lapides iaculetur aheno,
Discusset castella et ruptis agmina muris

and foliage withers, so that the tree, bereaved, grows dry, and, alas,   490
blasted by heat in leaf and bough, grieves, receiving no benefit
from irrigating streams. Therefore, extend high hedges in front of
it, join together the branches of dense stands of trees, and create
an obstacle with the shielding branches of laurel facing opposite
and a shade-bearing squadron of oaks.

Topiary

But if neither an interest in fruit nor a concern for profit from   495
your garden will be a motive, but only the pleasure of the orchard
is your object, and shady bowers known for their various shapes,
you should first find a place near which a spring or gliding brooks
flow, whence a stream of water may be drawn, or where a well   500
burbles nearby, lest perchance the tree should languish and die in
the heat, or later a harsh cold scorch it dry, and your toil and your
project of a proud orchard be wasted. Next, create a walled enclosure, warding off future storm winds ahead of time; afterward,
make squares, lay out ditches, arrange the spaces, and ring the   505
rows with trenches. Then plant the tender shoots, sow them in
regular furrows, and fasten them with cords, so that from an early
age they may learn the tasks to be carried out, each one in its own
space and place. Then, when, through the continual cultivation
and work of the gardener, as adult trees, they extend branches and   510
unravel foliage, single out each one for its task, arrange their
shapes—a pleasing work—and summon the shapeless flock to
handsome forms. Let this one rise up into a high tower or turrets,
another stretch a bow and put forth arrows; let one fortify ditches   515
with a rampart and build a ring of walls, another one summon
armed men with a trumpet and call the troop to arms, and yet
another one propel rocks from a bronze siege machine, smash
fortresses, and, once the walls have been breached, send in troops.

Immittat, factaque acies — immane! — ruina
520 Irrumpat portis et congrediatur apertis,
Diruat et captam irrumpens exercitus urbem.
Ars igitur tempusque et vis innata perenni
Cura hominum nemora in lanas vertere, ut in hortis
E foliis ramisque et diversis contextis
525 Iam videas fulgere novis aulea figuris.

Arbores citrios diutius vivere

Nec vero spacium vitae breve seu breve tempus
Est citrio, aeternum genus, immortalis origo,
Et species aeterna quidem. Stirps citria longum
Ipsa manet secla exuperans, et iungere seclis
530 Secla parans trunco extincto mox surgit et alter,
Inde alter victrixque diu sua robora servat.
Sic placitum Veneri et Parcae statuere faventes,
Quae rerum seriem et fatorum arcana ministrant.
Nanque ferunt rursumque colos et stamina retro
535 Coepisse et versos rursum in contraria fusos
Volvere fatorum dominas, quo lucis in auras
Extinctum revocent vitaeque ad munera Adonin,
Et Veneris dulces iterum instaurentur amores.
Non passa est dea, dum versum in nova corpora monstrat,
540 Dum foliis simul et pomis longum optat honorem.
Illae igitur properare manu atque evolvere pensa,
Tenuia pollicibus formabant ducta supinis
Atque eadem impressis purgabant morsa labellis.
Discolor at positis variatur lana canistris,
545 Coerulaque viridisque alboque insignis et aureo.
Coerula dum digitis intorquent fila virensque
Subtegmen neitur, stipes se subiicit, alti
In latum pandunt rami et nova provenit arbos,

After they have wreaked destruction (savage!), the gates opened, 520
let the vanguard rush in and engage the enemy, and let the army
burst into the captured city and destroy it. Thus artifice, time, and
the force inherent in the ceaseless attentions of men have transformed orchards into wool, so that in gardens you may now see 525
tapestries resplendent with novel shapes woven out of diverse
leaves and boughs.

The long lifespan of orange trees

Nor indeed is the course of life or the time of life short for the
orange tree; it is an everlasting species, its origin is immortal, and
its beauty is truly everlasting. The very stock of the orange tree
endures a long time, outlasting lifetimes, and after the trunk is
dead, another soon rises up, preparing to join generations to gen- 530
erations, and then another again, and it long preserves the vigor of
its wood, triumphant. Such was Venus' decree, and so it was established in propitious agreement by the Parcae, who manage the
succession of events and the hidden truths of destiny. For they say
that the mistresses of fate began to turn their distaffs and threads
backward, to turn their spindles back in the opposite direction, in 535
order to call the dead Adonis back into the airy realms of light and
back to the tasks of life and the sweet love of Venus might be renewed again.[39] The goddess did not allow it, instead showing him
transformed into new bodily form, choosing an honor long-lasting 540
in leaves and fruit. They therefore hurried at their task and spun
out their allotments of wool, they shaped and guided the fine wool
with upturned thumbs, and they cleansed the same bits of wool by
pressing their lips on it. But when the baskets were set out, the
wool was contrasting and varied in color, dark blue and green with 545
flashes of white and gold.[40] As they twisted the dark blue threads
with their fingers, as the verdant yarn was spun, the trunk shot up,
high branches expanded far and wide, and the newly created tree

Ac sensim patulis adolescit frondibus umbra.
550 Inde canunt: 'Cresce aeternum victura, perenne
Servatura decus foliorum et divitis umbrae,
Ornatura domos procerum atque palatia regum
Materiamque datura sacris post vatibus, arbor.'
Atque hinc candentis deducunt vellera lanae
555 Divinumque labris stillant fragrantibus himbrem,
Stamina quo intincta et fusi simul omne volumen
In flores vertuntur, opacaque silva nitescit
Candore, et viridi miscent se ebora indica gemmae,
Aemulaque Assyrios spirant pomaria odores.
560 Ipsae autem tenerum solantur voce laborem:
'Fundite odoratos flores, nemora inclyta luxu
Perpetuo et ramis semper florentibus horti,
Semper odore novo semperque virentibus umbris,
Aeternum Veneris monumentum insigne et amorum.'
565 Mox et sepositis educunt fila quasillis,
Aurea fila, cavumque rotant implexa sub orbem.
Illicet Hesperiis illa intumuere volemis,
Pomaque pensilibus micuerunt aurea ramis;
Insolitum radiat folia inter opaca orichalcum.
570 Tum Parcae auspicio cecinerunt omnia laeto:
'Et fructu felix et flore et fronde recenti
Vive, arbor, supera et seclis labentia secla,
Hortorumque honor et nemorum ac geniale domorum
Delicium; tua vel reges umbracula captent,
575 Ipsaque continuis iuvenum celebrere choreis;
Te convivia, te thalami nuptaeque frequentent;
Semper ament quicunque tua versantur in umbra;
Assiduum referant frondes ver; aemulus aurum
Foetus et argento niteat flos concolor albo.'
580 Sic placitum, sic fata neunt, Amathuntidi sic stat.

came forth, and gradually shade spread as its leaves unfolded. Then they sang: "Grow and live forever; you will always keep the glory of your leaves and rich shade, always adorn the homes of princes and palaces of kings, and ever afterward provide subject matter for holy bards, O tree." Then they spun finely the pieces of the white wool, and they let fall drops of divine moisture from their fragrant lips; infused with this, the threads and everything wound around the spindle were transformed into blossoms, the shady forest gleamed with brightness, and Indian ivories were combined with green emerald. The orchards in rivalry breathed forth Assyrian fragrances. But the Parcae solaced their tender labor with song: "Pour forth fragrant flowers, O groves famous for perpetual luxuriance, O gardens with ever-flourishing boughs, with fragrance always fresh and shade always green, the eternal memorial of Venus and symbol of her love." Then they took out threads from special baskets, golden threads, and turned and twisted them on the curved wheel. Immediately, these swelled with Hesperian fruit, and golden fruit gleamed on hanging branches; an unfamiliar copper shone amid the shady leaves. Then the Parcae sang all things of propitious augury: "Live, tree, abundant in fruit, blossom, and fresh foliage, and outlast the gliding centuries with centuries more, the grace of gardens and groves, the festive delight of houses. May even kings seek out your shady bowers; may you be celebrated by ceaseless dances of the young; may banquets, bedrooms, and brides make frequent use of you; may all those who spend time in your shade always love you; may your leaves bring continual spring; may the gleam of your fruit rival gold, the sheen of your blossom resemble bright silver." Thus they ordained, thus the Fates spun their threads, thus stood the determination of the Amathusian goddess.[41]

Ergo agite, o tenerae colitis quae flumina nymphae
Fundana et Lamios rivis trepidantibus hortos,
Phormiades nymphae, quae roscida culta Suessae
Quaeque Amalpheos saltus fulgentiaque auro
585 Sirenum rura et fulvis sata saxa metallis.
Hoc agite, o roseae mecum sua serta puellae
Ferte deae, varioque halent altaria flore,
Spiret et e nitidis genialis amaracus aris.
Magna Iovis proles eadem pulcherrima mater
590 Aeneadum, tibi nos meritos largimur honores,
Idalii regina, tuos nos pangimus hortos
Et tibi Arangaeae crescunt ad flumina silvae
Moeriadum et litus felix Bereniciaque arva.
Tu stirpem, dea, tu citrios defende comantis,
595 Arce aestum, compesce nives et frigora pelle,
Siste et ab arctoo perflant qui cardine venti,
Perpetuum Niasaea decus frondescat ut arbos.
Haec ego; vos autem, placidissima numina, nymphae,
Oscilla e summis suspendite mollia ramis,
600 Formosumque sonent et ripae et litora Adonin.
Pars choreas agitate deumque ad festa vocate:
'Pulcher ades felixque ades ad tua munera, Adoni,
Et cape partheniae nectunt quae texta puellae,
Texta auro radiata et flore nitentia verno,
605 Quae referant veteres formosae Amathusidis ignes.'
Nos canimus, favet en facilis cantantibus echo,
Et divina procul responsant antra sororum.

Come, then, tender nymphs who inhabit the streams of Fondi and Lamian gardens with their rushing rivulets, nymphs of Formia, nymphs who inhabit the dewy fields of Suessa Aurunca, and those who dwell in the groves of Amalfi, the lands of the Sirens 585 shining with gold, and the rocks with their harvest of tawny metals.[42] Do as I say, O rosy girls: accompany me in bringing the goddess her garlands, let the altars be fragrant with diverse flowers, and let nuptial marjoram waft from the gleaming altars. The great offspring of Jove and most lovely mother of Aeneas' descendants, on you we bestow well-deserved honors, O queen of Idalium, we 590 compose verses about your gardens, and for you, Arangaean groves grow by the streams and fertile shore of the Moeriads and the fields of Berenice.[43] You, goddess, defend the shoot, defend the leafy orange trees, ward off the heat, check the snow and drive 595 away the chill, and still the winds that come blowing from the arctic pole, so the Niasaean tree may put forth leaves, an undying glory.[44] Such is my prayer. You, however, nymphs, gentlest of deities, hang fluttering masks from the top branches, and let the 600 banks and shores echo the name of beautiful Adonis. Some of you lead dances, and summon the god to the festivities: "Be present, beautiful Adonis, be a happy presence at your festival, and take the textiles the Parthenian maidens weave for you, textiles shot through with gold and gleaming with flowers of spring, textiles to 605 recall the old flame of the beautiful Amathusian goddess."[45] We sing, and behold, an obliging echo favors us as we sing, and far off, the divine grottoes of the sister nymphs echo in response.

LIBER II

Iamque alios vocor ad cultus aliumque laborem
Hortorum; neque enim simplex genus unave stirpis
Hesperiae soboles ratio aut tantum una colendi.
Acrumen genus omne novo sub nomine pluris
5 Diditur in partes, uno quae cortice foetus
Dant alios tamen atque alio se stipite tollunt.
Pars exacta quidem prima est. Nunc o mihi, natae
Pleiones, astate atque aspirate canenti;
Vester honos agitur, vestro sub numine crescit
10 Hoc opus et vestris mea tempora cingite sertis.
Vos quoque adeste simul facilesque estote, puellae
Hortorum memores: tuque o mihi culta Patulci,
Prima assis primosque mihi, dea, collige flores
Impleat et socios tecum Antiniana quasillos.
15 Sic tibi perpetuum spiret rosa, floreat urna,
Scilicet urna tui qua conditur umbra Maronis,
Ambrosiae fundat rivos, det nectaris amnes
Mincius et niveos semper tibi pascat olores
Et laetata suos iteret tibi Mantua cantus,
20 Mantua dives avis, dives Gonsagide prole,
Ac nova Lucrinae stupeant ad carmina cautes
Sistat et ipsa suos mirata Neapolis amnes.
   Tu quoque partem hanc Phaurusii ne despice ruris,
Francisce, armorum et studiis quandoque remissis,
25 Neu tibi displiceant silvae Stachiritides aut te
Non capiant fulvis radiantia poma corymbis.
Mars, belli decus, ipse deus bellique repertor
Et Venerem atque hortos amat atque hortensia dona.
Exemplumque dei sequere armipotentis et artes;
30 Nanque tibi Aethiopum e campis, Garamatide ab ora

BOOK TWO

Now I am summoned a second time to the cultivation, a second
time to the work of gardens. For there is not just one type or single offspring of the Hesperian line, nor is there only one method
of cultivation. The whole genus of agrumes, to use a new name, is   5
divided into many species, which, though they have the same bark,
produce different fruit, and rise up from a different trunk.[1] Indeed, the first part has been completed. Now, O daughters of
Pleione, stand by me and inspire me as I sing: yours is the honor,
under the influence of your divinity this work rises up; with your   10
garlands encircle my brow.[2] You, too, be present and show favor,
maidens who are mindful of gardens. May you, my cultivated Patulcis, come first, gather the first flowers for me, goddess, and may
Antiniana fill shared baskets with you: so may the rose breathe its   15
fragrance perpetually for you, the urn put forth flowers, no doubt
the urn in which the shade of your own Maro is buried.[3] May
Mincio pour forth rivulets of ambrosia, produce streams of nectar
and ever maintain snow-white swans for you, and may Mantua,
rejoicing, repeat her songs for you, Mantua, rich in ancestors, rich   20
in the family of Gonzaga.[4] But may the Lucrine rocks gape in astonishment at new songs, and may Naples herself, amazed, cause
her rivers' flow to cease.[5]

You, too, Francesco, do not despise this region of Pharusian
land, and, whenever you have put aside your keen pursuit of warfare, do not be displeased by forests of the river Stachir, nor may   25
you be unimpressed by the fruit gleaming in golden clusters.[6]
Mars, the glory of warfare, the very god and inventor of war, loves
Venus, gardens, and the gifts gardens give. Follow the example and
the practices of the god powerful in arms; for I bear you fruit from   30
the fields of the Ethiopians, from the Garamantian shore, fruit

Poma fero, poma excubiis vigilata draconum,
Herculeae meritum clavae, nova munera gentis
Romulidum aetheriis famam quae sustulit astris.
Ecce autem, num ne haec coelo delapsa liquenti
35 Stella nitet? Num forte novum sese exerit astrum,
Et felix astrum et nostris aura addita coeptis?
En virides citro silvae, en limonia rura
Praetendunt frondes? En quae panduntur et umbrae?
Quique aurum luci nemora et generosa metallum
40 Irradiant? Quibus ipsa nitent ramalia gemmis?
An coniux Ariadna viri memor et memor horti
Sese offert? O hortensis miserata labores,
Uxor, ades: cape rastra simul, cape sarcula et ipsis
Innitens incumbe bidentibus et frondosas
45 Falce premas citros simul et rorantibus urnis
Funde amnes; spument plenis stagna ipsa lacunis;
Ac tandem iuvet optatos decerpere flores
Et fructus legere atque aestus vitare sub umbra
Ducentem socias nympharum ad plectra choreas.
50 Vos mecum Uraniae Aonium instaurate laborem
Ac mecum auricomas citrorum pangite silvas.

De citro et eius cultu

Hesperidum in silvis Niasaei et margine fontis
Nec fructu nec odore citro nec munere mali
Praestat adhuc arbor; tantum sibi sumpsit honoris,
55 Si sit et ipsa arbor. Nam stipite debilis imo
Nec cono insurgit nec in aera tendit apertum,
Viribus at defecta suis aliena moratur
Praesidia et vallis adiuta potentibus alte
Explicat et ramos et sese extendit in arctus,
60 Insignis fronde et fragrantis imagine pomi.

guarded night and day by the vigils of dragons, the prize of Hercules' club, new gifts for the race of the Romulids, which has
raised its fame as high as the stars in heaven. But look! Can this   35
be a gleaming star, descending in the clear sky? Can it be, perchance, that a new star has risen, a star bringing good fortune, a
breath of inspiration added to my undertaking? Behold, do groves
blooming with citron, fields planted with lemon trees, stretch forth
their leaves? What shade unfolds? What groves and noble woods
gleam with metal and gold? With what gems do the very twigs   40
glisten? Or is it, rather, that my wife Ariadne, remembering her
husband and her garden, shows herself? O wife, show sympathy
for my horticultural labors, and be present. Take up rakes and hoes,
lean with all your weight onto two-pronged mattocks, cut back the   45
leafy citron trees with a scythe, and pour out streams from watering urns, let the irrigation pools themselves foam with full ditches;
and may it please you at last to pluck the blossoms you desire, pick
fruits, and, in the shade, avoid the heat, leading shared dances
with the nymphs to the music of the lyre. May you all begin anew   50
with me the Aonian labor of Urania, and compose with me verses
about orchards of citron trees with their golden foliage.[7]

The citron and its cultivation

No tree in the groves of the Hesperides, by the bank of the Niasaean spring, either in its yield, its fragrance, or in the gift of its
fruit, has so far surpassed the citron; so much honor has it received — if indeed it be a tree at all. For, weak at the base of its   55
trunk, it neither rises to a cone, nor stretches outward into the
open air, but, feeble in its own strength, detains the protection of
others, and aided by powerful fortifications, it unfolds its boughs
from on high, and branches out into limbs, eminent for its foliage   60
and the appearance of its fragrant fruit. For Atlas, weighed down

Tanta etenim coeli mole ac vertigine pressus
Atlas, dumque humeris timet et prospectat Olympo,
Innisus citro et femur et vestigia firmat,
Inconcussa tenens firmatis terga lacertis,
65   Suffecitque honeri et mundum cervice refulxit.
Hinc manet accurvata et palmite flexilis arbos
Testaturque senis cedentia membra labori;
At divum meritis et fructu et fronde superbit
Indignata umbras nemorum cavaque antra ferarum.
70   Ergo illam quernis in postibus inque dolato
Robore constitue et multo cum vimine vinci
Immissisque hastis traiecta consere canna
Apricum ad solem, avertens Boreamque nivemque,
Effunde et laticum scatebras; ne absiste novare
75   Tellurem radice procul, neu neglige campae
Ingluviem cohibere manu seu carmine dicto
Pellere limitibus magicoque avertere cantu,
Ter quod anus succincta irato immurmuret ore
Invocet et manes Lethaeae et numina ripae.
80   Prima igitur florum tibi cura supersit et omne
Impende huc studium; nam si te gloria rerum
Delectet iuvet Hesperii et praestantia ruris,
Nec mora dum gravidos honeret vindemia ramos
Grandiaque infixis mirere et mala columnis,
85   Ut timeas pendentem alta de mole ruinam,
Ut mediis persaepe decembribus inque furenti
Solis anhelantis rabie sit cernere gentem
In florem ruere et fructus properare recentis.
Annua quanquam et bima simulque et menstrua pubes
90   Pendeat huberibus fraternaque brachia late
Diffundat, domus alta novis laetatur alumnis;
Usque adeo furit in venerem generosa propago
Natorumque et amor trahit et cura illa nepotum.

by the great mass of the whirling heavens, as he feared for his
shoulders and looked after the heavens, leaned on a citron tree and
steadied his thigh and feet, keeping his back unshaken, his arms
held firm; he was sufficient to the burden and the firmament   65
shone on his neck.[8] For this reason, the tree remains bent and
crooked in its boughs, testifying to an old man's limbs yielding to
the labor, yet it takes pride in its fruit, its foliage, and the rewards
of the gods, despising the shade of the woods and the hollow caves
of wild beasts.

Therefore, set it up on oaken posts and hewn wood, bind it   70
with a good many osier twigs, and, after threading a reed through
the posts you've put in place, plant it facing the open sun, warding
off Boreas and snow, and pour out gushing water. Don't refrain
from turning over the earth, keeping well away from the root;
don't neglect to keep off the caterpillar's maw with your hand, or,   75
by saying a spell, drive it away from the boundaries, avert it with a
magical incantation, the kind of thing an old woman with skirts
tucked up mutters thrice in angry tones, summoning the ghosts
and spirits of the banks of Lethe.

Lavish your attention first on blossoms, then, and expend all   80
your energy on this. For if the splendor of things should please
you, and the excellence of the Hesperian field delight you, it won't
be long until the harvest weighs down heavy boughs and you gaze
in wonder at fruit so large that, though support posts have been
planted in the ground, you fear the collapse of the mass hanging   85
high above, and quite often you can see the trees rush into flower,
hastening their still green fruit, both in the middle of December
and under the raging fury of the fiery sun. Although the one-year-
old, two-year-old, and month-old trees hang down with clusters of   90
fruit and spread wide their fraternal limbs, the high house rejoices
in new nurslings; to such an extent does the noble sapling rage to
reproduce, driven by the love of offspring and that well-known
yearning for progeny. Come, then, protect the growing offspring

Ergo age crescentem prolem a borealibus auris
95 Et culmis tueare iniecto et mergite farris
Aut gravido centone aut vimineo contextu,
Frigora ne perimant, pereat labor irritus anni.
Nec pigeat scenam frondentem aestate superne
Iniicere et ramis prohibere tenacibus aestus,
100 Ferventis aestus rapidi et fera vulnera Cancri,
Quanquam sole suo gaudetque calentibus arvis
Et patriam Aethiopem meminit Maurisiaque arva.
Sterne et humi calidumque fimum lapidesque recoctos,
Dum coelum riget; ast utroque in tempore largos
105 Funde himbris, inverge urnas et flumina sicca.
Vere autem cum priscus honos hortis redit, et cum
Garrula limosas sedes molitur irundo
Ac tenui solitum frustratur voce laborem,
Falce premes citri silvas annosa recidens
110 Brachia; non tamen ista tibi sit ut annua cura.
Tum fragmenta lege et ramos secerne valentis
Obliquosque infige solo, tamen ut capite extent,
Stipitis aut truncum gladioque et falce dolatum
Infode et in tenui nudatum contege sulco.
115 Continuo ingentem vicino ex amne paludem
Elice diluvioque comas immerge salubri.
Haud multum fluet, emerget vastissima silva
Solaque praecultis regnabit citrus in hortis,
Pendebunt gravidis tabulata aurata racemis,
120 Quae mox lecta tibi natalibus annua festis
Ornentur mensis circumque domestica pubes
Libet et ante focum melle illita et undique turba
Clamet: 'Io, bonus annus eat.' Tu, flatibus Euri
Ne noceant, memor anteveni sive obiice firma
125 Praeruptorum operum longive crepidine saxi,
Aut adversa procul depulset verbera laurus,

from cold north winds with straw, and cover it by throwing spelt   95
overtop, or cover it with an abundant quilt or woven wicker-work,
lest the cold destroy it, and the year's work perish uselessly. In the
summer, don't be reluctant to cast over it from above a bower
made of leaves, and ward off the heat with clinging branches, the   100
burning heat and savage wounds of blazing Cancer, although the
citron rejoices in the sun of its own land, the heat of the fields,
and remembers its Ethiopian homeland and the fields of Mauretania. Also, scatter on the ground hot manure and heated stones
during cold weather; but in either hot or cold weather, pour gener-   105
ous amounts of water; empty watering urns and dry up streams.
But in the spring, when their former glory returns to gardens, and
the chattering swallow works at building its muddy house, and
with meager voice distracts itself from its habitual task, you should
prune the stands of citron with the scythe and cut back the aged
boughs; but you need not have this as an annual task. Then,   110
gather the cuttings and put to one side the strong boughs. Plant
them crosswise in the ground, yet so that they protrude at the
end, or hew the trunk of the plant with blade and scythe and bury
it, stripped, covering it in a shallow furrow. Right away, draw a   115
large pool of water from a nearby stream, and submerge the leaves
in a healthful flood. Hardly much time will pass, and an immense
grove will rise up and the citron tree alone will rule in the highly
cultivated gardens; golden rows of branches will hang heavy with
abundant clusters. You should then pick the fruit from these trees   120
to adorn the festive tables on your birthday every year, and all
around let the household staff make libation and smear honey
before the hearth, and the whole company shout out on all sides:
"Hurrah, may the year be successful!" To prevent southeast winds
from doing harm with their blasts, don't forget to take action in
advance: shelter the tree with a stable enclosure of steep walls or   125
tall stone, or let a laurel standing opposite drive the winds' blasts

Aut circum ramosa abigens testudine cinge;
Atque Austro tueare una atque uredine salsa
Defensor nemorum generosique incola ruris,
130 Si te cura movet tantorum et fama laborum.
Sin forte in varias iuvet et te ducere formas
Nascentem citrum mutato et corpore mala,
Tu faciem e ligno, argillae aut de cespite ductam
Subiice et infantem tenerum nutricis amato
135 Conde sinu. Paulatim arctus formabit et inde
Ducet inumbratos signato in cortice vultus,
Occultas natura hominum miretur ut artes,
Spectatum veniant non nota ut poma Napeae,
Ut Pomona suo laetata assurgat honori
140 Exultansque novis plaudat Zephyritis alumnis.
    Est nemus extremis Calabrum inviolabile terris
Dis sacrum patriis multa et pietate verendum,
Arborei dives foetus volucrumque rapinis
Opportuna domus tuta et spelea ferarum.
145 Hoc nemore ex ipso lucisque horrentibus olim
Advectam memini stirpem, quae citron ab omni
Parte et odore quidem foliisque et flore referret,
Sed fructu variata et longe aliena figura:
Vix orbem retinens protento at corpore longos
150 Sese agit in ductus varia et trahit agmina cauda.
Quid moneam ne te capiat tam indigna cupido
Hortensis monstri caelatam implere tabellam?
Ah procul infamemque notam atque averte pudendum
Dedecus. En formosus adest chorus, ecce puellae
155 Iam cupiunt legere Idalios et iungere flores:
Ne prohibe Idalias carpendo a flore choreas
Infami portento aut seva ab imagine terrae,
Neu pudor inficiat, neve ora tenerrima pallor
Deformet, suppressa tegant ne lumina palmae.

far away, or ring it round with a shelter of boughs to ward them off. May you guard the trees from the southeast wind and the sharp bite of blight, as a defender of groves and inhabitant of a noble land, if concern for the trees and the glory of such great   130
tasks motivate you. But if perchance you should enjoy forming the growing citron tree and its fruit into various shapes, transforming its body, set up a mold made out of wood or from a clump of clay, and bury the tender infant in the beloved bosom of its nurse.⁹ Little by little it will form tendrils, and thence, a shade-covered   135
likeness imprinted on the bark, so that Nature marvels at the hidden arts of men; the dell nymphs come to gaze at the unfamiliar fruit; Pomona, delighted, yields before her own glory; and the   140
goddess of Zephyrium exults in her new charges and applauds.¹⁰

There is an inviolable grove in the furthest lands of the Calabrians, sacred to the ancestral gods, worthy of being revered with great piety, rich in its progeny of trees, a dwelling place suitable for the prey of birds, offering safe dens for wild beasts. I recall that   145
from this very wood, from these bristling groves, a shoot was brought long ago, which resembled the citron in every part, in fragrance, leaves, and blossom, but was different in fruit and far different in shape: barely preserving a round form, it extends in long lines with drawn-out body, and trails a dense mass of various   150
branches at its tail.¹¹ Why should I warn you not to be seized by so unworthy a desire to fill an engraved tablet with a horticultural monstrosity?¹² Ah, keep this mark of infamy, this shameful disgrace, far away! See, the beautiful dancing troop is here, see, the   155
girls yearn now to gather and weave together Venus' flowers. Do not let Venus' dancers be prevented from gathering flowers because of an obscene monstrosity or crude image made of earth, lest shame tinge and paleness disfigure their most delicate faces, their palms cover and block their eyes. If you heed my warning,

160 Aeternum tibi sic niteat ver, aurea semper
Mala assint, spiret Syrios procul hortus odores,
Nullo et Acidalii desint tibi tempore rores.

Tu vero, prolem ut teneram tueare benignis
Indulgens studiis maioraque corpora formes,

165 Fige trabes, tabulata simul dispone et in altis
Infantes insterne cubilibus et frondoso
Siste toro: ducent placidam per amica quietem
Ocia, ut ignavos sopor et cibus impleat arctus.
Si curae tibi sit lecta e frondentibus hortis

170 Servare, ut viridem teneant annosa vigorem,
Hoc age: carpe manu in tenebris, in nocte maligna,
Frondentem ramum frondenti et palmite mala,
Palmite cum valido frondem retinentia ramumque,
Et tibi nulla suas ostendat luna tenebras,

175 Luna soporiferis sub terras abdita bigis;
Mox illa in latebris unco suspende tenaci
Et blandire manu et ventorum averte procellas
Aut paleis strata et stipulis arentibus; inde
Servabunt nitidam propria cum fronde senectam.

Quo differat citrius a citro

180 Hoc vero differt citrio citrus: illa superbos
Sese agit in ramos procero et stipite surgit,
Termite at haec fragili lentoque cacumine terras
Prona petit fixisque cadens incumbit in hastis;
Huic maior foliis odor est et foetibus, illi

185 Floribus; aeterna silva vestitur uterque
Stipes et aeternam ducit sub fronde iuventam;
Flos illi albescens medioque interlitus auro,
Hunc inspersa notat postremo purpura limbo.
Ergo ab odoratis maturo tempore ramis

may spring shine perpetually for you, may you always have golden   160
fruit, may your garden waft Syrian fragrances for you from far
away, and may you never lack Acidalian dewdrops.[13]

But in order to guard over the tender shoot, indulging it with
benevolent attentions, and make it grow taller, plant beams in the   165
ground, set up a platform on them, and lay down the young plants
in a high bed, set them in a leafy couch. They will enjoy easy tran-
quility amid pleasing leisure hours, so that sleep and nourishment
fill their indolent limbs. If you should have a care to preserve se-
lected plants from your flourishing gardens, so they maintain   170
green vigor when they are full of years, do the following: in the
darkness, during the hours of spiteful night, pluck a leafy bough
and fruit on a leafy shoot, fruit that still cling to the foliage and
bough with sturdy shoot, and do not let any moon show you its
darkness, hidden beneath the earth in its sleep-bringing chariot.   175
Right afterward, hang them up in a covered place on a hook with
firm grip, caress them with your hand and keep off windstorms, or
lay them out on chaff and dry straw. In this way, they will stay
sleek in old age and keep their foliage.

How the orange tree differs from the citron

This is how the citron tree differs from the orange tree. The   180
orange tree branches up into haughty boughs and rises with noble
trunk, whereas the citron tree, with fragile branches and pliant
summit, bending downward, seeks the earth, and, descending,
leans on stakes fixed in the ground. The citron tree is more fragrant in its leaves and fruit, the orange tree in its blossoms;
each tree is clothed in perennial foliage and maintains perpetual   185
youth beneath its leaves. The orange tree's blossom is white inter-
mixed with gold in the middle; the citron's has hints of purple
marked on its furthest edge. Therefore, when the time is ripe,

190 Aurea poma legunt plenisque relata canistris
Suffigunt laribus divumque altaria donant
Primitiis sertisque deos halantibus ornant;
Sepositas etiam vestes, Lucensia texta,
A tineis tutantur odore medentur et ipso
195 Arcent et Tyrios tetra a rubigine comptus.
Munere quin etiam mali frondentis ab alto
Oceano (nam prisca quidem sic credidit aetas)
Pleias Alcione Neptunum ad litora traxit.
Multa querens fragilemque fidem thalamosque negatos
200 Et sibi praepositos Stachirae Phaurusidos ignes
Clamabat, dextraque et serta et poma tenebat
Infelix coniux; ac nunc miseranda papillas
Nudabat roseoque sinu invitabat amantem,
Nunc exerta genu primasque illapsa per undas
205 Candida reiectis ostentat crura coturnis,
Nunc effusa comas scopuloque insignis ab alto
Crudelem vocat ac vires superante dolore
Labitur exanimis siccaque insternitur halga.
Sensit fragrantem extremo de litore ramum
210 Neptunus captusque aurati munere mali
Et serto insigni, lacrimis quoque victus amantis,
Currit in amplexum cupidisque extollit in ulnis.
Illa viri ut gremio intepuit, calidusque per ossa
Ignis it, amplexu et tenero fovet ora mariti,
215 Ornavit serto caput atque Cloneide fronde
Implevitque sinum pomis felicibus, auraque
Extinctos revocat praerepti coniugis ignes.

De limonibus et earum cultu

Tertia iam superat limonis cura colendae,
Et rarus labor et coepti meta ultima nostri.

they pick the golden fruit from the fragrant boughs, and, carrying   190
it in full baskets, hang it up in the house; they bestow the first-
fruits on the altars of the gods, and they adorn the gods' statues
with fragrant garlands. These fruit protect stored clothing, textiles
from Lucca, from moths; they work as a remedy by their very
odor, and they protect Tyrian hair ornaments from rust.[14] Indeed,   195
by the gift of the leafy fruit (for so antiquity believed), the Pleiad
Alcyone enticed Neptune from the deep Ocean to the shore.
Much-complaining, she decried breakable trust, marriage refused,
and the flame of Pharusian Stachir preferred to herself.[15] In her   200
right hand, the unhappy spouse was carrying garlands and fruit;
and now, the pitiable woman was baring her breasts, and inviting
her lover with rosy bosom; now, baring her knee, gliding over the
tops of the waves, she cast off her boots, and was showing him her   205
white legs; now, letting her hair flow down, conspicuous, from a
high rock, she summoned her cruel lover, and, as pain overcame
her strength, fell down unconscious, and lay collapsed on the dry
algae. Neptune smelled the fragrant bough from the edge of the
shore, and, seduced by the gift of the golden fruit and the impres-   210
sive garland, conquered as well by the tears of his lover, ran into
her embrace, and raised her up in his desirous arms. As she heated
up in the embrace of her man, as a blazing fire pervaded her
bones, and as she warmed her husband's face with her tender
arms, she adorned his head with a garland and leaves of the Clo-   215
nian tree and filled his lap with abundant fruit, and their fragrance
rekindled the once extinguished flames of her stolen spouse.[16]

Lemons and their cultivation

There remains still our third subject, cultivation of the lemon, an
uncommon pursuit and the final turning point of our undertaking.

220 Assitis, nymphae Cyrenides, o mihi, nymphae
Masitholae, aspirate, o quae, Paliurides, umbra
Gaudetis, iuvat et fluvios habitare recessus
Et citri iuvet umbra, iuvent limonides aurae,
Hesperidum et veteres cantu renovemus honores.
225 In manibus nemus auricomum Chariteiaque arva,
Vestrum opus, o Charites; vestro nam munere quondam
Itala limonem noverunt litora; nam vos
Et causam meministis eam et memorare potestis,
Nec vestris meritis aeternae aut parcite famae.
230 Fonte Niaseio sese Venus aurea quondam
Laverat et pexos comebat nuda capillos,
Purpureo Charites pingebant ora colore
Ambrosio et niveas afflabant rore papillas.
Ecce puer passis volitans super aera pennis
235 Laetus adest; matrem amplexus nova gaudia portat:
'Te Sireneis felix Hymeneus in oris
Expectat thalamosque parat magnetis Amalphis;
I, propera Italicos illic molire triumphos,
Mater; ament et saxa.' Atque haec effatus hiulco
240 Ore simul genitricis et ora et labra momordit.
Surrisit dea et allectis Tritonibus altum
Ire parat. Dum colla Venus, dum pingit et ora
Ad thalamos ventura, et Amor dum territat arcu
Semideos maris et ponto minitatur et undis,
245 Interea Charites limonia dona pararunt
Quae ferrent nuptae: triplex genus, altera foetu
Exiguo atque acrem gustu referentia sensum;
Altera quae fructu maiore et rorida succo
Huberiore, sed oblongo tamen utraque ductu;
250 Tertia quae grandi fulgent honerata volemo
Ac citrii referant sinuosa ab imagine formam,
Sed succo ingrato quemque ora offensa recusent.

May you be present, nymphs of Cyrene; inspire me, O nymphs of 220
the Masitholus; and you, O nymphs of the Paliurus, who rejoice
in the shade, whom it pleases to inhabit the recesses of rivers, may
you also take delight in the shade of the citron, in the fragrance of
lemon trees; and let us renew in song the ancient praises of the
Hesperides. Your work, O Charites, is in hand, the gold-leafed 225
grove and the Charitean fields.[17] For once, by your gift, the shores
of Italy came to know the lemon; for you both remember the cause
and are able to tell of it. Don't be overly modest about your merits
or eternal fame.[18]

Once, golden Venus had washed herself in the Niasaean spring 230
and was combing and arranging her hair, nude; the Charites were
painting her face with purple color and perfuming her snow-white
breasts with ambrosial dew. Look, her boy, cheerfully flying
through the air with wings extended, arrived, embraced his 235
mother, and brought new joys: "Well-omened Hymenaeus is
awaiting you on the Siren's shore, and is preparing the marriage of
Amalfi, famed for the magnetic compass.[19] Go, hasten to celebrate
Italian triumphs there, mother; make even the rocks fall in love."
After speaking these words with open mouth, he bit his mother's 240
face and lips. The goddess laughed, and after selecting sea gods to
accompany her, prepared to embark on the deep. As Venus painted
her face and neck—for she was going to attend a wedding—and
as Love terrified the demigods of the sea with his bow and men-
aced the waves and water, the Charites, meanwhile, prepared gifts 245
of lemons to bring to the bride.[20] The species of lemon trees is
threefold: one type has very small fruit and has a bitter taste; a
second type has larger fruit, and drips with a richer juice; each of
these first two, however, is of oblong shape. Lemon trees of the 250
third type gleam, weighed down by large fruit, and with their
rounded shape recall the form of the orange in appearance, but
they have displeasing juice, which the mouth, offended, shrinks

Hic tamen admotusque foco sensimque recoctus
Instillante anima ac tenuem conversus in amnem,
255 Ora puellarum maculis lavit et candorem
Inducit nitidis per colla argentea guttis.
Ergo ubi concinuit festis Hymeneus, et ipsa
Fessa est assiduis ludens Cytherea choreis,
Munere felici Charites Nereida Amalphin
260 Donarunt, fuit et teneris sua gratia verbis.
Hinc rarum accessit decus hortis et nova silvis
Gloria, gemmiferis fontes nituere sub umbris,
Candidaque auratis fulserunt litora ramis;
Hinc et stirpis honos, hinc et chariteis Amalphis
265 Munere limonum et nemorum redolentibus auris
Ornavit thalamos, felixque Hymeneus et aras
Pinxit flore novo sparsitque Atlantide fronde,
Et passim stratis laetata est halga metallis.
Quod vero aut viridem trahit a radice colorem
270 Frondibus ac fructu, aut acuit sensumque palatumque,
Hinc nomen dubia certum sub origine mansit.
Est idem cunctis cultusque et cura, et iniquum
Coelum indignantur frigusque aestumque gravantur
Masitholae limones, at humida flumina poscunt
275 Auxilio et densas laurorum in prelia turmas.
Sed minor illa quidem cultu maiore tuenda;
Nanque tegenda hiemi tecto ac stipanda maniplis
Et circum tabulata fimo iungenda tenaci,
Ne coeli rigor aut Boreas immanior urat.
280 Nam neque sic thalamis clausis assueta puella,
Fota sinu genitricis et ostro induta nitenti,
Aut timet obstrictas gelidis Aquilonibus auras
Frigoris aut rabiem sub iniqui sidus Aquari.
Iccirco solem spectet, post terga virenti
285 Seu lauro seu rore maris cingenda, nec unquam

from. This juice, however, when it is brought near to the hearth, gradually cooked while being exposed to the air, and boiled down to a small amount of liquid, washes girls' faces clean of blemishes 255 and introduces whiteness to silvery necks with its gleaming drops. Therefore, when Hymenaeus sang at the celebration, and the Cytherean goddess herself grew tired from playing in continual dances, the Charites gave the Nereid Amalfi a propitious gift, and 260 their own quality of grace infused tender words of gratitude.[21] Hence a rare adornment was added to gardens, a new glory to orchards; the fountains glittered in the jewel-studded shade, and the shores shone bright with golden boughs. Hence came the glory of the tree, hence Charitean Amalfi adorned her bedroom with the 265 gift of lemons and the redolent airs of lemon groves; and Hymenaeus joyfully ornamented the altars with a new flower, sprinkled them with the foliage of Atlas, and the seaweed rejoiced in golden ore strewn everywhere. Either because the lemon draws a *meadowgreen* color from its root to its leaves and fruit, or because it stimu- 270 lates the *appetite* and palate, its name, despite the uncertain origin, has remained fixed.[22] The cultivation and care for all types of lemon trees are the same: Masitholean lemon trees resent and are vexed by adverse weather, cold, and heat, whereas they demand moistening streams as an aid and dense squadrons of laurels to do 275 battle with bad weather.[23] But when young, it must be guarded with greater care: in winter, it must be covered with an enclosure and surrounded with bundles of hay, and around it, planks must be joined with sticky manure, lest the weather's chill or Boreas scorch it too savagely. For not even the girl accustomed to the cozy 280 bedroom, cherished in the lap of her mother and clothed in gleaming purple, is so afraid of breezes allied to the chill north winds, or the ferocity of the cold under the constellation of adverse Aquarius.[24] For this reason, let the tree face the sun; let it be ringed 285 round behind its back with verdant laurel or rosemary, and you

Sola hiemi credenda tibi Chariteia limon,
Et florem semper parituraque semper honorem
Aurati foetus ramo et placitura comanti.
Qualem praerupti sub vertice montis adeso
290   Litore secessu in molli sub rupe cavata
Et Baccho felix, felix Amathuside myrto,
Frondenti et lauro Neptunnia Mergilline
Laeta colit; non aestus eam, non frigora tentant;
Non rivi crepitantis opem, non fictilis urnae
295   Exoptat sitiens large quam Thespias unda
Actiaque Aoniis irrorent dolia lymphis.
Ah fatum crudele hominum et sors invida votis:
Ignotos nunc per populos, per Gallica regna,
Horrentem ad Rheni ripam atque ad Norica saxa
300   Exulat oceanique vada ad squalentia tabo
Navifragum, extremos queritur Sincerus ad Anglos.
Interea sitiunt citri ac limonide in umbra
Torpet humus, decor ille horti fragrantis et aurea
Pleiadum intereunt mala, ac sine honore relictum
305   Litus et errantem dominum lacrimantur arenae.
At nympha e scopulis summique cacumine saxi
Incusatque deos coelumque et sidera damnat,
Et saxa et miserae responsant antra puellae.

De insitione

Iam reliqua insitio est hominumque industria: nunc tu
310   Huc adverte animum et veterum cape dicta virorum.
Citrigenum species cum sint et germine et ipso
Cortice tam similes cognato et semine iunctae,
Hospitia hinc sociis iungunt communia tectis
Affines ramos et dant capiuntque vicissim
315   Et mutant proprios alterno foedere fructus.

must not consign to the winter the Charitean lemon tree on its
own. Thus will it always bring forth flowers, always bring forth the
splendor of its golden fruit, and always give delight with its leafy
bough. This is the kind of tree Neptunian Mergellina grows pro-
lifically, beneath the peak of a steep mountain on the wave-worn
shore, in a pleasant retreat beneath the hollowed-out rock — Mer-   290
gellina, fruitful in the grapevine, fruitful in Amathusian myrtle
and leafy laurel. Neither heat nor cold assail it here; it does not
yearn with thirst for the aid of a burbling stream or a clay urn,
since the Thespian wave and Actian jars generously irrigate it with   295
Aonian waters.[25] Ah, cruel fate of men, and destiny hostile to our
prayers! Now, among unknown peoples in Gallic realms, by the
rough banks of the Rhine and the rocks of Noricum, by Ocean's   300
shores filthy with the rotting flesh of shipwrecked sailors, he lives
in exile, and amid the furthest Angles, he laments — Sincerus![26]
Meanwhile the citron trees are thirsty, and the ground in the shade
of the lemon trees is hard. The beauty of the fragrant garden and
the Pleiades' golden fruit are perishing, and the sands and aban-   305
doned shore, deprived of glory, shed tears for their exiled owner.
But from the rocky crags, from the peak of the highest rock, the
nymph finds fault with the gods, condemns the sky and stars, and
the rocks and grottoes echo back a response to the wretched girl.

Grafting

Grafting and human diligence still remain to be discussed. Pay at-   310
tention now to this and receive the sayings of men of old. Since
the species of citrus trees are so similar in bud and bark, and are
joined by kindred seed, shared hospitality accordingly joins their
related boughs in common residences, and they give and take by
turns, and exchange their own fruits by reciprocal agreement.   315

Non unae hinc species, sed misto semine plures
Scinditur in partes nemus et sua nomina miscet.
Accipit et citrium limon, limonaque citrus
Hospitio, et sociis ineunt convivia mensis;
320   Accipit et thalamo citrium citrus, et sua tractant
Iura simul, iunctisque toris accumbit uterque.
Hinc species mistis crescit variata figuris.
Ergo nunc ramos libro demitte sub hudo
Artifici dextra, fixo nunc iniice ligno,
325   Atque alte impacto cuneo insere alteriusque
Cortice cum iunge et cera mox illine adacta
Ulmeaque obsaeptis constringe et vincula plagis,
Arceto et pluviam coniecti cespitis haerba.
Nunc et crescentem vicino e margine virgam
330   Admove et inciso laevi sub vulnere libro
Sic fige, ut lento desint ne cingula nodo;
Aut et eam transmitte forato ad viscera trunco
Mirantem latebrasque cavas et operta viarum,
Qualis et Heleis longe delata sub antris
335   Miratur maris occultos Arethusa meatus
Et coelum suspirat amicae et litora terrae
Quaeque Syracusiis spirant de fontibus aurae.
Neve excide illam; sinito de matre propinqua
Hauriat ut succos solitos, solita hubera lactet,
340   Donec eam grandem natu longeque valentem
Atque novercales stringentem enisius ulnas
Videris et proprio meditantem vivere succo;
Tunc abrumpe manu materna et stirpe revelle:
Crescet et immensum ducet late aucta cacumen.
345   Interea laeto surgit dum surculus auctu,
Saepe riga, saepe eductas de stipite gemmas
Evelle et duris inverte ligonibus arva
Et matri blandire, sua dum prole repulsa

Therefore, they are not wholly separate species, but rather the seed is mixed together and the grove branches off into multiple parts and intermingles its names. The lemon tree receives the orange, the citron the lemon, in hospitality, and they join dinner parties with shared tables. The citron accepts the hand of the orange tree 320 in marriage, and together they exercise their marital rights, and both types of tree lie down in shared beds. Hence the genus develops diversified by mixed forms. Now, therefore, place branches under the moist bark with artful hand: put them in the pierced wood and insert them with deeply driven wedge; join them with 325 the bark of a second tree; then apply and smear on wax. Once the wounds are closed off, tie on elm-wood fastenings, and keep off the rain with a heap of grassy turf. Now also bring close a growing branch from the bordering vicinity, and after cutting a notch be- 330 neath the smooth bark, insert it so that the bindings do not fail the pliant knot; or, piercing the trunk, transfer it to the guts of the tree, where it gazes in amazement on the hollow hiding places and secret inner pathways, just as Arethusa, submerged deep be- neath the caves of Elis, gazed in amazement at the hidden pas- 335 sageways of the sea and sighed in yearning for the sky, the shores of friendly earth, and the breezes that waft from Syracusan fonts.[27] Do not cut it off; let it drink from its nearby mother the usual sap and suck from familiar teats, until you see that it is ma- 340 ture in age, very strong, clinging more strenuously in its step- mother's arms, and getting ready to live by its own sap; then break it off by hand and tear it away from its mother's trunk. It will grow, and, spreading out wide, project a vast tree top. Meanwhile, 345 while the scion rises up with abundant increase, often water it, often tear off buds that have risen up from the trunk, turn the soil with hard mattocks, and soothe the mother who is resentful at

Cogitur indignans alienos pascere foetus.
350 Quin et surgentem sobolem defende sub umbra
Frondentis rami, dum sol furit et furit aestas
Victa siti; idem ipse in glacie tege tecta superne
Insternens crassa e stipula cannave palustri,
Urat ne teneros rabies Aquilonia thyrsos.
355 Cum primis valida nitatur surculus hasta
A vento tutus longeque urgente procella,
Et nunc scalpello tenui, nunc molliter ungui
Detondens prima luxum compesce iuventa.
Utendum parce ferro; sed nec tamen ipsa
360 Luxuries toleranda; parens nam crimine in ipso
Haud natos miseratur, at acri percitus ira
Increpat et dictis et poena crimen acerbat.
Atque equidem memini, tantum se industria prompsit,
Qui diversa quidem parva sed semina in urna
365 Condat et educens collo breviore stolones
Subducatque arctetque manu ac sub vincula cogat
Crescentis; hi tandem uno se stipite miscent
Atque uno obducunt se cortice. Neve flagella
Dilabi sinito; neu summa cacumina ventus
370 Divellat, cera linito, aut diducat adulta,
Unguine dum proprio corpus iunguntur in unum
Atque operit lentum sub eodem codice gluten.
Postquam alta steterit radice infossa et opimum
Raptarit stirpes succum, mirabere poma
375 Plenaque grataque, non uno tamen una sapore.
Sunt qui diversos ramos, sed cortice raso,
Coniungant stringantque simul quo glutine misto
Increscant aeque; ac fixo mox stipite iunctos
Infigant pariter, tum vulnus rite coronent
380 Et fallax opus admota tueantur ab arte,
Quo ramo ex uno atque uno de palmite fructus

being forced to reject her own offspring and feed others' children.
You must also protect the rising shoot under the shade of a leafy   350
branch when the sun rages, when the summer rages, overcome by
thirst; and in the icy cold you must cover it, laying overtop a roof
of thick straw and swamp reed, lest the fury of the North Wind
scorch the tender stalks. In particular, let the scion be propped on   355
a strong post, safe from wind and from storm bearing down far
and wide, and gently pruning it now with a slender penknife, now
with your fingernail, check luxuriant growth in its early youth. You
should use the blade sparingly. Nonetheless luxuriance must not   360
be tolerated. For the parent hardly pities his children when they
have committed an offense, but moved by bitter rage, rebukes the
crime with words and makes it bitter by punishing it. Indeed, I
recall a man (so far has diligence advanced!) who would plant different seeds in the same small pot, and then, guiding the shoots   365
from its narrow neck, draw them forth, compress them by hand,
and force them together under bonds as they grew. These, at last,
merge into one trunk and are covered over by one bark. Don't let
the shoots fall asunder; smear them with wax, so the wind does not   370
tear apart their highest tops or separate them when fully grown, as
they are joined by their own sap into a single body, and sticky gum
covers them beneath the same bark. After it has come to stand
upright, planted in the ground with deep root, and its trunk has
seized rich nourishment, you will be amazed to see abundant,   375
pleasing fruit, yet not all with the same flavor. There are some who
join and press together different boughs with their bark stripped
off, so that the boughs grow in tandem with the help of glue.
Soon, they fasten the joined branches together onto a stable trunk.
Then they duly wrap the wound and look after the deceptive work   380
by applying artifice, so that from one bough and one branch more

Non uni veniant, sit honosque et gloria ruri,
Gaudeat insolito natura adiuta favore.
Sed nec defuerint scisso qui codice adacto
385   Dilatent vulnus cuneo, mox vulnere crudo
Includant gemmas alienae stirpis alumnas,
Mox tenui obstringant vitta: non fit mora, longos
Emittunt ramos et silva litus obumbrant
Exciso et veteri cono sua brachia fundunt,
390   Ac dorso alterius (mirum) nova pullulat arbos.
Quin etiam alterius nudato cortice plantam
Vidimus alterius frondente cacumine ramos
Erigere ingentem e tunica et subolescere silvam
Et stirpem infamem nemora in generosa novari.
395   Ergo castanea e molli, e praestante sagitta
Laudatae genitricis adulto et germine virgam
Exuito, exuvias gemmisque oculisque nitentes
Seligito; his sterili spoliatum cortice truncum
Degenerem induito vincloque urgente ligato,
400   Quo sese et pluvia et solis tueatur ab aestu.
Nec te blanda manus sinito frustretur inertem,
Aut ludat tunica vitiosum arente flagellum.
Iam videas docili e planta pubescere prolem
Frugiferam; tunc carpe manu, tunc erue ferro
405   Quod superat matre e sterili et blandire novellis:
Mira fides, nitidis palmes se tollet alumnis.

Laudes industriae humanae

Scilicet ut Iove nata Fides tellure relicta
Detestata hominum mores secessit Olympo,
Illicet emersit Fraus, admonituque deorum
410   Destitit assuetas Tellus producere fruges
Sponte sua, nullis hominum ante obnoxia curis.

than one type of fruit come, and it is a source of glory and honor for the orchard, and nature, aided by an unusual source of support, rejoices.[28] But there will be no lack of those who widen the wound by splitting the bark and driving in a wedge, and then, in the still raw wound, insert foster buds from another trunk; then they bind them with a slender band. Without delay, they send out long branches, extend shade over the riverbank with their foliage, and after the old tree top has been pruned, pour forth their boughs, and (amazing!) a new tree sprouts up on the back of another. Why, I have even seen a tree of one type, its bark stripped, raise up branches of another variety with leafy peak, and a vast wood grow up from the bark's membrane, and a disreputable stump transformed into a noble grove. Therefore, from the soft chestnut, from an outstanding offshoot of the lauded mother, remove a branch with mature buds, select spoils gleaming with gems and eyes. Remove the barren bark from a trunk that has fallen into decline, clothe it with these, and bind it with tight bonds so that it may be protected from the rain and heat of the sun. Do not, through lack of vigilance, let a flattering branch trick you, or a faulty shoot with dry membrane deceive you. At length, from the amenable graft you should see fruit-bearing offspring grow to maturity. Then pluck with your hand, dig up with iron blade, what survives of the sterile mother, and fawn over the young shoots: amazing to believe, the sprout will rise up with flourishing foster children.

The praises of human diligence

When Trust, daughter of Jove, after abandoning the earth and abominating the ways of men, withdrew to Olympus, Deceit, of course, appeared right away, and on the advice of the gods, Earth ceased to produce her accustomed fruits spontaneously, Earth, who previously was not subject to any efforts of men. To her aid

Cui Labor impatiensque oci languentis Egestas
Auxilio occurrere et fato Industria maior.
Haec Indo advexit merces pelagoque negatum
415 Stravit iter secuitque cavis liquida aequora velis;
Haec armenta boum domitans summisit aratro
Invertitque solum, cultis dominetur ut arvis,
Praescripsitque ovibus carpsitque e vellere lanam
Nudaque textilibus velavit corpora pannis
420 Construxitque domos, frigus quis arcet et aestus;
Quaeque olim sterilis fuit arbor et horrida cultu,
Hanc ferro domuit vertitque ad munera frugum,
Insitio ut plantas foecundet et imperet hortis,
Degenerent ne poma genusque in secla propagent.
425 Non igitur tantum pratis armenta, nec haerbae
Himbribus, aut apium debent examina rori,
Quantum de rebus merita est Industria nostris.
Cuius ope ingenium sese extulit et caput astris
Admovit, maria ac terras sibi subdidit, ut nil
430 Liquerit intentatum, ut summo e vertice Olympi
Traxerit attonitas citrii ad spectacula Musas.

De citriorum sapore duplici, acri ac dulci

Quando autem est citrio duplex sapor, acer ab ipsa
Natura ductus, dulcis ne ex arte magistra
Venerit, in dubio est. Nam tempora longa frequensque
435 Protulit insitio genus et decus; ars quoque multa
Usus et experiens reperit simul, haec quoque ut ipsa
Mala colore aurum, sed mella sapore referrent.
Nec vero non et veteres voluere coloni
Punica de fibris quondam crescentia amaris
440 In dulcem mutata saporem, lotia postquam
Senserunt hominum ardenti concocta calore.

came Toil, and Need, impatient of languid leisure, and Diligence
more powerful than fate. Diligence imported merchandise from
India, laid down a path despite the sea's refusal, and cut through   415
the watery waves with billowing sails. Diligence, taming herds of
cattle, made them submit to the plow, turned the soil to gain control over cultivated fields, gave orders to sheep and gathered wool
from fleece, covered naked bodies with woven garments, and con-   420
structed houses, with which it wards off cold and heat. The tree
that once was barren and scraggly in appearance Diligence tamed
with steel and turned to the production of fruit so that grafting
might render the shoots fertile and rule over gardens, lest the fruit
degenerate, so that they propagate their stock for generations to
come.[29] Flocks therefore do not owe as much gratitude to mead-   425
ows, nor grass to rainfall, nor swarms of bees to dew, as Diligence
has earned in our affairs. With her help, human intellect has ex-
alted itself and raised its head to the stars, subjected lands and
seas to itself, so that it has left nothing untried, and has dragged   430
the astonished Muses from the highest peak of Olympus to gaze
in wonder upon the orange tree.

The two flavors of oranges, sour and sweet

But while the orange has a twofold taste, it is uncertain whether
the sour taste derived from Nature herself and the sweet taste
came as the result of masterful skill. For long periods of time
and frequent grafting have advanced the species and its splendor.   435
Art and enterprising experience have also invented many things,
including how to make the fruit themselves resemble gold in
color, but honey in flavor. Indeed, cultivators of old also wanted
pomegranates, which once grew from bitter filaments, to be   440
changed to a sweet flavor after being treated with human urine
boiled with blazing heat. Poured out by hand in large amounts

Quae postquam diffusa manu multumque diuque
Igne suo acremque attactu domuere saporem
Concoctum et virus calido infregere liquore,
445 Transiit in lenem sensum purgatus amaror.
An ne hoc ipso etiam mutata et citria baccho
Silvestrem posuere animum et fregere rigorem?
Quo non ars penetrat? Palmes caedatur et ipse
Crassior, in palmumque cavetur et undique labris
450 In gyrum ductis nec pollice crassius; illuc
Infer mella liquata et grandi contege saxo
Quod solem avertat. Postquam arida suxerit arbor
Inclusum humorem et sitiens nova pocula gliscit,
Mella cavo immersans flaventibus imbue rivis
455 Rursus et evacuam Thymbraeo nectare cellam
Distende ac latices humano e corpore fusos
Mollibus irrora radicibus. Interea ne
Neglige frondosas toto de stipite gemmas
Vellere, Mesopius ni qua liquor implet et ipsa
460 Labra trahunt dulcem mulsi de fonte liquorem.
Illas tu gemmas illaque et germina serva
Et blandire manu et ventorum averte procellas,
Arce hiemes, funde Hyblaeos et largiter amnes.
Non derit tanto felix fortuna labori,
465 Crescet et immensum sata melle Cleartias arbor
Ornabitque hortos, ac tanto munere laeta
Divinas natura hominum mirabitur artes,
Quanquam adversa viris et fortibus invida coeptis.
Sunt qui lecta manu sollerti et semina cura
470 Contingunt mulsa Siculo aut madefacta liquore;
Postquam autem traxere ipsum ad praecordia rorem
Sedaruntque sitim medicato nectare, terrae
Infodiunt et culta rigant; ea denique fructu
Iam referunt tenerum quem quondam hausere saporem

over a long period, it tamed the pomegranate's bitter taste with its fiery contact, boiled down and mitigated the sharpness with its hot liquid, and its bitterness, after being purged away, changed to 445 a mild taste. Might it be the case that oranges, as well, put off their woodsy character, and diminished their roughness, after being changed by this very liquid? Where does art not enter?[30] Let a branch, a fairly thick one, have a cut made in it; let a hollow passage be made to a palm's depth, with the edges shaped on all sides 450 into a circle, yet no wider than a thumb; there pour liquefied honey and cover it with a large rock to keep away the sun. After the dry tree has sucked up the enclosed liquid and yearns thirstily for fresh cups, pour honey into the hollow, saturating it again with yellow streams; fill the empty storeroom with Thymbraean nectar 455 and irrigate the soft roots with liquid voided from the human body. In the meanwhile, do not neglect to pluck off the leafy buds from the whole trunk, except where the Mesopian liquid fills it and the lips draw the sweet nectar from the font of honey water.[31] 460 Keep those gems, those buds, intact; caress them gently with your hand, ward off windstorms, keep away winter weather, and generously pour streams of Hyblaean honey. Such great labor will not lack a prosperous outcome: the Cleartian tree sown with honey 465 will grow to a vast height; it will adorn gardens, and nature, happy with so great a gift, will wonder at the divine arts of men, despite being adverse to them and envious of their brave undertakings.[32] There are those who choose seeds with a skillful hand and sprinkle them with honey water with care, or soak them with Sicilian 470 honey. But after they have brought the dew itself into the seeds' innards and slaked their thirst with the honey-infused nectar, they bury them in the earth and water the ground. Subsequently, those seeds recall in their fruit the delicate flavor they once drank in

475　Quemque et arundineo duxere e palmite succum.
　　　Quando et inexpertum nihil ars sinit, hoc quoque et hortis
　　　Accedat, vel dictu etiam mirabile, de quo
　　　Quamvis longe audax, quanquam sibi conscius Usus
　　　Addubitet: ramum foecunda e matre revulsum
480　Decutiens capito; caesum mox undique librum
　　　Aequatis ferro spaciis dextraque volentem
　　　Exuito; inde pari confossum vulnere dorsum
　　　Stipitis alterius nudato et veste recenti
　　　Induito, ut coeant extremis partibus orae
485　Vestis et e lento mollescant vulnera limbo;
　　　Ulmea dehinc teneris indatur cingula plagis
　　　Vinculaque ingentis committant vulneris ora
　　　Vestiat et frondens truncum toga, pellat ut himbres,
　　　Arceat ut soles et sevae uredinis iram.
490　Di, facinus mirandum: haerenti e cortice cortex
　　　Ipse novus victum medius rapit atque supernis
　　　Instillat ramis, quaeque in sua pabula traxit
　　　Exuriens alimenta, suo ut de fonte refusa
　　　Ipse suis infundat alumnis, ipse et amicum
495　Irroret lac, ut sensim in sua nomina vertat
　　　Ramosque frondesque et eodem semina foetu,
　　　Ante quater nidum in tignis quam figat irundo
　　　Et quater extincti renovet quam funera nati:
　　　Tantum ars ipsa valet, tantumque industria pollet.

De utilitate horum pomorum

500　Omnibus his usus suus est. Seu forte voluptas
　　　Quaeratur, seu certa salus studiumque medendi
　　　Praecipue pueris, semen lege, coniice lectum
　　　In cyatho, et latices ad summum infunde liquentis,
　　　Sub Iove quos tacitae contingant frigora noctis;

and the sap which they drew from the reedy shoot. Since art al-   475
lows nothing to go untried, let this also be added to gardens, a
thing amazing even to speak of, a thing which Experience, although very bold, although conscious of its powers, would hesitate
to try: knock down and seize a branch torn from its fertile mother;
next cut off the bark on all sides, making the spaces even with the   480
blade, and remove the willing bark by hand; then pierce and strip
the back of another tree with a wound of equal size, and clothe it
with the fresh attire so that the garment's borders merge with its
furthest edge, and the wounds grow soft from the pliant band.   485
Next let a ring of elm wood be applied to the tender scars, let its
bindings compress the openings of the great wound, and let a
gown of leaves clothe the trunk to drive off rains, keep away the
sun and the rage of savage blight. O gods, what an amazing ac-   490
complishment! From the clinging bark, the new bark in the middle
takes sustenance and instills it into the branches above, so that the
bark itself pours back from its own font and infuses into its foster
children the food that, in its hunger, it took for its own nourishment. It diffuses into them the welcome milk, and gradually con-   495
verts to its own name the branches, leaves, and seeds of the same
fruit, all before the swallow affixes her nest to the roof beams four
times, and four times renews lament for the death of her perished
son.[33] So much power has art, such strength has diligence.

The usefulness of these fruits

All these fruits have their own specific use. Whether perchance   500
pleasure be sought, or good health and the pursuit of a medical
cure are wanted, especially for children, choose a seed, then cast
the chosen seed in a cup, and pour in flowing waters up to the
brim, waters that are exposed to the chill of the silent night under

505 Mane autem puero instilla: bibet acre venenum
Lumbricis, stomacho (mirum) medicabitur aegro:
Quin et arundineis mala ipsa liquoribus ante
Arte quidem medicata coquunt, ac laenibus inde
Intingunt succis et vase madentia servant,
510 Auxilium latura et opem languentibus aegris
Regalisque epulas vario affectura sapore.
Quid quod et in calidis fornacibus igne tepenti
Saepe liquant lectos flores et in horrea condunt
Vitrea odoratos latices, suffimina nota;
515 Saepe et fictilibus in lancibus himbre recenti
Dimensis spaciis macerato cortice, melle
Contingunt Siculove premunt concocta liquore,
Atque hos atque alios convertunt citria in usus.
Caetera te antiqui doceant exculta Salerni
520 Pectora, quis artis medicas monstravit Apollo,
Quis rerum notae causae, quorum inclyta in agris
Silva nitet fulgentque auro radiantia culta,
Ac nemora Hesperiis vinci indignantur ab hortis.
     Hoc sat erit, nymphae Sebethides. O mihi si quae,
525 E vobis si quae, nymphae Sebethides, hudam
Benaci de fonte ferat Parmesida laurum,
Qua manes spargam magni senis eque sepulchro
Eliciam felicem umbram ac venerabile numen,
Quo nemora Italiae senserunt Pana canentem
530 Et mirata suos requierunt flumina cursus,
Quo laetae in campis segetes, quo munera Bacchi
Ditarunt colles, nec non coelestia dona
Stiparunt liquidas divino nectare cellas.
Salve, o et gregibus decus et decus addite silvis,
535 Quo ductante Italae fremuere in bella cohortes,
Martiaque horrifico sonuerunt cornua cantu,
Audiit et Triviae longe lacus, audiit et Nar,

the open sky. In the morning, pour it in the child's mouth; the 505
child will drink a strong drug for intestinal worms, and — behold! — it will cure a sick stomach. Why people even cook the
fruit themselves, artfully sprinkled with cane-sugar juices before-
hand, steeping them in the mild liquors and keeping them soaking
in a dish both to bring help and aid to languid invalids and to 510
grace regal feasts with diverse flavor. Then there's the fact that in
warm ovens with low fire they often melt down the blossoms they
have picked, and keep in glass storehouses the fragrant liquid, a
well-known type of incense. Often, after macerating their rinds 515
with fresh rainwater on earthenware dishes for measured intervals,
they sprinkle the fruit with honey, or cook them with Sicilian
nectar and press them. They apply oranges to these and other
uses. The rest may you learn from the learned spirits of ancient
Salerno, to whom Apollo revealed the arts of medicine, to whom 520
the causes of things are known, in whose territory the famous
wood gleams, the fields are radiant with the sheen of gold, and the
groves refuse to be defeated by the Garden of the Hesperides.[34]

This will suffice, O nymphs of the Sebeto. If only anyone
among you, if only any of your company, nymphs of the Sebeto, 525
would bring me a moist Permessian laurel branch from the spring
of Benacus that I might sprinkle with it the great old man's shade
and draw forth from the grave his blessed soul and revered spirit,
through whom the groves of Italy heard Pan singing and the rivers, 530
amazed, stopped their own currents, through whom crops flourished in the fields and the gifts of Bacchus enriched the hills, and
heavenly gifts crammed the cells with the flow of divine nectar.[35]
Hail, O glory bestowed on flocks, bestowed on forests: under your 535
guidance Italian cohorts roared into battle, and the horns of Mars
sounded out with chilling cry; the lake of Diana heard from afar,

Ac trepidae matres pressere ad pectora natos;
Salve iterum et nato felix et, Mantua, vate,
540   Felix et populis et tanto principe felix,
Quo Gonsaga domus spoliis exultat opimis
Gallorum, cum excussa metu tremit Itala tellus,
Summittitque humiles Alpina ad gesa secures.
Te duce discussere iugum, Francisce, superbum
545   Insubrium attonitae gentes, quique ora Timavi
Amne lavunt populi, quos et rigat Abdua dives
Gurgitibus, longe et cultis Mela inclytus arvis;
Per te a servitio caput eximit accola Parmae,
Et quas saxosi vexat ripa aspera Rheni
550   Sollicitas urbes, quas et de montibus actis
Turbat Senus aquis campo inferiore vagatus;
Et tibi nimbiferum inclinat caput Appenninus
Communi pro libertate et fortibus ausis,
Teque et arundineo incinctus veneratur amictu
555   Eridanus, late irriguis plaudentibus undis
Pro decore Italiae et Belgis belli arte repressis.
Macte animo, Francisce, et macte ingentibus orsis,
Assurgit cui felici Campania tractu,
Assurgit latis venerata et Daunia campis,
560   Quaeque nitet pigro tellus madefacta Galeso,
Quodque mare Italiam supra quodque alluit infra.
Ecce autem insignis cantu atque insignior armis
Bellorum et laude et multis spectata triumphis
Parthenope tibi laeta canit, quod te auspice regno
565   Reddita sit, quodque e solio venerabilis aureo
Imperitet populis sublato et Marte triumphet.
Non tamen Hesperidumque hortos, Berenicia rura,
Iccirco aut Libycos tu dedignabere saltus,
Quos olim excisorque Hydrae domitorque leonis

the Nar heard, and fearful mothers pressed their children to their breasts.³⁶ Hail once again, Mantua, who are happy in your native son and bard, happy in your peoples, and happy in so great a ruler, through whom the house of Gonzaga exults in spoils of honor taken from the Gauls, at a time when the land of Italy has been shaken and trembles with fear, and submits its humbled axes before Gallic javelins from the Alps.³⁷ Under your leadership, Francesco, the terrified peoples of Insubria cast off the arrogant yoke, as did those who wash their faces in the stream of Timavo, and those whose fields are irrigated by the Adda, rich in waters, and by the Mella, very famous for its cultivated lands. Through your help, the inhabitant of Parma raises up his head from servitude, along with the anxious cities that the harsh bank of the rocky Reno harasses, and the cities that the Senio troubles by straying in the valley below when its waters have been driven down from the hills. And before you the Apennine range bows its storm-bearing head in the name of the shared cause of liberty and daring deeds; you the Po venerates, wrapped round in its garment of reeds, its flowing waters applauding far and wide, cheering the cause of Italy's glory and the suppression of the Belgae through the art of war.³⁸ Bravo for your spirit, Francesco, and bravo for your massive undertakings, before whom Campania with its fertile expanse shows deference, and Apulia revered for its broad fields, along with the land that flourishes irrigated by the sluggish Galeso's waters, and the sea that flows above Italy and the one that flows below it.³⁹ But behold, famous for song and even more famous for her achievements and glory in war, of proven merit with her many triumphs, Parthenope sings to you joyfully because, under your auspices, she has been returned to power: treated with reverence, she rules over peoples from her golden throne, and with war brought to an end, celebrates triumphs.⁴⁰ You will not for that reason disdain, however, the gardens of the Hesperides, Berenician fields, nor the groves of Libya, once visited by Alcides, the beheader of the

540

545

550

555

560

565

570 Alcides adiit, quibus et splendescere iussit
Phormiadumque et agros et litora iuncta Vesevo,
Quos et Sirenes scopulos, quae saxa frequentant,
Aequanique serunt colles Meteiaque arva,
Quosque secat Sileris frondoso margine campos,
575 Aenarie quos nostra colit, colit aspera et Ansur,
Atque Suessa vago Liris quam temperat alveo.
    Nec mihi Naiades in tanti parte laboris
Abnuerint viridem salicis de fronde coronam,
Nec mihi culta suos neget Antiniana recessus,
580 Quis superat vites Hermi atque rosaria Pesti
Quaeque et Idumeas mittunt palmaria bacas.

Hydra and tamer of the lion. With such groves he also bade the   570
fields of Formia and the shores neighboring Vesuvius to shine, and
the crags, the rocks, which the Sirens frequent. Such groves the
hills of Aequana sow, and the fields of Meta, and the fields the
Sileris cuts through with its leafy bank; such groves our Ischia   575
cultivates, and rough Terracina and Suessa Aurunca, which the
Liris tempers with its wandering river bed.[41]

Neither may the Naiads, in return for so great a labor, deny
me a green garland made from foliage of willow, nor may my cultivated Antiniana deny me her retreats, with which she outstrips   580
the vineyards of Hermus, the rose beds of Paestum, and the palm
groves that produce the fruit of Idumea.[42]

Note on the Texts

Near the end of his life, Pontano sent to Aldus Manutius in Venice the autograph manuscripts of his *Hendecasyllabi* and his hexameter works, including *De hortis Hesperidum* and *Eclogae* 1–4 (Monti Sabia 1969). These final autograph manuscripts were subsequently lost. For the *Eclogae* and the *De hortis Hesperidum*, therefore, the Aldine editions of 1505, 1513, and 1533 (and in the case of *Eclogae* 5 and 6, Summonte's 1507 edition: see below) are the authoritative witnesses to the text, as they were based on the final autograph manuscripts produced by the poet at the end of his life. In each case, however, other surviving manuscripts complicate the picture.

ECLOGUES

For Pontano's *Eclogae*, I have adopted the text of Monti Sabia 1973. My comments on the text in this instance will therefore be brief; for a more detailed discussion, I refer the reader to the discussion in the introduction to Monti Sabia's edition (Monti Sabia 1973). Pontano's final manuscripts, as mentioned, formed the basis for the 1505 and subsequent Aldine editions. *Eclogae* 5 and 6 were discovered by the Neapolitan humanist Pietro Summonte among Pontano's papers and sent to Aldus, who, however, declined to publish them. Summonte therefore published them as an addendum to his Neapolitan edition of Pontano's prose works (Sigismund Mayr, 1507). No manuscripts of the *Eclogae* survive except for the *Coryle*. Manuscripts 3413 and 9977 in the Biblioteca Palatina in Vienna include autograph copies of sections of the eclogue as well as another section copied by an unknown hand, but corrected and revised by the author's hand (Monti Sabia 1973, 12–13). Therefore, Monti Sabia bases her text primarily on Aldus' and Summonte's printed editions, but for the *Coryle*, she also takes into account the manuscript copies in the Biblioteca Palatina. Some typos in Monti Sabia 1973 have been corrected in this volume and minor adjustments have been made to punctuation and orthography, especially substituting *v* for consonantal *u*.

GARDEN OF THE HESPERIDES

The only modern text of the *De hortis Hesperidum* is that of Soldati 1902, which, however, is marred by errors and does not follow a coherent orthographical practice.[1] I have therefore established the text of the *De hortis Hesperidum* on the basis of the Aldine editions as well as a single surviving manuscript in the Biblioteca Provinciale di Avellino discovered by Mauro de Nichilo (1977). In De Nichilo's assessment, which I find convincing, the manuscript is an apograph representing not the final, but perhaps the penultimate, version of the poem; it is not in Pontano's hand, but it appears to have been copied by a member of Pontano's humanist circle in Naples sometime near the end of the poet's life. There are numerous minor differences: the section headings in the Aldine editions are missing from the Avellino manuscript; while paragraphs are marked by larger initial capital letters projecting into the left margin, these do not always correspond to the paragraph divisions of the Aldine; the title and the dedication of Book 2 are also missing. In all these instances, the Aldine edition is to be followed. While it cannot be ruled out that Aldus added the section headings for the benefit of the reader, there is no justification for removing them, given Aldus' access to Pontano's final autograph manuscripts. More substantively, some twenty lines present in the Aldine editions are missing from the Avellino apograph (1.209–31). The missing lines correspond to a poetic digression on the citrus trees that line the banks of the Lago di Garda, which, in Pontano's explanation, were a special gift from the goddess Venus to the region in honor of the love poet Catullus, who came from Verona and owned a villa on the island of Sirmio. This passage can be easily understood as a later insertion by Pontano, possibly to appeal to Pontano's Mantuan patrons, Francesco Gonzaga and his wife, Isabella d'Este (De Nichilo 1977, 244–45). Here too the Aldine edition is clearly to be followed.

Most other differences among the witnesses are due to obvious slips or orthographical variations. De Nichilo 1977 (237–44) identifies three true variants, but the Aldine readings are to be preferred in each case: see Notes to the Text. Adopting a consistent editorial policy regarding Pontano's orthography is notoriously difficult. The humanist had strong ideas about orthography but was inconsistent in his application of these notional norms. Editors are thus left in a quandary. I have adopted a compromise position. In instances where Pontano has a known preference, I have used that preference to decide between variants. In instances where there is no known preference, I have favored the Avellino manuscript's readings, which more often represent his known orthography. As De Nichilo 1977 (236–37), has remarked, the Avellino manuscript is particularly useful for stripping away the orthographical "incrustations" of the Aldine editions, which impose their own sometimes peculiar norms. However, in cases where the Aldine editions and the Avellino manuscript agree, I have refrained from imposing a correction based on a notional orthographic system that was inconsistently applied. The punctuation and capitalization of the text have been modernized; diacritical marks have been excluded.

The following chart represents variations among the Aldine editions (1505, 1513, 1533), the Avellino manuscript, Soldati's edition, and the present edition, with the exception of the missing lines, paratextual differences, and orthographical variations. This list is not exhaustive. For example, as De Nichilo 1977 (233n37), points out, the Avellino copyist often omits the diacritical mark indicating the dipthong *ae*; such lapses have not been included. Also, a few of the errors in the Aldine recorded here were subsequently corrected in the *errata corrige*.

Line	A 1505	A 1513	A 1533	Avell.	Soldati	I Tatti
1.63	triplici et	triplici	triplici	triplici et	triplici	triplici et
1.85	candor	candor	candor	candore	candor	candor
1.91	lachhymis	lacrymis	lachrymis	lacrimis	lacrimis	lacrimis
1.194	diffluat	defluat	defluat	diffluat	defluat	diffluat
1.196	nunc	nunc	nunc	tunc	nunc	nunc
1.197	mensibus	mensibus	mensibus	[omitted]	mensibus	mensibus
1.222	etiam	edam	etiam	[omitted lines]	etiam	etiam
1.297	tetra	terra	tetra	tetra	tetra	tetra
1.302	sqnalid	squalida	squalida	squalida	squalida	squalida
1.373	et in	et	et	et	et	et
1.395	reseus	roseus	roseus	roseus	roseus	roseus

Line	A 1505	A 1513	A 1533	Avell.	Soldati	I Tatti
1.398	pupureis	purpureis	purpureis	purpureis	purpureis	purpureis
1.415	permeet	permeet	permeet	permeet	permeet	permeet
1.419	Tu	Tu	Tu	In	Tu	Tu
1.432	beata	beata	beata	beta	beata	beata
1.463	laetus	laetus	laetus	ramove	laetus	laeta
1.467	sin	sin	sin	sim	sin	sin
1.504	fossas	fossa	fossas	fossas	fossa	fossas
1.533	menistrant	ministrant	ministrant	ministrant	ministrant	ministrant
2.23	dispice	despice	despice	despice	despice	despice
2.44	innitens	immitens	innitens	innitens	innitens	innitens
2.45	rorantibus	rorantibus	rorantibus	rurantibus	rorantibus	rorantibus
2.50	Uranie	Uranie	Uranie	Uranie	Uraniae	Uraniae
2.63	innisus	invisus	invisus	innisus	invisus	innisus
2.65	refulxit	refluxit	refluxit	refulxit	refulxit	refulxit
2.68	divem	divem	divum	divum	dives	divum
2.111	se cerne	secerne	secerne	secerne	secerne	secerne
2.124	firmo	firmo	firmo	firmo	firmo	firma
2.150	in ductus	in ductus	in ductus	inductus	in ductus	in ductus
2.195	tetra	terra	tetra	tetra	tetra	tetra
2.212	ulnis	ulnis	ulnis	ulmis	ulnis	ulnis
2.228	memenistis	meministis	meministis	meministis	meministis	meministis
2.231	pessos	pessos	pexos	pessos	pexos	pexos
2.234	passis	passis	passis	pasis	passis	passis
2.263	fulserunt	fulserunt	fulserunt	fulserunt	fulxerunt	fulserunt
2.301	ad Anglos	ad Anglos	ad Anglos	ad axes	ad axes	ad Anglos
2.346	eductas	eductas	ductas	educta	eductas	eductas
2.355	valida	valida	valida	validis	valida	valida
	hasta	hasta	hasta	hastis	hasta	hasta
2.368	flagella	flagella	flagella	fragella	flagella	flagella
2.379	coronent	coronent	coronent	cororent	coronent	coronent
2.397	oculis	oculisque	oculisque	oculisque	oculisque	oculisque
2.402	ludat	ludat	ludat	luda	ludat	ludat
2.402	flagellum	flagellum	flagellum	fragellum	flagellum	flagellum
2.411	spote	sponte	sponte	sponte	sponte	sponte
2.417	ut	ut	ut	et	ut	ut
2.418	carpsit	carpescit	carpsit	carpsit	carpsit	carpsit
2.444	virus	virtus	virtus	virus	virtus	virus

Line	A 1505	A 1513	A 1533	Avell.	Soldati	I Tatti
2.448	caedatur	caedatur	caedatur	cedatur	caedatur	caedatur
2.464	deerit	dederit	deerit	derit	derit	derit
2.493	rafusa	refusa	refusa	refusa	refusa	refusa
2.505	are	are	acre	acre	acre	acre
2.512	et in	et in	et in	et	et in	et in
2.524	siqua	siqua	siqua	si quae	siqua	si quae
2.525	siqua	siqua	siqua	si quae	siqua	si quae

NOTES

1. The text edition with French translation included in the thesis of Georges Tilly (2020, published online April 2021) appeared too late to be considered in this volume.

Notes to the Text

De hortis Hesperidum 1.463: The Avellino apograph offers *ramove* instead of *laetus* (Aldine editions). I follow De Nichilo 1977 in viewing *laetus* as preferable. It conforms with other similar uses of *laetus* in the poem (e.g., 2.293, *laeta colit*), where, in agreement with the subject, it has a quasi-adverbial sense. The point is that *prolific* growth occurs after pruning; *ramove* adds little to the picture. However, the gender of an adjective describing a tree, as De Nichilo 1977 points out (238), should be feminine. With some hesitation, I have therefore emended to *laeta*.

De hortis Hesperidum 2.68: The 1505 and 1513 Aldine editions read *divem meritis*, which makes no sense; the Avellino apograph and the 1533 Aldine edition read *divum meritis* (rewards of the gods). Soldati's conjecture of *dives* makes acceptable sense, but it is not necessary.

De hortis Hesperidum 2.124: I have emended *firmo* to *firma* to allow agreement with *crepidine* in line 125. An adverbial *firme* would also be possible.

De hortis Hesperidum 2.301: The phrase *extremos ad Anglos* (among the furthest Angles), found in the Aldine editions, is potentially problematic: Sannazaro's exile was in France, not England. The Avellino apograph, by contrast, reads *extremos ad axes* (at the furthest poles). I am convinced, however, by the arguments of De Nichilo 1977 in favor of retaining *ad Anglos*. Pontano, who died in 1503, would not have known the full itinerary of Sannazaro's completed journey (1501–5) and thus could not be expected to document its precise geography. The apograph appears to have been a copy of the penultimate draft made by a member of Pontano's circle. Summonte was presumably consulting a similarly penultimate draft when he wrote the correction *ad axes* onto his copy of the Aldine text (De Nichilo 1977, 243). Furthermore, the idea of Britain as the remote edge of the world is a classical topos, notably in Catullus (*ulti/mosque Britannos*, c.11.11–12).

231

De hortis Hesperidum 2.355: The Avellino apograph reads *validis . . . hastis* instead of *valida . . . hasta* (Aldine editions). Once again, I agree with De Nichilo 1977 that the Aldine is to be preferred. The singular post suits a single shoot.

Notes to the Translations

❦❦❦

ECLOGUES

I. Lepidina

1. The Eclogue is named after the character Lepidina, a pregnant shepherdess married to the shepherd Macron. In Latin, *lepidus* (charming, attractive) is related to *lepos* (charm, attraction, wit). Both words were used frequently by Catullus.

2. As Monti Sabia 1973 notes, ad loc., Pontano's phrase (*haec farta*) is vague. She translates: "questo canestro colmo di ricotte fumanti." Casanova-Robin 2011 translates "farcis fumants." Du Cange 1884, s.v. *fartum*, offers *praedium rusticum*. Alternately, one could translate "these [foods] stuffed in a steaming basket."

3. The phrase has pastoral associations: Vergil, *Eclogues* 9.20, *viridi . . . umbra*.

4. A perfect example of the Platonic "soul kiss" so frequent in neo-Latin lyric: see Gaisser 1993, 249–54; Casanova-Robin, 2011, ad loc. Orcus is the god of the underworld, personifying death. He is the "shaggy monster" of line 24 below.

5. The siren Parthenope personifies Naples: see Introduction.

6. Sebeto: the main river of Naples in antiquity. Its presence was significantly diminished with the development of the city, and by Pontano's time, was more myth than reality.

7. *Anas*: "duck." Pontano's story is suggestive of an Ovidian bird metamorphosis. On "Dogliolo," see Introduction. Parthenope bathing at Poggioreale and her marriage to Sebeto symbolize the connection between the Aragonese regime and Naples' water system (Hersey 1969; Modesti 2014).

8. "Dog": The word *pilaster* is otherwise unknown. I follow Casanova-Robin 2011, ad loc., in taking it as a pejorative term for dog.

9. Hymen and Hymenaeus are variant names of the Roman god of marriage and weddings.

10. Willows are associated with the pastoral world, while myrtle is the plant of Venus.

11. The Graces, the daughters of Venus, bathed in the Acidalian font in Boeotia. Hence "Acidalian" is an epithet of Venus.

12. Pausilype is the Greek name for the coastal district of Posillipo: see Introduction.

13. Crambane represents S. Giorgio a Cremano, southeast of Naples (Monti Sabia 1973, ad loc., drawing on Summonte 1512, ad loc.). The nymph Mergelline personifies the Mergellina district of Naples, the site of Sannazaro's villa: see Introduction, and on *Eclogae* 1.115, n. 12. Prochyte and Caprite represent, respectively, the islands Procida and Capri.

14. The noun *acta* ("shore"; compare Greek *aktē*) plays on Jacopo Sannazaro's academic name, Actius Sincerus; see also on *De hortis Hesperidum* 2.296, n. 25; compare Sannazaro, *Piscatory Eclogues* 2.44–45, 4.17–20 in Putnam 2009.

15. The nymph Sarnitis represents the Campanian river Sarno: see Monti Sabia 1973, ad loc.

16. The nymph Resina represents the town of the same name located at the base of Mount Vesuvius. As Monti Sabia 1973 notes, ad loc., the humanist Antonio Beccadelli (Panormita) had a villa here, called the *Plinianum*, where the Neapolitan Academy met: see Introduction.

17. Monti Sabia 1973, ad loc., drawing on Summonte 1512, ad loc., identifies Hercli with Monte Echia, located in the Neapolitan neighborhood of Pizzofalcone.

18. Triton: a sea god, son of Neptune and Amphitrite. Plural Tritons are generic sea gods. Here, a chorus-leader Triton is in dialogue with a chorus of Tritons.

19. The nymphs are topographical: The island of Capri faces the peninsula of Sorrento where Amalfi and Aequana (mod. Vico Equense) are located. The description that follows reflects the local landscape (Monti Sabia 1973, ad loc.).

20. On "the queen of the sea of Capri," see on *Eclogae* 1.183, n. 19. The Teleboans from Acarnania established a colony on Capri. The Garamantes were a North African people. "Cinyphian" refers to the river Cinyps (mod. Wady Khahan) in Libya.

21. Aenaria is a sea goddess personifying the island of Ischia. Both Aenaria and the goddess personifying Capri are represented as Nereids, daughters of the sea god Nereus.

22. Butine and Ulmia represent urban neighborhoods of Naples, associated with a meat market and bakeries, respectively. Ulmia may correspond to Piazza d'Ulmo, an area near Castel Nuovo (Monte Sabia 1973, ad loc.); the neighborhood corresponding to Butine is unknown. The neo-Latin phrase *intortis torallis* refers to the Southern Italian specialty of *taralli*—salty baked snacks, twisted or interlaced in shape, similar to a breadstick or pretzel (but much superior), and still popular today. Pontano's editor Pietro Summonte comments: "My good friend Pontano, insofar as he possessed the highest degree of authority regarding the Latin language, sought to admit an entirely new word into Latinity, and (so to speak) bestow on it Roman citizenship" (1512, ad loc.).

23. Theodocie personifies *Thuducium* (San Giovanni a Teduccio), a coastal area east of Naples (Monti Sabia 1973, ad loc.).

24. Compare Vergil, *Eclogues* 1.4–5, where the shepherd Tityrus sings of Amaryllis.

25. The nymph Pistasis, according to Summonte 1512, ad loc., refers to a fountain in Naples, probably in the present-day area of Forcella in the city center (Monti Sabia 1973, ad loc.).

26. The Laestrygonians are a race of cannibalistic giants in *Odyssey* 10 (80–132). The Cyclopes are one-eyed giants in Greek mythology (*Odyssey* 9.105–566). Both are paradigms of uncivilized barbarism, which included a lack of sexual restraint. Fauns cohere with the same idea of animalistic lack of self-control. The Laestrygonians and the Cyclopes were associated in antiquity with locations in Southern Italy and Sicily.

27. These heroic figures and their feats are invented by Pontano.

28. Drawing on Summonte 1512 and *De hortis Hesperidum* 2.580, Monti Sabia 1973, ad loc., identifies Hermitis with the Vomero hill. Conicle

NOTES TO THE TRANSLATIONS

represents an area north of central Naples called Conocchia. Olympias personifies a small district called *Il Limpiano* on the slopes of the Vomero.

29. Monti Sabia 1973, ad loc., suggests that Olympias may love horse competitions because the nearby Largo del Mercatello (mod. Piazza Dante) was known for horse training.

30. Formellis represents the fountain in the piazza of Porta Capuana; the word *formula*, or *formale*, referred to the branches of an aqueduct (Monti Sabia 1973, ad loc.). Next to the Porta Capuana is the Chiesa di Santa Caterina a Formiello. Formellis is appropriately the daughter of Labulla, who represents the Bolla aqueduct system (*Labulla/La Bolla*).

31. Pomon appears to have been invented by Pontano as a male equivalent to Pomona, the Roman goddess of fruit orchards: see further Tufano 2015, 148n84.

32. Fragola personifies Afragola, a town northeast of Naples; Acerra is a town in the same area; Casulla may represent Casolla, another town nearby (Monti Sabia 1973, ad loc.).

33. Monti Sabia 1973, ad loc., rightly sees here an autobiographical reference: Pontano came to Naples in 1447 and never left.

34. The maiden (*virginis*): presumably Parthenope. The Latin *virgo* glosses the meaning of Parthenope's name in Greek (maiden face). Compare *Eclogae* 1.27, 1.196, 1.587.

35. The goddess: Formellis.

36. Pontano quotes line 347 in the *Actius* as an example of the affective use of rhythm: "What is slower or tireder than these words and rhythms?" *Actius* 52, ed. Gaisser 2020. According to Summonte 1512, ad loc., the phrase "beneath this arch" alludes to Pontano's palazzo on the Via dei Tribunali in Naples, which incorporated a tower called the Torre ad Arco, featuring a splendid view of Naples. Note also the description of Pontano's house in the *Aegidius* 1, ed. Gaisser 2020. See Monti Sabia 1973, ad loc., and Introduction, n. 9.

37. Meliseus: Pontano's pastoral alias (see on *Eclogae* 2.1, n. 1). Phosphoris refers to his daughter Lucia Marza, who died in 1479 (Greek *phōs* and Lucia/*lux* = "light"); see Monti Sabia 1973, ad loc., and Summonte 1512,

ad loc. For the "high tower," see on *Eclogae* 1.346, n. 36. "A monument of cruel pain": compare Vergil, *Aeneid* 12.945.

38. Planuris represents Pianura, west of Naples (Monti Sabia 1973, ad loc.).

39. Paestum, a city in southern Italy, was (and still is) famous for its roses and its substantial archaeological remains (Vergil, *Georgics* 4.119).

40. Summonte 1512, ad loc., identifies Leucogis with the Leucogei mountains between Naples and Pozzuoli, linking the name (from Greek *leukós*) with their rocks' white appearance. This whiteness derives from the mountains' sulfurous volcanic exhalations (Monti Sabia 1973, ad loc.).

41. The entrance to the underworld was traditionally located in the area of the Campi Flegrei in antiquity. Local bodies of water evoke this region: Lago Miseno (*stagna Baulorum*) in Bacoli near the port of Misenum (Monti Sabia 1973, ad loc.); the nearby Lake Avernus in Pozzuoli (Vergil, *Aeneid* 3.442, 6.201); and the Arasso River (Pliny the Elder, *Natural History* 18.114), which Monti Sabia identifies with the modern Acqua dei Pisciarelli on the slopes of the Leucogei (see on *Eclogae* 1.370, n.40, above). Pontano infuses his gods of the underworld with the volcanic qualities of the local landscape.

42. The crypt, as noted by Summonte 1512, ad loc., refers to the Crypta Neapolitana, a passageway through the hill of Posillipo built by Agrippa in the classical period (ca. 37 BCE). In the Medieval period, it was believed to have been created by Vergil "the magician." Vergil's so-called tomb was located on the Naples end of the tunnel in the area called Piedigrotta. These Vergilian associations support the suggestion in Monti Sabia 1973, ad loc., that the name *Aeronius* recalls the legend of the bronze archer placed by the same sorcerer Vergil in front of Vesuvius to protect Naples from the volcano (Latin *aes, aeris,* "bronze").

43. Typhoeus was a rebel giant buried under Mount Etna. In a variant version, Typhoeus was buried under the volcanic Mount Epomeo on Ischia (Monti Sabia 1973, ad loc.).

44. According to Summonte 1512, ad loc., the "exquisitely clear stream" that "flows down below" refers to the Bolla aqueduct running underground beneath Naples. The "topmost window" refers to Pontano's house

ad Arco: see on *Eclogae* 1.346, n.36, and Monti Sabia 1973, ad loc. The figure in the "topmost window," Urania, is Pontano's personal muse, inspirer of his didactic epic on astrology *Urania*. As Summonte notes, Pontano did well to place her in his house and make her his *familiaris*. Moreover, as Lepidina's "older and more beautiful" sister, she represents Pontano's achievements in a higher-order genre.

45. The term Oriarch, "Lord of the Mountains," appears to be an invention of Pontano.

46. The giant Gaurus personifies an extinct volcano in the Campi Flegrei, Monte Gauro; his wife, Campe, personifies the fertile fields (*campi*) in the crater of Monte Gauro, an area called Campiglione (Monti Sabia 1973, ad loc.). Summonte 1512, ad loc., notes that the Via Campana, which runs between Pozzuoli and Capua, passes near Gauro.

47. Laboris personifies the Campi Leborii, the modern Terra del Lavoro; the Clanius, the modern Lagno, is a Campanian river; "Vulturnian" refers to the Volturno River; Ardea is a town south of Rome; the Lucrine Lake is located near Baiae. Pontano often invents his own postclassical adjectival forms (*Vulturnius, Lucrinis*: Montia Sabia 1973, ad loc.).

48. Summonte 1512, ad loc., identifies Ursulon with a chestnut grove near Antignano (the location of Pontano's villa), perhaps represented by the modern Via Orsolone northwest of the Vomero near Largo dei Cangiani (Monti Sabia 1973, ad loc.).

49. *Crumeram* at 1.421 presumably represents Pontano's variant orthography of *cumera*, "box or basket used to hold corn, etc., also ritual objects in a bridal procession" (*Oxford Latin Dictionary*, s.v. *cumera*) — a doubly appropriate sense here. Pontano employs a similar orthography in the *Actius* (see Gaisser 2020, 373n4). Some scholars take it as a variant spelling of *crumēna* (bag [of money]), but that would not fit the meter here, and the meaning is less apt. *Sorbinum* and *Viridiscum*, as noted by Summonte 1512, ad loc., are Latin terms coined by Pontano for Campanian wines; Monti Sabia 1973, ad loc., identifies them as Verdicchio and Asprino.

50. Marana represents Marano, located northwest of Naples near the area identified with her husband, Ursulon: see Monti Sabia 1973, ad loc.,

and on *Eclogae* 1.417, n. 48, above. In line 427, *macerum* is presumably equivalent to *maceratum*.

51. Misenius personifies the Capo Miseno (compare Vergil, *Aeneid* 6.234–35).

52. For "Sebeto," see on *Eclogae* 1.25, n. 6.

53. On "Acerra," see on *Eclogae* 1.321, n. 32. Pomelia personifies Pomigliano d'Arco, northwest of Naples (Monti Sabia 1973, ad loc.).

54. Pontano indicates the spider via its mythic originator, the Ovidian Arachne, a famous weaver: see Ovid, *Metamorphoses* 6.5–145; Arachne was Lydian (*Metamorphoses* 6.5).

55. Prochyteia personifies the island of Procida, located near her husband, who represents Capo Miseno: see on *Eclogae* 1.123, n. 13, and on *Eclogae* 1.437, n. 51.

56. Latona's daughter: that is, Diana, the moon.

57. Capimontius personifies Capodimonte, an elevated area northwest of Naples.

58. Marillia personifies Mariglianella, a town northeast of Naples (Monti Sabia 1973, ad loc.).

59. Maenalus was a mountain in Arcadia associated with Pan (Vergil, *Eclogues* 8.21–61). "Maenalian verses" are thus pastoral poetry.

60. In the ancient Roman wedding ceremony, "Fescennine" song was ritual joking or abuse alluding to the consummation of the marriage. It was thought to have originated in the Etruscan town of Fescennia (compare Seneca the Younger *Medea* 113: *festa dicax fundat convicia fescenninus*).

61. Ansatia, according to Monti Sabia 1973, ad loc., drawing on Summonte 1512, ad loc., personifies an area near Arzano once called Villa Lanzciasini. "Of Costalio": compare Vergil, *Eclogues* 3.37, *divini opus Alcimedontis* (the work of divine Alcimedon).

62. Montia Sabia 1973 translates "carezza al caprone," taking *viro* as the she-goat's mate (compare Vergil, *Eclogues* 7.7, *vir gregis*). Following *adiuvat*, however, and picking up on the reference to the husband's difficult labor,

this phrase more naturally refers to the husband. See also Casanova-Robin 2011 ("cajole son mari") and Tufano 2015, 211. Compare *De hortis Hesperidum* 1.315–35.

63. This use of *praescribo* (write before, in front of) is unusual. Pontano may have had in mind Vergil, *Eclogues* 6.12 (*praescripsit*). The artistic concept of tracing out a design may also be present (Pliny the Elder, *Natural History* 35.10.36, *praescripta lineamenta*).

64. Murro personifies the town of Castel Morrone, and his wife, Marcinis, the town of Marcianise—both rural communities near Caserta. "Tifatean": Tifata is a mountain in the same general area, near Capua (Monti Sabia 1973, ad loc.).

65. Caserta and Casora (mod. Casoria) are towns in the same fertile region: see on *Eclogae* 1.551, n. 64. Lenaeus, Euhius, and Lyaeus (the relaxer) are epithets and names for the wine god, Bacchus.

66. Pulvica personifies Polvica, north of Naples; Panicoclis personifies nearby Villaricca, previously Panicocoli; Cicala corresponds to present-day Castello di Cicala outside Nola (Monti Sabia 1973, ad loc., drawing on Summonte 1512, ad loc.). Capreo is an invention of Pontano. Vesuvius, of course, personifies the volcano, here curiously in a festive mood, oblivious of his previous devastating eruptions.

67. The name Amaryllis is reminiscent of Vergilian pastoral: see on *Eclogae* 1.260, n. 24.

68. The location of this marketplace has not been identified: see further Tufano 2015, 234.

69. "Little cabbages" (*brasiculis*): probably a coinage by Pontano. It also appears in his *Asinus*, sections 21 and 30 in Gaisser 2020. See Ramminger, s.v. *bras(s)icula*.

70. Porticia personifies Portici, a coastal town near Vesuvius; Carmelus is a fountain in Naples near the Chiesa del Carmine in Piazza Mercato (Monti Sabia 1973, ad loc.).

71. The Sarrastes were a Campanian people who lived near the Sarno River. Pontano uses an adjective derived from them to indicate the Monti Picentini near Sarno (Monti Sabia 1973, ad loc.). The personified Vesu-

vius' features correspond to features of the mountain itself. The use of the Latin word *sanna* (mocking grimace) to mean "tusks" or "fangs" is presumably modeled on the vernacular Italian *zanna*.

72. Casanova-Robin 2011, who sees *at* as oppositional and takes *non* with *mutuus*, translates: *varie en revanche un amour non partagé*. I see *at* as "introducing an apodosis" (Lewis and Short 1975, s.v. *at*, II.F), and follow Monti Sabia 1973 in taking *non* with *variat*.

73. For "Planuris," see on the prose introduction to the Fifth Procession, n. 38 above. For "Patulcis," see Introduction, n. 9.

74. Nesis personifies Nisida, a volcanic island off Capo Posillipo (Monti Sabia 1973, ad loc.).

75. Halantus is a minor maritime deity invented by Pontano. Platamonis personifies an area of Naples where, according to Summonte 1512, ad loc., artificial grottoes were excavated along the coast used for parties and other pleasurable pastimes — the modern-day Via Partenope and Via Chiatamone (Monti Sabia 1973, ad loc.).

76. A topographical love triangle. Nisa could be the same as Nesis, that is, a personification of Nisida (see on *Eclogae* 1.659, n. 74); a reference to Vergilian bucolic (*Eclogues* 8.26); or simply an invented character: see Casanova-Robin 2011, ad loc. Nivanus is probably Grumo Nevano, a town north of Naples (Monti Sabia 1973, ad loc.). An elegiac poem by Pontano (*Eridanus* 2.22 in Roman 2014), tells of the love of Patulcis and Nivanus.

77. Pansa and her spouse are characters invented by Pontano. For the postclassical coinage *liguris* ("chaffinch," Italian *lucherino*), compare Pontano, *De tumulis* 2.50, and see Monti Sabia 1973, ad loc.

78. Antiniana personifies Pontano's villa on the Vomero hill: see Introduction, n. 9. The "old man," as confirmed by Summonte 1512, ad loc., is Pontano himself. Summonte further states that the *allegoria* is continued throughout the entire passage.

79. A very close echo of Pontano, *Urania* 3.1349–50; see Monti Sabia 1973, ad loc. Note also the Orpheus and Eurydice theme in *Meliseus* (*Eclogae* 2.228–35).

80. Compare Vergil, *Eclogues* 8.43: *Nunc scio quid sit Amor* (now I know what Love is).

81. Monti Sabia 1973, ad loc., argues that Pontano continues here the autobiographical allegory begun in line 682 (see on *Eclogae* 1.680, n. 78). The *flumen Hymellae* mentioned at Vergil, *Aeneid* 7.714, can be identified, with Servius' help, with the modern Salto River in Umbria, near Pontano's birthplace. "Melidoxus" suggests a master poet ("teacher of song"), like the pastoral alias Meliseus (Casanova-Robin 2011, ad loc.; see on *Eclogae* 2, n. 1).

82. The mention of swans and supremacy in song evokes Vergilian pastoral: *Eclogues* 8.55, 9.29, 9.36. Swans also accompany mention of Vergil's birthplace, Mantua: *Georgics* 2.199, *Eclogues* 9.29. The latter passage is a model for Pontano's bilingual play on two different words for swan, *olor* and *cycnus*, of Italic and Greek derivation, respectively.

83. Antiniana, the nymph personifying Pontano's villa, here becomes his muse, setting the stage for the performance of the closing *pompa*, in which she will play a central role.

84. Hesperus, the planet Venus' manifestation as the evening star, ushers in the wedding night: Catullus 62.20, 26, 32; 64.329. The deity's Latin name is Vesper: Catullus 62.1.

85. This wedding chant, with evocation of the Roman god of marriage (Hymen or Hymenaeus), recalls similar Catullan refrains (e.g., 61.117–18, 62.5).

86. In ancient Rome, the *genius* was the protective deity of a person or place, especially of the *paterfamilias*; hence, the *genius* was often linked with the household.

87. There is similar attention to clothing and adornments at Catullus 61.6–10, including the *flammeum* (the flame-colored bridal veil) and distinctive footwear (*luteum . . . soccum*).

88. This epithalamial prophecy recalls Catullus 64, in which the Parcae (Fates) sing at the wedding of Peleus and Thetis, prophesying their future son Achilles' heroic career, *nascetur . . . Achilles* (Achilles . . . will be born, 338), and featuring the threads of destiny in a refrain, *currite ducentes*

subtegmina, currite, fusi (run, spindles, run, as you draw the woof threads, 64.327; compare Vergil, *Eclogues* 4.46–47). The other major intertext is Vergil's Fourth *Eclogue*, which predicts a future golden age connected with the birth of a mysterious *puer* (boy), anachronistically identified as Christ in the Renaissance. In Antiniana's prophecy, the *proles* (offspring) of the marriage of Sebeto and Parthenope will be the city of Naples itself and her people, with specific attention to Naples' achievements under Aragonese rule: agriculture and viticulture (724–26), spinning and textile production (729–31), warfare (734–37), monarchy and the rule of law (740–42), poetry (745–75).

89. "Quincunx": that is, the shape of the five dots on a die; the usual pattern for planting vines.

90. For "Tritons," see on *Eclogae* 1, Fifth Procession, n. 18. For the "land of the Sirens," see on *Eclogae* 1.25, n. 5, and Introduction. Pontano's *aclidibus* (darts) is a postclassical spelling of the rare *aclys, aclydis*.

91. Mopsus and Meliboeus are herdsmen-singers in Vergilian pastoral (*Eclogues* 1, 5, 7).

92. This figure is the poet Vergil, who, born near Mantua, came as a "stranger" to the region of Naples. See Summonte 1512, ad loc.: *P. Virgilium Maronem intelligit.* Damon and Alphesiboeus (Eclogue 8), Menalcas (Eclogue 9), and Tityrus (Eclogue 1) are figures from Vergilian pastoral. For other Vergilian reminiscences in these lines, see *Eclogues* 1.39, 1.56, 7.3, 8.4; *Georgics* 2.199. On rivers ceasing to flow, compare *De hortis Hesperidum* 2.22, n. 5, and 2.530, n. 35. See also Poliziano's *Manto*, which likewise adapts Vergil's prophetic frameworks in *Eclogues* 4 and the *Aeneid* to predict the birth of Vergil himself; note also Pontano, *Eridanus* 1.14, on Vergil's birth, in Roman 2014. See further Monti Sabia 1983 on the "Neapolitanization" of Vergil.

93. This second "stranger" is the Umbrian-born Pontano, who viewed himself as an adoptive Neapolitan like Vergil: see on *Eclogae* 1.754, n. 92. As noted by Summonte 1512, ad loc., "Pontano portrays himself" (*se ipsum Pontanus depingit*). Whereas Vergil merely *wrote* about agriculture, Pontano proudly notes that he is the "sower of his own garden"—i.e., at Antignano (see Introduction). For other Vergilian reminiscences in these

lines, see *Eclogues* 5.51–52, 6.84 (being conveyed to the stars), 2.34 (wearing down one's lip with a reed), 5.72 (Damoetas and Lyctian Aegon); for "swans," see on *Eclogae* 1.694, n. 82. Lyctus is a town in Crete; hence Lyctian can mean simply "Cretan." For "Amaryllis," see on *Eclogae* 1.260, n. 24. For "Urania," see on *Eclogae* 1.399, n. 44.

94. The old man is Pontano himself, who, like Vergil, will one day have a tomb venerated by successor poets: see Introduction; compare *De hortis Hesperidum* 2.15–16. For Pontano's tomb as the site of his posthumous fame, compare *Urania* 5.912–82.

95. Having honey smeared on one's lips was a metaphor in antiquity for poetic eloquence. In his response, Macron takes the figure literally, admiring Antiniana's apicultural wealth.

96. *Cirneus:* "Corsican," from the Greek name for the island of Corsica (compare Vergil, *Eclogues* 9.30). For "snub-nosed (*simae*) she-goats," see Vergil, *Eclogues* 10.7 (Monti Sabia 1973, ad loc.). "While tawny otherwise . . .": compare Horace, *Odes* 4.2.59–60, of a calf to be sacrificed: *qua notam duxit, niveus videri, / cetera fulvus* (snow-white where it has a mark, elsewhere tawny). "Laconian dogs": a well-known Spartan breed in antiquity. "Arctos": the constellation of the Great and Little Bear; the adjective *arctous* means "northern." "Teatine" refers to the Apulian town of Teate (mod. Chieti). *Inenarrabile textum* (work of indescribable weave): compare Vergil's description of the shield of Aeneas (*non enarrabile textum: Aeneid* 8.625).

97. *Lepos* (charm, grace): see on *Eclogae* 1, prologue, n. 1, above.

98. An echo of the eclogue's opening lines (*Eclogae* 1.1–2); compare Vergil's citation of the opening of his *Eclogues* in his *Georgics* coda (4.565–66).

II. MELISEUS

1. Pontano's wife, Adriana Sassone, died in 1490. He built the Cappella dei Pontano in her honor: see Introduction. As both Monti Sabia 1973, ad loc., and Casanova-Robin 2011, ad loc., observe, there are many connections between this poem and Eclogue 12 of Sannazaro's *Arcadia*. In his poetry, Pontano writes his wife's name as Ariadne/Ariadna, sometimes

taking advantage of the name's mythological associations. Meliseus: Pontano himself; see on *Eclogae* 1.693, n. 81.

2. The names Faburnus and Ciceriscus, which recall *faba* (bean) and *cicer* (chickpea), suggest a rural agricultural milieu.

3. Phosphoris: Pontano's daughter Lucia: see on *Eclogae* 1.355, n. 37 above.

4. Corydon, Thyrsis, and Amyntas are figures from Vergil's *Eclogues* (2, 3, 5, 7, and 10).

5. Patulcis personifies Pontano's villa at Posillipo: see Introduction, n. 9. Daphnis is a figure from both Vergilian and Theocritean pastoral. Monti Sabia 1973, ad loc., suggests that Daphnis stands for Jacopo Sannazaro, who had a villa nearby at Mergellina. On the theme of poets' tombs, see Introduction, and on *Eclogae* 1.775, n. 94; compare *De hortis Hesperidum* 2.15–16.

6. A common technique of winnowing in the ancient world.

7. *Teges*, in classical Latin a "covering or mat," in medieval Latin can refer to a cottage for guardians of vineyards or shepherds (Du Cange 1884, s.v. *teges*).

8. For *liguris* (chaffinch), see on *Eclogae* 1.670, n. 77. For "sugar cane honey" (*mellis arundinei*), or molasses, see Tufano 2015, 351.

9. "Sun's grief": the hyacinth (i.e., the grief of Apollo for his young lover Hyacinthus: Ovid, *Metamorphoses* 10.162–219). "Weeping boy's love": narcissus (i.e., the mythological figure Narcissus, Ovid, *Metamorphoses* 3.339–510). "Locks plucked from Venus' forehead": maidenhair (see Isidore, *Origines* 17.9.67, and Monti Sabia 1973, ad loc.).

10. The word *coma* (both "hair" and "foliage") nicely suits the personification of trees here.

11. On Pontano's use of *citrius* to refer to orange trees, and their importance for Pontano and the Aragonese monarchy, see Introduction; compare *De hortis Hesperidum* 1.311–35. It is uncertain exactly which herb corresponds to *sisymbrium*: *mentha aquatica* is one possibility (Du Cange 1884, s.v. *sisimbrium*).

12. Pontano identifies himself with Orpheus mourning his wife, Eurydice (Vergil, *Georgics* 4.315–547).

13. A rural divinity of Sabine origin: see Horace, *Epistles* 1.10.49; Ovid, *Fasti* 6.307–8; Pliny the Elder, *Natural History* 3.12.17 (109); and Casanova-Robin 2011, ad loc.

14. The waters, like Meliseus' emotions, have reached a point of equilibrium—neither too low nor swollen with rains.

15. Pontano often mixes georgic and pastoral material—normally kept separate in classical poetry. For the resumption of rural tasks as a distraction, compare Vergil, *Eclogues* 2.70–72.

III. Maeon

1. Syncerius here stands for Sannazaro (Actius Sincerus): see on *Eclogae* 1.126, n. 14. Monti Sabia 1973, ad loc., suggests that Zephyreus is Pontano. Paolo Attaldi was a doctor and philosopher from Aversa who participated in Pontano's academy. Monti Sabia suspects that the prose introduction to this and the following eclogue were added by the editor Aldus. The name Maeon belongs to a priest of Apollo, god of healing, in Statius' *Thebaid* (2.693, 4.598). The eclogue combines the pastoral subgenres of epicedion and singing contest.

2. Monte d'Ocre, south of Aquila, and the Matese massif in the Campanian Apennines are cited here for their impressive altitude. Pontano also plays on the word *ocris*, which in classical Latin refers generically to a rugged, stony mountain. For the phrase *vale aeternum*, compare Vergil, *Aeneid* 11.97–98, and Pontano, *Eclogae* 2.101, 180.

3. The female names recall the generic, often Greek-derived names in Latin poetry: e.g., Phyllis (Vergil, *Eclogues* 3.78; Horace, *Odes* 4.11.3); Philaenis (Martial 2.33). Lychnis resembles the Greek word for "lamp" (see Casanova-Robin 2011, ad loc.), an important item in ancient erotic poetry.

4. The constellation of the Dog, associated with the hottest period of the summer.

5. The "god": presumably Pan, the pastoral deity *par excellence*.

6. Lucania: a region of southern Italy. "Hercules' bull": the Cretan bull, which was captured by Hercules, became the object of Pasiphae's passion and was at last sacrificed by Theseus.

7. The closure of the pastoral day coinciding with the closure of the poem is a motif adapted from Vergil, *Eclogues* 10.75–77; compare Martial, *Epigrams* 4.89.1–2. The name Saturisca plays on the theme of satiety (*satur/satis*) present in both Martial's and Vergil's closural passages.

IV. Acon

1. On the prose summary, see on *Eclogae* 3 (*Maeon*), n. 1. The name Nape suits the character's transformation into a turnip (Latin *napus*: Monti Sabia 1973, ad loc.). Vertumnus is a god of Etruscan origin associated with the changing seasons and with change generally (Propertius 4.2; Ovid, *Metamorphoses* 14.642–771). For "Meliseus," who stands for Pontano, see on *Eclogae* 2, n. 1. Petasillus recalls the word *petasus*, a broad-brimmed hat (Casanova-Robin 2011, ad loc.). "Saliuncus" resembles *saliunca*, a fragrant plant (Vergil, *Eclogues* 5.17).

2. *Ruptare* here is equivalent to *ructare* (belch): see Monti Sabia 1973, ad loc., and line 59 (*ruptat*); Ramminger, s.v. *rupto*.

3. Ariadne: Pontano's wife, Adriana; see on *Eclogae* 2, n. 1.

4. Arangas: a mountain of Inner Libya (Ptolemy 4.6.12); compare Monti Sabia 1993 in Monti Sabia et al. 2010, 1147; *De hortis Hesperidum* 1.592. *Nigirides*: an adjectival form invented by Pontano to indicate the region near the river Niger (Tufano 2015, 452n32). These references cohere with Pontano's association of Africa with the mythical Garden of the Hesperides.

5. Falernian territory in Campania was a famous wine region in antiquity. For "Asprino," see on *Eclogae* 1.423, n. 49.

6. *Scrutum* in later Latin, like *scrutulus*, often refers to sausage (Monti Sabia 1973, ad loc.). For *ruptat* (belches), see on *Eclogae* 4.23, n. 2 above.

7. Hybla was a city in Sicily famous in antiquity for its honey. *Libyscis*: an adjectival form coined by Pontano (Monti Sabia 1973, ad loc.).

8. On "Gaurus," see on *Eclogae* 1.423, n. 46; for "desolate Cumae," compare Juvenal 3.2. The *cryptae* are the caves excavated by the Romans along the shores of the lake (Monti Sabia 1973, ad loc.); see on *Eclogae* 1.659, n. 75. Lake Avernus, near Pozzuoli, was the mythical entrance to the underworld (Vergil, *Aeneid* 6.201). Monti Sabia 1973, ad loc., identifies *antraque Musconis* with Moschiano in the province of Avellino. Tubenna is modern-day Monte Tubenna near Salerno; the *sepulcra* would refer to the so-called catacombs of the Church of S. Agnese a Sava, northwest of Tubenna.

9. A well-known type of hunting dog in antiquity.

10. The reference to the cave of Vulsone is uncertain. The name recalls the Umbrian warrior Volso at Silius Italicus 10.142 (Monti Sabia 1973, ad loc.). Mopsus is a figure from Vergilian pastoral: 5.1, 8.26. Salento is a region in southern Apulia. In all three cases, Monti Sabia sees references to episodes in Pontano's career.

11. For "Dogliolo," see on *Eclogae* 1.30, n. 7, and Introduction. Minio may refer to the Etruscan river Mignone: see *Aeneid* 10.183, and Monti Sabia 1973, ad loc.

12. The "nightingale": in classical myth, King Tereus of Thrace raped his wife Procne's sister Philomela. When Procne found out, she killed her son Itys and fed him as a meal to the unknowing Tereus. The gods transformed Procne into a swallow, Tereus into a hoopoe, and Philomela into a nightingale (Ovid, *Metamorphoses* 6.424–674). Pontano here makes Philomela into the mother who mourns her murdered son (Monti Sabia 1973, ad loc.).

13. The generic sense of *brigantes* is "brigands," but the term can refer to the French: compare *De hortis Hesperidum* 1.329. The "theft" refers to the 1494 French invasion (Monti Sabia 1973, ad loc.); see Introduction. The *impluvium* in a classical Roman house is an opening in the roof of the atrium located over a basin for catching rainwater.

14. *Attonitu*: a postclassical, fourth-declension noun: Forcellini 1771, s.v. *attonitus*; Venantius Fortunatus *Carmina* 8.6. For "Lyaeus," see on *Eclogae* 1.560, n. 65.

15. Pales is a Roman deity who protects shepherds and flocks.

16. *Intendo* is sometimes used of "stretching" the strings of a musical instrument: Vergil, *Aeneid* 9.776; Persius, *Satires* 6.4.

17. *Boleti*: mushrooms especially prized by the ancient Romans.

V. Coryle

1. Coryle is a name based on the Latin word for hazel tree, *corylus*. The hazel tree has a special connection with the love of Pontano and his wife, Adriana. Compare *Eclogae* 2 and the eclogue in Pontano's dialogue *Antonius*, where Amaryllis appears to correspond to Adriana: see Gaisser 2012, 267–71, and Monti Sabia 1973, ad loc. Actius Syncerus Sannazarius is Jacopo Sannazaro: see on *Eclogae* 1.126, n. 14.

2. For "Meliseus," see on *Eclogae* 2, n. 1; and for "Patulcis," see Introduction, n. 9. For the lines referring to Adriana's death, compare *Eclogae* 2.4.

3. For "Sebeto," see on *Eclogae* 1.25, n. 6. The Latin adjective *Circeis* is Pontano's invention. The witch Abelle recalls the town of Abella in the province of Avellino, known for its hazel trees (Monti Sabia 1973, ad loc.). With line 16 (*quo non penetrat livor?*), compare Ovid, *Ars Amatoria* 3.291, and *De hortis Hesperidum* 2.448.

4. Tityrus, Corydon, Alexis, and Damon and Alphesiboeus are all figures from Vergilian pastoral (*Eclogues* 1, 2, 8).

5. Tityrus, who "first" (*primum*) composed Latin pastoral song, probably represents Vergil; Corylenus, his successor, would then correspond to Pontano (compare *Eclogae* 1.745–67 and nn. 92, 93, 94); his beloved "Aridia" represents a satirical version of Pontano's wife, Adriana. For more detail, see Monti Sabia 1973, ad loc. Compare the physical description of Pontano in the dialogue *Antonius* in Gaisser 2012, 256–57. Monti Sabia attempts to identify the singer Amilcon with a Neapolitan humanist who flourished prior to Pontano, such as Panormita or Battista Spagnuoli. However, Pontano may have created a deliberately ambiguous allegory, anticipating that his text, like Vergil's, would one day become the object of learned speculation and commentary.

6. The nymph personifying Pontano's villa at Antignano: see Introduction.

7. Difficult lines (Monti Sabia 1973, ad loc.). The subject of *referret* in line 48, awkwardly omitted, must be Antiniana, who is introduced here as a new speaker with significant emphasis, and who, in the seventh procession of the *Lepidina*, was similarly responsible for an extended section of embedded song. In line 159, Pontano makes it clear that Antiniana has told the story.

8. Pontano embeds an elegiac poem within a pastoral frame. This combination of dactylic hexameter and elegiac couplets has no classical precedent. The basic premise recalls Ausonius' *Cupid Crucified* (Monti Sabia 1973, ad loc.). Pontano may also have been influenced by multilayered, experimental poems from the classical period: e.g., Catullus 68, or Vergil's *Sixth Eclogue* (a bound Silenus; embedded song).

9. Both Paphos and Cnidos are places associated with the cult of Aphrodite.

10. This scene recalls Pontano's *Lullabies* (*Naeniae = De amore coniugali* 2.8–19 in Roman 2014); e.g., 2.17.20, where Pontano's son reaches for his mother's breasts in his sleep.

11. A nymph personifying the Sebeto River (Vergil, *Aeneid* 7.734, *Sebethide nympha*).

12. Pontano often uses the Greek name of Charites for the three Graces.

13. For "Dogliolo," see on *Eclogae* 1.30, n. 7.

14. Monti Sabia 1973, ad loc., is surely correct in attributing lines 85–88 to Antiniana as an anticipative expression of empathy for Cupid, not to Sebethis. Sebethis has just abandoned the boy and is now wholly distracted by her own erotic emotions.

15. The famous mistresses of classical elegy take revenge on the god who persecuted them: Corinna appears in Ovid's *Amores*, Cynthia is Propertius' mistress, Lesbia is Catullus' lover, and Nemesis is Tibullus' mistress in his second book of elegies.

16. Ariadne: that is, Pontano's wife, Adriana: see on *Eclogae* 2, n. 1. He offers her the compliment of being mistaken for the goddess Venus by Cupid himself.

17. Love is blindfolded, hence the need for recognition by touch.

18. Compare *Aeneid* 6.190–204, where a pair of Venus' emblematic doves similarly help her son Aeneas find the golden bough.

19. Antiniana predicts Pontano's future poetic career: compare *Eclogae* 1.745–67 and nn. 92, 93, 94.

VI. Quinquennius

1. The five-year-old boy (*quinquennius*) is Pontano's son, Lucio; his mother, Pelvina, whose name recalls *pelvis/pelvinum* (a basin for domestic tasks: Casanova-Robin 2011, ad loc.; Tufano 2015, 549), corresponds to Pontano's wife, Adriana. As Monti Sabia 1973, ad loc., aptly notes, the poem is not so much a pastoral poem as "un delizioso mimo." There is a comparable story about Lucio in Pontano's *Aegidius*, section 13 in Gaisser 2020.

2. There is a similar depiction of Orcus—here an ogre rather than the classical god of the underworld—in Pontano, *De amore coniugali* 2.14, in Roman 2014.

3. On Pontano's coinage *brasicula* (little cabbage), see on *Eclogae* 1.596, n. 69.

4. *Praecoqua* are a type of peach (*pesche percoche*). I follow Monti Sabia 1973 in translating *citriolum* as "cucumber" (Italian *cetriolo*, derived from the diminutive of *citrium*, "gourd"). Unctilia's name is related to the verb *unguor*, "to anoint or cover with oil."

5. *Micturio* (make water, urinate) is a rare verb that occurs twice in Juvenal (6.309, 16.46)

GARDEN OF THE HESPERIDES

Book I

1. For "the gardens of Dogliolo," see on *Eclogae* 1.30, n. 7, and Introduction. Note also Summonte 1512, ad loc., who comments that the *fons* of Dogliolo is near Naples on *Via Acerrana* and that Alfonso, duke of Calabria, adorned it with sumptuous structures and had it renamed Poggioreale. Maro: the poet Vergil. For the plants that make up his poetic garland, see *Georgics* 4.183; *Eclogues* 5.38, 7.6; *Aeneid* 11.69. On "Sebeto," see on *Eclogae* 1.25, n. 6.

2. For "green shade" as a pastoral topos, see on *Eclogae* 1.3, n. 3.

3. For "Urania," invoked here as Pontano's Muse, see on *Eclogae* 1.399, n. 44. Idalium is a town on Cyprus associated with the cult of Venus.

4. This précis of Pontano's astrological poem echoes its proem (*Urania* 1.1–10).

5. Apollo is Urania's half brother, as they share Zeus as their father.

6. For "Antiniana," the personification of Pontano's villa, see on *Eclogae* 1.680, n. 78, and Introduction. For "Patulcis," see on *De hortis Hesperidum* 2.16, n. 3, and Introduction, n. 9.

7. Bianor: the legendary founder of Mantua. The battle of Fornovo took place near the Taro River; see Introduction. "Feretrian" refers to the Roman tradition of dedicating the so-called *spolia opima* (richest spoils) in the temple of Jupiter Feretrius. The reference to Hercules' club perhaps alludes to a story about Vergil: accused of plagiarizing Homer, he replied that it was easier to steal Hercules' club from him than to steal a single line from Homer (Donatus, *Life of Virgil* 46). I owe this suggestion to Coleman Connelly.

8. The Nias is a river in interior Libya (Ptolemy 4.6.7); Pontano elsewhere uses "Niasaean" to refer to the orange tree. Summonte 1512, ad loc., calls it "a river of the Hesperides." In antiquity, Africa was sometimes specified as the location of the mythic garden of the Hesperides. Citrus trees were also associated with North Africa (Pliny, *Natural History* 13.91). On the term *citrius* (orange), see Introduction. For *arboreae . . . praeconia palmae* (heralding of the arboreal prize), compare Ovid, *Heroides* 17, 207; Pliny, *Natural History* 31.41.2.

9. This initial description of the orange tree (*citrius*) recalls Vergil's description of the citron (*Georgics* 2.126–35). See Caruso 2013, 15, and Iacono 2015, 17–18.

10. Pontano's story of Venus and Adonis is based on that of Ovid's *Metamorphoses* (10.519–59, 708–39) as well as his narrative of Daphne and Apollo (see on *De hortis Hesperidum* 1.76, n. 11) and Apollo and Hyacinthus (*Metamorphoses* 10.162–219).

11. Apollo pursued Daphne, daughter of Peneus, and she was trans-

formed into a laurel tree—an emblem of Apollo and symbol of poetic inspiration (Ovid, *Metamorphoses* 1.457–567). Note in particular the tree's beauty and its status as perpetual memorial (*semper . . . semper*: *Metamorphoses* 1.558, 565), and as memorial of grief (*Metamorphoses* 10.725–27).

12. To explain the fruit's arrival in Italy, Pontano inserts his myth of the orange tree among Hercules' labors: the theft of the fruit of the Hesperides, his slaying of the three-bodied monster Geryon in Spain, and his killing of the ogre Cacus (the Italian monster) near the future site of Rome (Livy 1.5; Vergil, *Aeneid* 8.184–279). The phrase *procul orbe subacto* (a far-off region having been subjugated) presumably refers to Hercules' defeat of the Amazons and his retrieval of Hippolyta's belt in the "far-off" land of Themiscyra on the Black Sea (Apollonius of Rhodes, *Argonautica* 2.965), prior to his slaying of Geryon. Alternately, it could refer to the world "having been raised up far off [in the Garden of the Hesperides]" on Hercules' shoulders.

13. Formia, Gaeta, and Amalfi are southern Italian coastal towns associated with citrus groves. [H]ormiala is a nymph personifying Formia. Lamus is the legendary founder of Formia, supposed to have been the home of the savage Laestrygonians of Homer's *Odyssey* (10.80–132). Fundanus is a lake near Fondi, represented here by the place-nymph Fundania. The Liris River, now called the Gargiliano, flows by the Latian town of Suessa Aurunca (compare Pliny, *Natural History* 3.59.7). The Sirens were emblematic of Naples: see on *Eclogae* 1.25, n. 5. For "Niasaean," see on *De hortis Hesperidum* 1.53, n. 8. "Forest of Zephyrium's goddess": that is, the forest of Venus, who created the orange tree. See on *De hortis Hesperidum* 2.140, n. 10. Alternately, *Zephyritide* could be an adjective coined by Pontano, "relating to Zephyr," the West Wind.

14. Throughout the poem, Pontano imitates exhortative phrases typical of classical Latin didactic (e.g., *nunc, age,* "come, now . . . ," e.g., Vergil, *Georgics* 4.149–50) as well as the series of indirect questions summarizing didactic content (compare *Georgics* 1.1–5).

15. There is a nearly identical phrase in Columella (*fossus gracilis imitatur harenas* 10.6–8). *Imitatur* (imitates) signals the imitative intention; com-

pare *similis* at 1.60 with n. 9, and *veterum admonuit . . . amorum* (reminded her of an earlier love story) at 1.74 with n. 11.

16. For "Niasaean," see on *De hortis Hesperidum* 1.53, n. 8. *Mersatilis* (irrigating) appears to be a Pontanian coinage: see the comment of Monti Sabia in Arnaldi et al. 1964, 781n145; compare *De hortis Hesperidum* 1.444, *roratilis*.

17. The Sithonii dwelled in Thrace. Lycaonia was a mountainous region in Asia Minor. Both areas were known for bleak, cold climates.

18. Compare Columella, *On Agriculture* 10.27–28. "Othrysian" refers to Othrys, a mountain in Thessaly sometimes ascribed to Thrace by imperial Latin poets.

19. The term *Aeneadae* (descendants of Aeneas) means "Romans": the founder-hero Aeneas was the son of Venus.

20. The sun is in the sign of Cancer at the summer solstice.

21. That is, at the vernal equinox. Compare Columella on the autumnal equinox: *paribus Titan orbem libraverit horis* (*On Agriculture* 10.42).

22. The Adda, Ticino, and Mincio Rivers are tributaries of the Po in northern Italy and modern-day Switzerland. These lines allude to Francesco Gonzaga of Mantua (compare 1.50), Vergil, and perhaps also the poet called Mantuan (Battista Spagnuoli, 1447–1516).

23. Clonia is the Latin name for a lake in the interior of Libya; compare Summonte 1512, ad loc.: "a swamp (*palus*) in the region of the Hesperides." See on *De hortis Hesperidum* 1.53, n. 8.

24. Benacus is the Lago di Garda. *Charidae* is an adjective, apparently coined by Pontano, meaning, "relating to the Charites," that is, the Graces; see on *De hortis Hesperidum* 2.225, n. 17. It may also play on "Garda."

25. The poet Catullus (named at 1.229) came from Verona; for *vatem egregium* (extraordinary poet), compare Juvenal 7.53. Salò is a town in Brescia on the Lago di Garda. The river Adige flows south past Verona to the Adriatic. Cythera was an Aegean island famous for the worship of Venus.

26. Dione is the mother of Venus: for the adjective *Dionaea*, compare, for example, Vergil, *Aeneid* 3.19.

27. Cyrene is a town in Libya: see on *De hortis Hesperidum* 1.53, n. 8. Catullus owned a villa on the island of Sirmio in the Lago di Garda. *Volemus*, which occurs only once in classical Latin, seems to refer to a type of large pear (Vergil, *Georgics* 2.88).

28. This phrase (*venti excutiant*, "winds tear up") echoes the closing words of the metamorphosis of Hyacinthus in Ovid (*Metamorphoses* 10.739).

29. In mythology, the Thracian Procne was turned into a swallow. Daulis was a city in Thrace. See on *Eclogae* 4.129, n. 12.

30. For "Idalian," see on *De hortis Hesperidum* 1.28, n. 3. Pontano's wife, Adriana Sassone, died in 1490.

31. Pontano refers to the death of his son, Lucio, in 1498 and the French invasion of Naples in 1495 that brought down the Aragonese dynasty and ended Pontano's public career. The Penates were gods of the inner part of the house in classical Roman religion, here standing for Pontano's Neapolitan *patria*, contaminated by the French presence.

32. Pontano employs an archaic form of the negative purpose clause with *ut + ne*.

33. *Lamiae [urbis]* presumably refers to Formia, founded by Lamus. Compare *De hortis Hesperidum* 1.582 (*Lamios . . . hortos*) and see on *De hortis Hesperidum* 1.124, n. 13.

34. The Portuguese expedition of Vasco da Gama in 1497–98, which sailed to India by circumnavigating Africa, is believed to have brought back sweet oranges to Europe.

35. Prassum is the present-day Cape Delgado (Ptolemy 4.8.1); Rhapton is the promontory of Ras Utontwe (Ptolemy 9.1; 4.7, 12, 28); and *barabaricum fretum* is the Indian Ocean. See Heinz Hofmann, "*Adveniat tandem Typhis qui detegat orbes*: COLUMBUS in Neo-Latin Epic Poetry (15th–18th Centuries)," in *The Classical Tradition and the Americas, Volume 1: European Images of the Americas and the Classical Tradition, Part 1*, ed. Wolfgang Haase and Meyer Reinhold (Berlin/New York: Walter De Gruyter, 1994), 426n12. See also Monti Sabia 1993, 1143–45; Roellenbleck 1975, 108. Hymettus, a mountain near Athens, and Hybla, a mountain in Sicily, were famous for their honey in antiquity.

36. Cleonae was a small town near Nemea where Hercules obtained his famous lion skin. Paphos is a city on Cyprus known for its cult of Venus.

37. The Falernian region in Campania was famous for its wines in antiquity.

38. The archaic infinitive *dominarier* (lord it over) occurs once in classical Latin literature, at *Aeneid* 7.70, where Vergil describes the prodigy of a swarm of bees that lands on a sacred laurel tree in King Latinus' palace — a suitably arboreal intertext.

39. The Parcae are the Roman goddesses of destiny. In the passage that follows, Pontano imitates the song of the Parcae in Catullus 64, which emphasizes the weaving of destiny and tells the story of a hero's life and untimely death. See further on *Eclogae* 1.721, n. 88.

40. The lengthening of *–que*, in imitation of Greek metrics (*te . . . te*), typically occurs in a verse-initial sequence with double *–que* in Vergil. See Vergil, *Aeneid* 8.425, and C. J. Fordyce, *Virgil: Aeneid VII–VIII* (Bristol: Bristol Classical Press, 1986), ad loc. Note also the synizesis with *aureo*, again recalling Vergil: see on *De hortis Hesperidum* 2.565, n. 40, and on *De hortis Hesperidum* 2.576, n. 41.

41. The town of Amathus on Cyprus was a cult center of Venus.

42. For "Fondi," "Suessa Aurunca," "Amalfi," and "Lamian gardens" (i.e., in Formia), see on *De hortis Hesperidum* 1.124, n. 13.

43. For "Idalium," see on *De hortis Hesperidum* 1.28, n. 3. The phrase *tuos nos pangimus hortos* has a double sense, corresponding to Pontano's role as gardener and poet: either "we compose [verses about] your gardens" or "we plant your gardens." Mount Arangas was a mountain in interior Libya. Moeris was an Egyptian king believed to have excavated an artificial lake named after him; hence, "the Moeriads" are Egyptians (cf. *Aeneadae*). Alternately, *Moeriadum* might refer to the nymphs of Lake Moeris. These geographical references, in combination with the town of Berenice in Egypt, evoke the mythic African origins of citrus fruit. At the same time, *Arangaeae* plays on words for "orange": see Ramminger, s.v. *arantium, arangia*; Italian *arangio*; compare the variant adjectival form at *Eclogae* 4.33.

44. For "Niasaean," see on *De hortis Hesperidum* 1.53, n. 8.

45. The festival of the Adonia, celebrated annually in ancient Greek communities in June. For the practice of hanging up masks on trees in honor of a god, which wave in the wind (*oscilla*), compare Vergil, *Georgics* 2.389. The term *partheniae* could be Pontano's adaptation of the Greek adjective *parthenios* (maidenly) or might refer to the Monti del Partenio in Campania (cf. Tilly 2020, 424, "les nymphes du Partenio"). The word *parthenos* also recalls Parthenope, the siren symbolizing Naples.

Book II

1. The medieval Latin *acrumen* refers to sharp or piquant foods and herbs. Pontano here appears to coin a new usage based on the Italian *agrume* (citrus).

2. The Pleiades were the daughters of Atlas and Pleione and thus shared a father with the Hesperides. In his discussion of the Pleiades in the *Urania*, Pontano assimilates them to aspects of the Hesperides' mythology, associating them with their Garden and its golden fruit: 3.769–71, 804–5. Here, they also assume the characteristics of Muses.

3. Antiniana and Patulcis personify Pontano's villas; see on *Eclogae* 1.680, n. 78, and Introduction, n. 9. "Maro's urn" refers to the so-called tomb of Vergil outside Naples: see Introduction.

4. Mantua is Vergil's town of origin and the city ruled by Francesco Gonzaga. The Mincio, a tributary of the Po that flows past Mantua, is honored in each of Vergil's major works: *Eclogues* 7.12–13, *Georgics* 3.12–15, *Aeneid* 10.205–6.

5. Lake Lucrinus: modern Lago Lucrino, near the Campanian coast (compare Juvenal 4.141). For streams ceasing to flow, compare Vergil, *Georgics* 1.479, and *Eclogues* 8.1–5; Pontano, *Eclogae* 1.753; and *De hortis Hesperidum* 2.530.

6. The Pharusii were a people in Mauretania; compare Summonte 1512, ad loc.: "a people by the Hesperian sea." The Stachir was a river in Libya (Ptolemy 4.6–8); compare Summonte 1512, ad loc.: "The river Stachir

flows into the Hesperian sea." For citrus fruit and North Africa, see on *De hortis Hesperidum* 1.53, n. 8.

7. On *pangite* (compose/plant), see on *De hortis Hesperidum* 1.591, n. 43. Aonia, a region in Boeotia, was associated with poetic inspiration in the classical tradition since Hesiod (*Theogony* 1–34). The plural *vos* possibly includes all of Pontano's poetic supporters and Muses addressed in this proemium: the Pleiades, Antiniana, Patulcis, Francesco, and Adriana, his wife.

8. The unclassical form *refulxit* is an orthographical variant on *refulsit* from *refulgeo* (shine). I cannot rule out that Pontano may have been using the likewise unclassical *refulcio* ("prop," cf. *fulcio*), in which case this clause would be translated: "and he held the firmament propped on his shoulders."

9. That is, plant the seed in the ground.

10. Pomona is a goddess of fruit orchards. Zephyritis, the cult title of Arsinoe/Aphrodite at Zephyrium, here refers to Venus, creator of the citrus tree; cf. Catullus 66.57. Alternately, it may refer to Flora, goddess of flowers and bride of Zephyr.

11. Pontano here Latinizes the Greek word κίτρον for citron (Latin *citrus*). The word *cauda* (tail, extremity) can also refer to the penis. This seems to trigger the subsequent prohibition on obscene images in gardens, as with statues of Priapus in antiquity. For *agmina cauda*, compare Vergil, *Georgics* 3.423 (*agmina caudae*, a snake's coils — an aptly phallic allusion).

12. An "engraved tablet" sounds like a relief carving, yet the obscene image is made of soil (*seva ab imagine terrae*); perhaps *caelata tabella* is a mold used to shape earthworks.

13. Acidalian: see on *Eclogae* 1.92, n. 11.

14. Lucca was known for its textile industry and silk trade. Pontano no longer explicitly distinguishes between orange and citron here, but may have citron in mind: note Pliny, *Natural History* 12.7, on citron used to protect clothing; compare Theophrastus, *Enquiry into Plants* 4.4.2.

15. Libya, daughter of Epaphus, was impregnated by Neptune with twin sons; for "Pharusian Stachir," see on *De hortis Hesperidum* 2.23, n. 6. Al-

cyone was one of the Pleiades. The mythological love triangle and Alcyone's use of citron to entice Neptune are inventions of Pontano, despite his apparent "citation" of antiquity: *nam prisca quidem sic credidit aetas*.

16. Clonian: see on *De hortis Hesperidum* 1.204, n. 23. Line 216 is hypermetric; compare *De hortis Hesperidum* 1.106, 1.437, 2.173, 2.270.

17. Cyrene was a city in Libya. The Masitholus (Ptolemy 50.4) and the Paliurus (Ptolemy 4.4, 4.5) were rivers in Libya. Compare Summonte 1512, ad loc., who identifies Masitholus as a river that flows into the Hesperian sea and Paliurus as a "swamp of the Hesperides." "Charites" is the Greek name for the three Graces. Both the name Charites and the associated adjectival form—e.g., *Chariteia*, 225, apparently coined by Pontano—recur frequently throughout this passage (2.225, 226, 232, 245, 259, 264, 286); for the adjective, compare Pontano, *De tumulis* 2.52.7; *De amore coniugali* 2.7.69 and *Eridanus* 1.36.31 in Roman 2014. Since Venus was closely associated with the Graces in antiquity, Summonte 1512 suggests that the adjective refers to Venus and Pontano's newly-invented myth of her creation of the citrus tree. He further suggests that this play on "Charites" alludes to the Neapolitan humanist Benedetto Gareth (*Chariteus*, or "Il Cariteo"); compare *Aegidius*, sections 40–45 in Gaisser 2020, where Pontano and Pardo's discussion of *carentia* (absence, lack) possibly also plays on Cariteo's name.

18. Compare Vergil, *Aeneid* 7.645–46.

19. For the "Niasaean spring," see on *De hortis Hesperidum* 1.53, n. 8. For the "Siren's shore," see on *Eclogae* 1.25, n. 5. The town of Amalfi was credited with the invention of the compass, although it had already been in use in China for centuries.

20. Oranges and lemons in the Renaissance were often associated with marriage.

21. Hymenaeus: Roman god of marriage; see on Eclogae 1.82, n. 9. Cytherean: see on *De hortis Hesperidum* 1.211, n. 25. On "Amalfi," here personified as a nymph, see on *De hortis Hesperidum* 1.124, n. 13. *Gratia* (gratitude) plays on the Graces' name.

22. "Foliage of Atlas": the foliage of citrus trees, because Atlas was the father of the Hesperides. In Ancient Greek, *leimōn* means "meadow," and

limos "hunger": see Summonte 1512, ad loc. The humanists, like classical authors, were fond of such playful etymologies.

23. For "Masitholean," see on *De hortis Hesperidum* 2.21, n. 17.

24. Pontano alludes to a passage on windy weather in Hesiod's *Works and Days* (1.519–25).

25. On "Amathusian," see on *De hortis Hesperidum* 1.580, n. 41. Thespiae is a town near Mount Helicon in Boeotia; see on *De hortis Hesperidum* 2.50, n. 7. "Actian" refers to the humanist poet Jacopo Sannazaro ("Actius Sincerus" by his academic name), the owner of a villa at Mergellina: see on *Eclogae* 1.122, n. 13, and on *Eclogae* 1.126, n. 14. Compare Summonte 1512, ad loc., who identifies Mergellina as the location of Sannazaro's villa "near the *Crypta Neapolitana*."

26. Sannazaro followed Frederick of Aragon into exile in 1501.

27. Arethusa was an Arcadian nymph who was pursued by the river god Alpheus and transformed by Artemis into a stream. She flowed underground and undersea to the island of Ortygia in Syracuse, re-emerging as the freshwater Fount of Arethusa (Ovid, *Metamorphoses* 5.572–641).

28. The phrase "deceptive work" echoes Propertius' characterization of love elegy (*fallax opus*, 4.1b.135).

29. Compare Vergil's discussion of how a tree's fruit degenerate without the help of grafting (*pomaque degenerant: Georgics* 2.57–60).

30. Compare Ovid, *Ars Amatoria* 3.291.

31. "Thymbraean nectar": *Thymbraeus* is an epithet of Apollo, the father of Aristaeus, who, in Vergil's *Georgics*, miraculously created honey bees from the carcasses of cattle (4.528–58); see *Georgics* 4.323, *pater est Thymbraeus Apollo*. "Mesopian liquid": Attic honey was famous; Pontano's adjective refers to an old name for Attica, Mopsopia, with a variant orthography.

32. Cleartus is a lake in Marmarica, Libya; compare Summonte 1512, ad loc.

33. On Procne's transformation into a swallow, see on *Eclogae* 4.129, n. 12; she murdered her son Itys to avenge herself on her husband, Tereus.

34. The famous medical school at Salerno, the first in Europe.

35. On "Sebeto," see on *Eclogae* 1.25, n. 6. Permessus was a river of Mount Helicon associated with poetic inspiration. Benacus is the Lago di Garda near Mantua. The "old man" is Vergil; on his so-called tomb in Naples, see on *De hortis Hesperidum* 2.15–16, n. 3, and Introduction. Pontano here outlines his *Eclogues* (Pan singing, amazed rivers), *Georgics* (agriculture, viticulture, apiculture), and *Aeneid*; compare Columella, *On Agriculture* 10.1–5; Vergil, *Georgics* 1.1–5, 4.1, 4.164; *Aeneid* 1.432–33. On song's power to stop rivers, see on *De hortis Hesperidum* 2.22, n. 5; compare *Eclogae* 1.753.

36. These lines summarize the *Aeneid* with specific verbal echoes: e.g., *Aeneid* 7.519–20, 11.474–76. Compare *Eridanus* 1.14.36–56 in Roman 2014; Propertius 2.34.61–84.

37. The "native son and bard" is Vergil, and the "ruler," Francesco Gonzaga, celebrated for his victory at the Battle of Fornovo: see Introduction. On "spoils of honor," see on *De hortis Hesperidum* 1.49, n. 7. "Axes" (*secures*) represent the sovereign authority of Italian cities: bundled rods and axes (*fasces*) were carried by the lictors, who accompanied Roman magistrates. The *gaesum* is a Gallic javelin. Compare Caesar, *The Gallic Wars* 7.77, [*Gallia*] . . . *securibus subiecta* (where the situation is reversed).

38. On "the Adda," see on *De Hortis Hesperidum* 1.200, n. 22. Insubria was a region near Milan: alternately, "the arrogant yoke of the Insubrians," because Milan was initially allied with the French; but the point here seems to be that Milan switched sides before the battle of Fornovo. The Timavo is a river near Trieste; the Mella is a river near Brescia. The Reno is a small Po tributary, and the Senio a tributary of the Reno. The Belgae, a tribe of northern Gaul, stand for the French forces by synecdoche.

39. Southern Italy is likewise grateful for Francesco's victory: the Galeso is a river in Calabria (Vergil, *Georgics* 4.126); the seas "above" and "below" the Italian peninsula are, respectively, the Adriatic and Tyrrhenian seas (*Aeneid* 8.149).

40. On "Parthenope," see on *Eclogae* 1.25, n. 5; compare Vergil, *Georgics* 4.564, as well as his description of Jupiter on his throne (*Aeneid* 10.116; Pontano imitates the phrasing and metrical synizesis). Pontano gives

Francesco Gonzaga credit for driving out the French forces, thereby returning Naples to Aragonese rule under Ferrandino and Federigo IV.

41. Berenice, or Berenicis, is a city in Cyrenaica, Libya; see on *De hortis Hesperidum* 1.53, n. 8. Alcides ("grandson of Alceus") is Hercules, who, according to Pontano, brought citrus fruit to Campania from the Garden of the Hesperides. On "Formia," "the Sirens," "Suessa Aurunca," and "the Liris," see on *De hortis Hesperidum* 1.124, n. 13. The Aequana mountains are located near Sorrento; compare Summonte 1512, ad loc., who identifies the region as the source of excellent wine. The Sileris is a river on the boundary of Campania and Lucania. Meta is a Campanian town; see Summonte 1512, ad loc.: *vicus est Surentinus*. Terracina is a coastal town in Lazio. "Our Ischia": Pontano owned a villa there. The phrase *temperat alveo* imitates Vergilian phrasing and metrical synizesis: *Aeneid* 7.33, *fluminis alveo*; compare *De hortis Hesperidum* 2.565 with n. 40.

42. On this passage generally, see Introduction. For "Antiniana," see on *Eclogae* 1.680, n. 78 and Introduction. For "Paestum," see on *Eclogae* 1.361, n. 39; compare Vergil, *Georgics* 4.118–19. On "Idumean palms," see *Georgics* 3.12. Summonte 1512, ad loc., identifies Hermus (Eramo in the vernacular) as the *mons sancti Hermi* to the west of Naples, renowned for its many villas, that is, the Vomero hill. Compare the nymph Hermitis at *Eclogae* 1.290 and Monti Sabia 1973, ad loc. Yet in this sequence of Vergilian allusions, "Hermus" surely also evokes the river of the same name in Aeolis in Asia Minor, famous for its gold deposits: see *Georgics* 2.136–38; *Aeneid* 7.721. The golden fruit of Antiniana's orchards thus surpass both the contemporary vineyards of the Vomero and the golden wealth of the river lauded in antiquity by Pontano's classical model.

Bibliography

EDITIONS OF PONTANO'S WORKS

Arnaldi, Francesco, Lucia Gualdo Rosa, and Liliana Monti Sabia, eds. 1964. *Poeti latini del Quattrocento*. Milano: Ricciardi.

Casanova-Robin, Hélène, ed. 2011. *Pontano: Églogues/Eclogae*. Paris: Les Belles Lettres.

Dennis, Rodney G., ed. 2006. *Giovanni Gioviano Pontano: Baiae*. I Tatti Renaissance Library 22. Cambridge, MA: Harvard University Press.

Gaisser, Julia, ed. 2012. *Giovanni Gioviano Pontano: Dialogues*. Vol. 1, *Charon and Antonius*. I Tatti Renaissance Library 52. Cambridge, MA: Harvard University Press.

———, ed. 2020. *Giovanni Gioviano Pontano: Dialogues*. Vol. 2, *Actius*; vol. 3, *Aegidius and Asinus*. I Tatti Renaissance Library 91 and 92. Cambridge, MA: Harvard University Press.

Manutius, Aldus, ed. 1505. *Pontani Opera. Urania siue de stellis libri quinque. Meteororum liber unus. De hortis Hesperidum libri duo. Lepidina siue pastorales, pompae septem. Item Meliseus, Maeon, Acon. Hendecasyllaborum libri duo. Tumulorum liber unus. Neniae duodecim. Epigrammata duodecim.* Venice.

———. 1513. *Pontani Opera. Urania, siue de stellis libri quinque. Meteororum liber unus. De hortis Hesperidum libri duo. Lepidina siue pastorales, pompæ septem. Item Meliseus, Maeon, Acon. Hendecasyllaborum libri duo. Tumulorum liber unus. Neniae duodecim. Epigrammata duodecim.* Venice.

———. 1533. *Pontani Opera. Urania siue de stellis libri quinque. Meteororum liber unus. De hortis Hesperidum libri duo. Lepidina siue pastorales, pompæ septem. Item Meliseus, Maeon, Acon. Hendecasyllaborum libri duo. Tumulorum liber unus. Neniae duodecim. Epigrammata duodecim.* Venice.

Monti Sabia, Liliana, ed. 1973. *Ioannis Ioviani Pontani Eclogae*. Testo critico. Naples: Liguori.

Oeschger, Johannes, ed. 1948. *Carmina: ecloghe, elegie, liriche*. Scrittori d'Italia 198. Bari: Laterza.

Roman, Luke, trans. 2014. *Giovanni Gioviano Pontano: On Married Love. Eridanus.* I Tatti Renaissance Library 63. Cambridge, MA: Harvard University Press.

Soldati, Benedetto, ed. 1902. *Ioannis Ioviani Pontani Carmina. Testo fondato sulle stampe originali e riveduto sugli autografi, introduzione bibliografica ed appendice di poesie inedite.* Firenze: G. Barbèra.

Summonte, Pietro, ed. 1507. *Pontani Actius de numeris poeticis et lege historiae. Aegidius multiplicis argumenti. Tertius dialogus de ingratitudine qui Asinus inscribitur.* Naples: Sigismund Mayr.

———. 1512. *Pontani De fortuna.* Naples: Sigismund Mayr. [At the end of this volume, Summonte appends a section entitled *loca quaedam in Urania, Hesperidum hortis, Eclogisque propter rerum novitatem alicui fortasse obscuriora.*]

LITERATURE

Bentley, Jerry H. 1987. *Politics and Culture in Renaissance Naples.* Princeton, NJ: Princeton University Press.

Caruso, Carlo. 2013. *Adonis: The Myth of the Dying God in the Italian Renaissance.* London: Bloomsbury.

Casanova-Robin, Hélène. 2006. "Les *Eclogae* de Pontano entre tradition et modernité: *imitatio et inventio.* L'exemple de *Lepidina.*" *Canadian Review of Comparative Literature* 33.1–2:21–45.

Celenza, Christopher S. 2004. *The Lost Italian Renaissance: Humanists, Historians, and Latin's Legacy.* Baltimore: Johns Hopkins University Press.

Chatfield, Mary P., ed. 2005. *Pietro Bembo: Lyric Poetry. Etna.* I Tatti Renaissance Library 18. Cambridge, MA: Harvard University Press.

Croce, Benedetto. 1948. *Storie e leggende Napoletane.* Bari: Laterza.

De Divitiis, Bianca. 2010. "Giovanni Pontano and His Idea of Patronage." In *Some Degree of Happiness: Studi di storia dell'architettura in onore di Howard Burns,* edited by Maria Beltramini and Caroline Elam, 107–31. Pisa: Edizioni della Normale.

———. 2012. "*Pontanus Fecit*: Inscriptions and Artistic Authorship in the Pontano Chapel." *California Italian Studies* 3.1:1–36.

———. 2015. "Memories from the Subsoil: Discovering Antiquity in Fifteenth-century Naples and Campania." In Hughes and Buongiovanni 2015, 189–216.

De Nichilo, Mauro. 1977. "Lo sconosciuto apografo avellinese del *De hortis Hesperidum* di Giovanni Pontano." *Filologia e Critica* 2:217–46.

Du Cange, Charles Du Fresne, et al. 1884. *Glossarium mediae et infimae Latinitatis*. Niort: L. Favre.

Fantazzi, Charles, ed. 2004. *Angelo Poliziano: Silvae*. I Tatti Renaissance Library 14. Cambridge, MA: Harvard University Press.

Figliuolo, Bruno. 2009. "Nuovi documenti sulla datazione del *De hortis Hesperidum* di Giovanni Pontano." *Studi Rinascimentali* 7 :11–15.

Forcellini, Egidio, Jacopo Facciolati, and Gaetano Cognolato. 1771. *Totius Latinitatis lexicon*. Padua: Typis Seminarii apud Joannem Manfré.

Furstenberg-Levi, Shulamit. 2016. *The Accademia Pontaniana: A Model of a Humanist Network*. Leiden: Brill.

Gaisser, Julia. 1993. *Catullus and His Renaissance Readers*. Oxford: Clarendon Press.

Germano, Giuseppe. 2015. "Giovanni Pontano e la costituzione di una nuova Grecia nella rappresentazione letteraria del Regno Aragonese di Napoli." *Spolia* 1:1–48.

Glare, P. G. W. 1968. *The Oxford Latin Dictionary*. Oxford: Oxford University Press.

Grant, W. Leonard. 1965. *Neo-Latin Literature and the Pastoral*. Chapel Hill: University of North Carolina Press.

Hersey, George L. 1969. *Alfonso II and the Artistic Renewal of Naples, 1485–1495*. New Haven: Yale University Press.

Hughes, Jessica, and Claudio Buongiovanni, eds. 2015. *Remembering Parthenope: Receptions of Classical Naples from Antiquity to the Present*. Oxford: Oxford University Press.

Iacono, Antonietta. 2015. "Il *De hortis Hesperidum* di Giovanni Pontano: tra innovazioni umanistiche e tradizione classica." *Spolia* 1:188–237.

Ijsewijn, Jozef, and Dirk Sacré. 1998. *Companion to Neo-Latin Studies. Volume 2: Literary, Linguistic, Philological, and Editorial Questions*. Leuven: University Press.

Kidwell, Carol. 1991. *Pontano: Poet and Prime Minister*. London: Duckworth.

Lewis, Charleton T., and Charles Short. 1975. *A Latin Dictionary*. Oxford: Clarendon Press.

Ludwig, Walther. 1982. "Neulateinische Lehrgedichte und Vergils *Georgica*." In *From Wolfram and Petrarch to Goethe and Grass. Studies in Literature in Honour of Leonard Forster*, edited by Dennis H. Green, Leslie Peter Johnson, and Dieter Wuttke, 151–80. Baden-Baden: V. Koerner.

Modesti, Paola. 2014. *Le delizie ritrovate: Poggioreale e la villa del rinascimento nella Napoli aragonese*. Florence: Leo S. Olschki.

Monti Sabia, Liliana. 1969. "Una schermaglia editoriale tra Napoli e Venezia agli albori del secolo XVI." *Vichiana* 6:319–36. Reprinted in Monti Sabia, Monti, and Germano 2010, 1:195–214.

——. 1983. "Trasfigurazione di Virgilio nella poesia del Pontano." In *Atti del Convegno virgiliano di Brindisi nel Bimillenario della Morte: Brindisi, 15–18 ottobre 1981*, edited by Francesco della Corte, 47–63. [Puglia]: Istituto di filologia latina dell'Università di Perugia. Reprinted in Monti Sabia, Monti, and Germano 2010, 2:1115–34.

——. 1993. "Echi di scoperte geografiche in opere pontaniane." *Columbeis* 5:283–303. Reprinted in Monti Sabia, Monti, and Germano 2010, 2:1135–57.

——. 1998. *Un profilo moderno e due vitae antiche di Giovanni Pontano*. Naples: Accademia Pontaniana. Reprinted in Monti Sabia, Monti, and Germano 2010, 1:1–32.

Monti Sabia, Liliana, Salvatore Monti, and Giuseppe Germano. 2010. *Studi su Giovanni Pontano*. 2 vols. Messina: Centro interdipartimentale di studi umanistici.

Nuovo, Isabella. 1998. "Mito e natura nel *De hortis Hesperidum* di Giovanni Pontano." In *Acta Conventus Neolatini Bariensis. Proceedings of the Ninth International Congress of Neo-Latin Studies. Bari, 29 August to 3 September 1994*, edited by J. F. Alcina, John Dillon, and Walther Ludwig, 453–60. Tempe, Arizona: Medieval and Renaissance Texts and Studies.

Pèrcopo, Erasmo. 1921. "Ville ed abitazioni di poeti in Napoli. I. La villa del Pontano ad Antignano." *Napoli Nobilissima* 2.2:1–7.

_____. 1938. *Vita di Giovanni Pontano.* Edited by Michele Manfredi. Naples: Industrie tipografiche editoriali assimilate.

Putnam, Michael C. J., ed. 2009. *Jacopo Sannazaro: Latin Poetry.* I Tatti Renaissance Library 38. Cambridge, MA: Harvard University Press.

Ramminger, Johann. *Neulateinische Wortliste: Ein Wörterbuch des Lateinischen von Petrarca bis 1700.* Online at http://ramminger.userweb.mwn.de.

Roellenbleck, Georg. 1975. *Das epische Lehrgedicht Italiens im fünfzehnten und sechzehnten Jahrhundert: Ein Beitrag zur Literaturgeschichte des Humanismus und der Renaissance.* Munich: Wilhelm Fink.

Roman, Luke. Forthcoming. "To Gaze in Wonder Upon the Orange Tree: Landscape, Nature, and Art in Giovanni Pontano's *De hortis Hesperidum.*" In *The Three Natures: Gardens and Landscapes of the Italian Renaissance,* edited by Anatole Tchikine. Philadelphia: University of Pennsylvania Press.

Soranzo, Matteo. 2014. *Poetry and Identity in Quattrocento Naples.* London and New York: Routledge.

Tateo, Francesco. 1960. *Astrologia e moralità in Giovanni Pontano.* Bari: Adriatica Editrice.

Tilly, Georges. 2020. *Un manifeste posthume de l'humanisme aragonais: le De hortis Hesperidum de Giovanni Pontano.* Thèse, Université de Rouen Normandie and Università degli Studi di Napoli Federico II. Thesis published online with HAL Archives Ouvertes (CNRS) in April 2021 at https://tel.archives-ouvertes.fr/tel-03197923/document

Trapp, J. B. 1984. "The Grave of Vergil." *Journal of the Warburg and Courtauld Institutes* 47:1–31.

Tufano, Carmela Vera. 2015. *Lingue, tecniche e retorica dei generi letterari nelle Eclogae di Giovanni Pontano.* Napoli: Paolo Loffredo.

Wilson-Okamura, David Scott. 2010. *Virgil in the Renaissance.* Cambridge: Cambridge University Press.

Index

❧❧❧

Abella (town), 249n3
Abelle (witch), 119, 249n3
Acarnania, 235n20
Acerra (town), 31, 41, 236n32
Acheron, 35
Achilles, 242n88
Acidalian font (Boeotia), 11, 13,
    197, 234n11
Acilla, 99, 107
Acon (character), xvi, 9, 105
Acqua dei Pisciarelli, 237n41
Acron, 37
Actian, 205. See Sannazaro, Jacopo
Adda (river), 159, 221, 254n22
Adige (river), 159, 254n25
Adonia (festival), xiv, 257n45
Adonis (beloved of Venus), xxi,
    xxiv, 149–51, 157, 159, 167, 171,
    181, 185, 252n10
Adriana. See Sassone, Adriana
Adriatic Sea, 254n25, 261n39
Aegean Sea, 254n25
Aegon, 69
Aenaria (sea goddess), 23, 235n21
Aeneadae, 157
Aeneas, 185, 244n96, 251n18,
    254n19
Aeolis, 262n42
Aequana (mod. Vico Equense),
    21, 223, 234n19
Aequana (mountains), 262n41
Aeron, 27

Aeronius, 37
Afragola (town), 236n32
Africa/African, xxii, 155, 247n4,
    252n8, 255n34, 256n43
Agrippa (Marcus Vipsanius
    Agrippa), 237n42
Albigena, 99
Alcidamas, 107
Alcides (Hercules), 221, 262n41
Alcimedon, 239n61
Alcon, 17, 107
Alcyone (Pleiad), 199, 258–
    59n15
Aldus Manutius/Aldine, xvi, xvii,
    xviii, xix, xx, 246n1
Alexis, 121, 249n4
Alfonso (duke of Calabria), ix,
    251n1 (Garden of the Hesperides)
Alfonso the Magnanimous (king
    of Naples), vii
Allegory, xiii–xiv, 241n78, 242n81,
    249n5
Alphesiboeus, 67, 69, 121, 243n92,
    249n4
Alpheus (river god), 260n27
Alps/Alpine, 155, 221
Aluntas the Red, 31
Amalfi (town; nymph), xxi, xxii,
    21, 147, 153, 185, 201, 203,
    234n19, 253n13, 259n19, 259n21
Amaryllis, 27, 49, 69, 235n24,
    240n67, 249n1

269

Epaphus, 258n15

Epic poetry, 219, 221, 261n36. *See also* Apollonius of Rhodes; Homer; Vergil: *Aeneid*

Epicedion. *See* Bereavement and poetic lament

Epomeo, Mount, 237n43

Erebus, 85

Este, Isabella d', xxix n28

Ethiopia/Ethiopian, 187, 193

Etna, Mount, 237n43

Etruscan, 239n60, 248n11

Euhius (deity), 47. *See also* Bacchus

Europe, 255n34, 261n34

Eurus, 155

Eurydice, 61

Experience and experimentation, 213, 217. *See also* Human artifice and industry

Faberonta, 49

Faburnus (character), 77–93, 245n2

Falernian (wine; wine-producing region), xvi, 109, 117, 175, 247n5 (*Ec. 4*), 256n37

Family life, viii, xvii–xviii, 131–41, 167, 175, 193

Fates. *See* Parcae

Fauns, 27, 35

Faunus, 19, 67

Federico IV (king of Naples), 262n40

Ferdinand I (king of Naples), vii

Feretrian (referring to Jupiter Feretrius), 147, 252n7

Ferrandino (Ferdinand II; king of Naples), 262n40

Fescennia (Etruscan town), 239n60

Fescennine verses, 45

Flora (deity), 258n10

Florentine Academy, xxi

Fondi, 185, 253n13

Forcella (area in Naples), 235n25

Formellis (nymph), xxix n22, 29, 31, 236n30, 236n35

Formia (town), xxi, 151, 185, 223, 253n13, 255n33

Formiello, fountain of, xv

Fornovo, battle of, xviii, xxiii, 252n7, 261nn37–38

Fragola, 31, 236n32

France/French, 147, 167, 248n13, 261n38, 262n40; invasion of Italy (1495), viii, xii, xviii, 248n13, 255n31

Frederick of Aragon, xviii, 260n26

French invasion of Italy (1494), viii, xii, xviii, xxvii n4, 115, 147, 167, 221, 248n13, 255n31, 261n38, 261–62n40

Fundania (nymph), 153, 253n13

Fundanus (lake), 253n13

Gaeta (town), 151, 253n13

Galeso (river; *Galaesus*), xix, 221, 261n39

Galicia/Galician, 169

Ganges, 21, 169

Garamantes/Garamantian (a people of North Africa), 23, 187, 235n20

Siren, land of (Naples), ix, 201,
  259n19
Sirens, 21, 65, 153, 185, 223, 253n13
Sirmio/Sirmione, xxiii, 161, 255n27
Sithonii/Sithonian, 155, 254n17
Sleep, 125
Sorrento, 234n19, 262n41
Southern Italy, 235n22, 235n26,
  237n39, 247n6 (Ec. 3), 261n39
South Wind, 177
Spagnuoli, Battista, xiii, 249n5
Spain, 253n12
Spartan, 113, 244n96
Spinning, 29, 31, 45, 49, 107, 113;
  associated with destiny or the
  Parcae (Fates), xxiv, 63–69, 81,
  83, 181, 183, 242n88
Stachir (river), 187, 199, 257n6
Statius (Publius Papinius Statius):
  Silvae, xiii; Thebaid, 246n1
Strozzi, Tito Vespasiano, xiii
Suessa Aurunca, 153, 185, 223,
  253n13
Summonte, Pietro, 235n22
Switzerland, 254n22
Syncerius (character), xiv, 95–103
Syracuse/Syracusan, 207, 260n27
Syria/Syrian, 145, 197

Taralli, 25, 235n22
Taro (river valley), 147, 252n7
Teate (town; mod. Chieti),
  244n96
Teleboan, 23, 235n20
Tempe, xxii, 147
Tereus (king of Thrace), 248n12,
  260n33

Terracina (town), 223, 262n41
Themiscyra, 253n12
Theocritus/Theocritean, viii, xii,
  xiv, xvii, 245n5; Idylls 1, xiv;
  Idylls 15, xiv
Theodocie, 27, 235n23
Theophrastus, Enquiry into Plants,
  258n14
Theseus, 247n6 (Ec. 3)
Thespiae/Thespian (town), 205,
  260n25
Thessaly/Thessalian, xxii, 147,
  254n18
Thrace/Thracian, 155, 254nn17–18,
  255n29
Thymbraean, 215, 260n31
Thyrsas, 99
Thyrsis, 79, 245n4
Tiber (river), 151
Tibullus (Albius Tibullus),
  250n15
Ticino (river), 159, 254n22
Tifata/Tifatean (mountain), 47,
  240n64
Timavo (river), 221, 261n38
Tityrus (shepherd), xiv, xvi, 67,
  121, 235n24, 243n92, 249nn4–5
Toil, 213
Tombs, ix, x–xi, xxiv, xxviii n11,
  xxix n39, 69, 79, 83, 89, 95,
  244n94, 244n1, 245n5; the
  so-called tomb of Virgil, x,
  xxiii, 219, 237n42, 257n3, 261n35
Torre ad Arco (part of Pontano's
  palazzo on Via dei Tribunali),
  236n36
Trieste, 261n38

Publication of this volume has been made possible by

The Myron and Sheila Gilmore Publication Fund at I Tatti
The Robert Lehman Endowment Fund
The Jean-François Malle Scholarly Programs and Publications Fund
The Andrew W. Mellon Scholarly Publications Fund
The Craig and Barbara Smyth Fund
for Scholarly Programs and Publications
The Lila Wallace–Reader's Digest Endowment Fund
The Malcolm Wiener Fund for Scholarly Programs and Publications